Komatipoort Bridge

by

Nick Brown

Komatipoort Bridge
Copyright ©Nick Brown 2024

All rights reserved, including the right to reproduce this book or any portion thereof in any form. No part of this publication may be reproduced, distributed decompiled, reverse engineered or stored, in any form or introduced into any information storage and retrieval system in any form or by any means, whether mechanical or electronic, without the express permission of the author.

Typesetting and Cover Design by: Levellers

Dedicated to my Great Grandfather Captain William Brown, late of the 97th Foot and the Queen's Own Royal West Kent Regiment and to all those who served in the 97th, the Queen's Own, The Queen's Own Buffs, The Queen's Regiment and the Princess of Wales' Royal Regiment.

Quo fas et Gloria Ducunt - Where right and glory lead

All the business of war, indeed, all the business of life is finding out what you don't know from what you do.

Arthur Wellesley
First Duke of Wellington.

Contents

CHAPTER ONE 11
London 1899 11
CHAPTER TWO 39
A surprise meeting 39
CHAPTER THREE 65
An explosive beginning 65
CHAPTER FOUR 87
RMS Goorkha 87
CHAPTER FIVE 111
Lourenço Marques 111
CHAPTER SIX 137
Breaking and entering 137
CHAPTER SEVEN 161
Incursion into Swaziland 161
CHAPTER EIGHT 187
Brown's rendezvous with Steinaecker 187
CHAPTER NINE 211
Battle in the Botanical Gardens 211
CHAPTER TEN 235
Malelane Bridge 235
CHAPTER ELEVEN 263
Holding up the train 263

CHAPTER TWELVE	289
Battle at Krokodil River	289
CHAPTER THIRTEEN	315
Komatipoort revisited	315
A Note About The Boer War and Bibliography	333

Acknowledgments

Many people have helped with this book, some passively most actively. First among the former is my wife Elizabeth who suffered through the course of the writing with great stoicism. Of the latter, Mike Inkster acted as inspiration, editor, cartographer and most of all military advisor. Ben Tophill encouraged me to keep going when I was struggling and my daughter Alexandra who is fluent in Afrikaans assisted with linguistics. Thanks too to my sister in law Beryl Brown who took time out from her own successful writing to offer advice.

Lastly but by no means least, the late Stephen Nicholl who offered professional advice and pointers despite being gravely ill

CHAPTER ONE

London 1899

Christmas 1899 in the City of London.

The City was the financial capital of England and the world and London was the beating heart of an empire that put all previous empires to shame.

The Roman may have had his *Mare Nostrum*, but the British Empire spanned all the continents of the globe. A Briton could hold his head up anywhere in the world and expect respect. To be born British was to win first prize in the lottery of life and truly, most Britons held this as an article of faith whether they served the Empire on her wild frontiers or in the merchant houses of Hong Kong and Singapore.

It was certainly what they taught in British schools and most if not quite all Britons believed it. Surprisingly, those who never left the British archipelago, perhaps toiling in the counting houses of the City of London, calculating the profits of imperial adventures or sweating in Northern mills and factories manufacturing the trade goods and arms that kept the flag flying, felt it even more keenly than their fellow countrymen overseas.

On this December day, as the church bells of the City struck noon, the insurance and shipping clerks, the bank tellers and the merchants emerged into the cold December air to grab a brief repast before returning to their labours.

On Cornhill, where the Royal Exchange stood in Greco-Victorian splendour across from the Bank of England, the crowds swirled out into the streets dodging between the steaming horses of the cabs and drays, pausing to gape at the sight of the almost completed underground railway and paying little heed to the news seller crying news of a so-called 'black week' in faraway South Africa where Britain was engaged in a war with the two Boer Republics. A war started by the Boers and which they were prosecuting with surprising success.

Among the crowd was a man that no casual observer would have remarked upon as being any different from any of the other office workers seeking refreshment or a break from the labours of the day.

A more interested watcher, a policeman say, might well have noted that he carried himself in the upright manner of a military man, which, he had once been.

His dark moustache, while less luxuriant than some, did nothing to dispel the impression. His attire was in keeping with the City but better cut and more expensive than those around him and he walked with purpose. An interested detective would have correctly guessed that he was, or had been, an army officer.

Making a path through the crowd, the man stopped to buy a newspaper then cut across Cornhill to St Michael's Alley and entered the Jamaica public house. As he entered, a group of young city clerks were hogging the space by the fire and being noisy enough to attract the watchful eye of Joe the barman.

Joe was a solid citizen in his middle age who sported splendid side whiskers and had a taste for brightly coloured waistcoats. Like many a publican, Joe too had spent some time in the army and was not having the peace of his respectable house disturbed by noisy, young idiots full of war talk. Particularly when an officer and gentleman had taken a place at his bar.

The youngsters were full of patriotic zeal encouraged perhaps by patriotic ale and were loudly announcing their intention to join the army before the war was won. Joe sighed and looked briefly away from the new arrival to give the rowdy youngsters the look he may once have reserved for errant soldiers. Sensing his baleful eye upon them, the young men turned, flushed and then quietened, at least for a time.

The arrival of the well-dressed man with his newspaper brought a smile to the barman who greeted him with a 'morning Captain' and an enquiry as to whether he would like a pint of ale, which was his usual drink of choice.

In truth, the Captain had never achieved greater rank than a lieutenancy in his Father's old regiment the 97th Foot later the Queens Own Royal West Kent Regiment but he didn't bother to correct the error.

Had a curious policeman made enquiry of Joe he would have discovered that despite being a relatively wealthy man, the Jamaica, respectable but a simple tavern nonetheless, was his customary lunchtime haunt rather than the lunch clubs favoured by his peers.

A more widespread and detailed enquiry might have established the following: Christened William Ferguson Brown, he was known to acquaintances and friends as Bill and scion of a military family yet he was the first of his family to have been granted the Queen's commission.

That was all in the past however. His brief military career had ended in the last Boer War, which had been brief and bloody; so brief in fact, that it was over before Lieutenant Brown and the 97th could come to grips with the enemy.

It was a short and embarrassing conflict for Britain because however you dressed it up, the Boers, and their civilian army had beaten British professionals. Fortunately, that memory had been largely swept under the carpet even with the present hostilities but those who were there like the former Lieutenant Brown remembered as they read the accounts of new defeats in their newspapers and wondered if history might be repeating itself.

Our policeman would not see any of that however, just a successful businessman and former soldier approaching forty. He might well wonder though, what wrought the transition from young army officer to prosperous city gentleman.

The inquisitive Peeler would not have known that over his solitary pint, Brown was ruminating over just the same thing. How he had started, where he had been and where he was now. It was not an everyday story but hardly unique either.

The British Empire afforded many opportunities for the talented and determined to make spectacular fortunes. Brown's was a modest fortune but a fortune none the less and he made it by using his brain and taking his chances and had you asked him, he would have agreed that while he had thought and worked hard, there were slices of luck involved too.

His father had been a regular soldier enlisting as a fourteen-year-old drummer boy to escape the poverty and hunger of the Ulster weaving community.

Through diligence and good sense, he retired from the army as a colour sergeant and a wealthy man. His wealth which marked him out from many of his peers was acquired during the Indian Mutiny when having fought the rebellious sepoys, British soldiers fought each other for the choicest pieces of loot from the palaces of wealthy Indians. Brown's father had kept his head and more surprising his loot, until it could be profitably disposed of to the jewellers of Bombay.

On his return to England, Brown senior determined that his two sons would live a better life than he had and after purchasing a pleasant but unostentatious cottage in the countryside near Maidstone, he put both his sons through good schools. So good in fact, that William Brown had followed his father into the army via the Woolwich Academy as an officer and gentleman.

Whatever illusions father or son may have had about their improved social status, died in the officer's mess of the 97th. His father's reputation was both asset and curse. His father had been much respected although the Colonel was probably the only officer to remember him, having fought alongside him at Lucknow. He was however, a ranker and old comrade or not, the Colonel would no more have eaten his dinner with him than he would his gardener. Officer or not, Brown was the son of a ranker, and the mess knew it before he even arrived at the Maidstone barracks.

Nothing was said, of course and Brown applied himself to soldiering and applied himself well, earning some respect from those of his fellows who took their soldiering seriously rather than as a way of passing the time between school and inheriting their father's farms or estates.

The men he commanded were wary at first and wondered what sort of hybrid was in charge of them. They complained to each other that he worked them hard but noticed that he worked hard himself. He also took the trouble to learn all of their names but never fell into the error of trying to be their friend.

He wasn't a martinet but no soft touch either. Within the customary limits of the ordinary soldiers' views of their officers, they respected him.

He learned his trade steadily and settled in to the routine of military life on home service. Soldiering kept him busy during the days but there was hunting in winter, cricket in summer and boxing and fencing if the mood took you. For many there was the social whirl of Kentish society and for the better off a short train journey to the West End of London. He certainly enjoyed the company of the young ladies that attended the local balls and parties but found himself tongue tied much of the time, leaving the field to his more self-assured colleagues.

This was something he could accept quite happily; it was his deficiency, and he could manage without being part of the county set. What was less easy to tolerate was the snobbery of mess nights when social divisions could be painfully exposed. The mess divided into a number of distinct parts presided over by the Colonel; a tall, slim figure with an iron grip on his regiment. The hair now thinning, the moustache still luxuriant but white. A stern disciplinarian possessed of a firm sense of the order of society and his place in it. When flogging was available as a punishment, he never shirked, yet, in his way he loved his men as part of his home, his regiment. Brave as a lion, the stories about him were legion not least how he and Brown's father had stood by the colour at Lucknow and fought off the mutineer rabble that tried to take it from them.

Now the Colonel presided over mess nights in Maidstone, holding his position as fiercely as any he had defended in India. Below the Colonel came the senior officers, white haired Majors and ageing Captains who had not had the fortune of any serious fighting and promotion opportunities. they mostly kept their own counsel and if they troubled a junior officer it was generally to have them pass the salt, or more frequently the port.

Then came the younger officers, Brown's contemporaries. They, in turn, divided into the wealthy, fast set with money to burn and grand social standing and the more humble officers. They lacked the advantages of the others but were not necessarily better or indeed worse soldiers than their wealthier brothers. Human beings, even soldiers, do not fit easily into pigeonholes. Thus some of the fast set were also not merely keen but excellent soldiers, while some of those who were soldiering for the salary and the status were less keen or effective.

Leading light of the fast set was a Captain Peter Fitzherbert. An old Etonian whose people owned a goodly piece of Ulster, possibly including the area where Brown's father had been born. Fitzherbert was beautifully dressed and spoken, had immaculate manners and had the ladies queuing up for dances. He was also highly intelligent, and a talented officer who was excellent at nearly all sports, not least because, in addition to a natural athleticism, he had a cool head and a killer instinct, whether sending down fast balls at cricket or slashing his way to victory on the fencing piste. Brown had bested him once with a sword but only by the skin of his teeth and a lucky hit. It was not an event that Fitzherbert would allow to be repeated.

For whatever reason, Fitzherbert, known to his friends as Fitz, went out of his way to be pleasant to Brown despite the social gulf between them. Brown was under no illusions that he had been invited to join Fitz's inner circle and in any case had no aspirations in that direction. Occasionally he wondered what caused such affability in the older man but decided that anyone that talented and wealthy could afford to be affable. Still, he treated Captain Fitzherbert with polite respect, opening the batting with him for the regimental cricket team but otherwise keeping a discreet distance.

Thinking about Fitz and listening to all the war talk in the pub, he couldn't help wondering where Fitz was now and remembered his own South African War such as it was. Ordering another pint, he recalled how just as he had settled into the routine of military life, enjoying the soldiering and enduring the social aspects rumours of a war against the Boers began to circulate. The rumour of war was sharpened by belief that if war came the 97th would be going. Brown had set about reading whatever he could find about the Boers and their history and the nature of the country where the regiment might be posted. He was keen to put his skills to the test but sensible enough to be apprehensive. He was unaware of the statement that knowledge is power but he knew that the Duke of Wellington had said that all the business of war is finding out what you don't know from what you do. Such material as he could find was meagre, but he managed to establish a few salient facts. The Dutch had first set foot on the Cape of Good Hope in the 1650's establishing a source of fresh water and food for the ships of the Dutch East India Company heading round the Cape to their Eastern colonies. The settlement had grown and had absorbed Protestant refugees from France and some Germans in addition to the Dutch. By the time the British arrived earlier in the early 1800's the settlers had developed an identity and culture of their own.

Brown was somewhat discouraged to learn that confronted with the realities of a British administration that told them they could no longer keep slaves or avoid paying taxes, the Boers moved *en masse* over mountains and desert, exposing their families to all manner of hardship including warlike tribes. In his view, this suggested a degree of stubborn refusal to accept anything imposed upon them but also a courage and tenacity that could prove difficult for even the British Empire to overcome. His research was terminated by the arrival of embarkation orders to the surprise of no-one. Brown had busied himself with lists of stores, ensuring his men had all of the necessary clothing and equipment and lastly looking to his own outfitting and provisions. His Mother fussed and worried while his father discreetly pressed some sovereigns and a rather fine pair of binoculars on him. Then suddenly the time arrived and the regiment was on board HMS 'Tamar' heading down the coast of Africa at a frustrating snail's pace and finally being discharged into the heat and humidity of the port of Durban on the Natal coast.

Having arrived more or less safely barring a few cases of seasickness and the consequences of being confined to a slow-moving troopship for some weeks, the regiment began its march towards the front lines. It was hot and uphill all the way. The railways were just beginning to be built in South Africa but the 97th would advance towards their foe on foot or in ox carts. Cursing the heat, the dust and the country they struggled forward to join General Colley's forces. Word had reached them of the defeat at Laing's Nek and imperialists at home might have expected the men of the 97th to be thirsting for revenge against the Boer. In one respect, they would have been correct. The men were permanently thirsty as they sweated their way on and over the hills. Had they had the time or the inclination to think about the broader war, no doubt they would have been keen to inflict a swift and crushing defeat on the enemy. Their feet and their bellies were their primary concerns but they cursed the Boers with the same fervour with which they cursed their officers, the heat, their cooks and anyone else they saw as contributing to their discomforts.

After some days of this they were halted near a river in the Natal Hills with an unpronounceable name preparing tents and fires for the night when a lone rider in khaki appeared over the skyline. Pausing from their various tasks, the soldiers watched as he trotted down into their midst and enquired as to the whereabouts of the Colonel. A soldier took his bridle and the man slid out of his saddle and was escorted by a Sergeant to where the ruddy faced Colonel was discussing supplies with the adjutant. He ignored the Sergeant and his companion until he had finished his discussion and then, with evident irritation, he turned to acknowledge their presence. The silence as the men had watched this individual's progress was now broken by muttered speculation as to its meaning. This in turn was swiftly quelled by various NCOs encouraging the men to return to work, not always gently.

Like his men, Brown too was distracted and while not an old sweat, he knew enough to realise that surprise visitors to commanding officers in times of hostilities were probably of some significance. Beyond that he was as uncertain as any but as an officer, it was his job to remain unruffled and to keep his men busy. This he accomplished with the help of a couple of burly corporals but naturally he and everybody else remained consumed with curiosity.

He didn't have long to wait. Within the hour, the officers were summoned to the Colonel's presence. Brown was surprised not to see the mysterious khaki rider but learned later that he had paused only long enough to deliver his message and to feed and water his horse, then had ridden on. The Colonel drew himself up to his full height and looking down his beak-like nose delivered the news. Like many messages in many wars, it was a mixed bag. The Boers had inflicted a significant defeat on General Colley's main force at a hill called Majuba causing many casualties, including the General who had been killed while trying to organise a fighting retreat. A ceasefire had been agreed pending negotiations for a more permanent peace. It was hard for anyone on the British side to see anything positive in what looked like a shattering defeat. Had the full extent of the shambles that was Majuba Hill been fully known, Brown and all of the 97th would have been appalled. Nearly three hundred British soldiers including their commander were killed, wounded and captured by a civilian army of farmers with hunting rifles. If there was a positive note in such a disaster, for Brown, it was the cessation of hostilities, not because he was a coward, he wasn't, but because he did not relish the thought of men under his command or brother officers being killed or mutilated in a war between two European or semi European tribes for control of African territory properly the manor of the black African tribes who had lived there for hundreds if not thousands of years. Listening to the young clerks in the pub under Joe's watchful eye, he thought back to that time and wished he could have shown them the dead horses, the fresh graves and broken gear around Majuba and Laing's Nek. Not, as he reflected that it would change their minds. Young men want to prove themselves and a war was a good place to do it, just so long as you came back intact.

When he had heard the news though, he kept his thoughts to himself. He had quite enough social problems in the mess without giving voice to what were largely just his personal musings. He wasn't against the Empire or even the idea of Empire. After all, the evidence was pretty clear that areas of the world ruled by Britain fared much better than those under the sway of corrupt local chiefs or worse, continental European countries. British territories, bar the odd famine or other disaster, often caused by the lack of education or fecklessness of the locals, generally thrived and prospered. Naturally, Britain took a slice of the prosperity but without Britain, where would they be? However, he couldn't help wondering what the natives felt about their protectors and whether they knew they were better off under British rule. Looking at the blacks he had encountered, they seemed friendly enough but it was only two years since a swarm of Zulus had massacred a British column at Isandlwana. They obviously hadn't appreciated the benefits of British rule. Whether reducing their capital Ulundi to a smoking ruin with artillery or exiling their king to London had done much to improve relations he couldn't tell but it seemed unlikely. He wasn't guilty of cowardice or even treason. If he was guilty of anything it was being thoughtful. It was not a quality to be greatly admired in the Victorian Army as he would soon learn.

Ruminating on his near brush with war in the safety of a city pub, he reflected that it was the disdain for any sort of thought or consideration of details or consequences that set him on an alternative path. He understood that the army needed unthinking obedience and he also understood that that was something he couldn't give. While in uniform, had he been ordered to charge an enemy position, he would have done it, but he would have been wondering if there wasn't a better way to do it. That sort of thinking can get you killed in battle. In the social conflict of the mess it could also draw unwelcome attention as he recalled without the warm glow of nostalgia.

Here in London, it was cold and damp, but he was thinking about the heat of Africa and instead of the tang of smoke, the curse of dust. Having arrived too late for the fighting, assuming the cease fire held, the question of what might happen next was on every man's mind. As Brown knew, the army might lack long term planning or introspection but it has a way of dealing with the short term very efficiently. Idle soldiers are soldiers that get into and cause trouble and in the absence of a peace treaty, the soldiers of the 97th were put to work building defensive works in Natal colony. When they were not thus engaged, there was football, tug of war and other athletic events against other regiments or just within their own.

Anything to keep the men occupied and out of trouble. Brown participated in the sporting events sometimes as administrator or referee, sometimes as a player in his own right, captaining the tug of war team that beat the artillery to the Colonel's great pleasure. Away from the playing fields of Natal, he worked his men hard but was not afraid to get his own hands dirty which won him their respect and a measure of condescension from his brother officers. In between supervising the construction of forts and the odd piece of civil engineering - road repair and similar tasks, Brown had taken to his horse, exploring as much as he could, shooting the odd antelope that crossed his path for the mess and generally enjoying the country and the freedom from the pettiness of military life.

The more he explored Africa, or at least the portion of Natal assigned to his regiment, the more Brown was taken by the sense of space and light, the purity of the air and the water in the streams and rivers. There was game enough too, although as human settlements increased so the game decreased but that had the advantage that natural predators were also few and far between, having followed their prey away to less crowded parts. The local farmers that he chatted to occasionally tried to frighten him with tales of killer leopards or hippopotami but while it paid to check rivers for crocodile, generally, he was safe enough.

With the threat of war with the Boers seemingly gone, and the Zulus licking their wounds from the 1879 invasion, Natal was a fine and happy place that winter of 1881. The talk having moved away from war, the country was full of the news of the diamond diggings in and around Kimberley. Diamonds had been found there ten years before, setting off a stampede of prospectors. The actual diamond fields were claimed by the two Boer Republics of the Transvaal and the Orange Free State, the British Cape Colony and the local black tribe, the Griqua. As the land lay at the edges of all of these estates and borders were far from well defined, each claim might have been considered reasonable but the Boers were unsophisticated and the Griqua bewildered at the negotiation process. Britain kindly arranged a mediation that was carried out by the British governor of Natal who demonstrated his impartiality by awarding the land to the Griqua. The Boers were naturally unhappy and when the Griqua promptly put themselves under British protection, equivalent to an annexation, their resentment knew no bounds. Even the compensation offered by London did little to offset the sense of having been cheated but they took it anyway.

Brown heard much of the diggings and the enormous fortunes being made there as he roamed the countryside. Because he was a thoughtful man, he often considered what it might be like to be rich like perhaps Peter Fitzherbert. He came from a comfortable background but not a wealthy one and he still had to deal with military snobs on a daily basis from the Colonel down.

Would money change any of that? Quite possibly, but the days of looting Indian palaces were over. To make any real money would mean leaving the Army and stepping into a strange new world where battles were conducted with cash and balance sheets. His older brother Bob had gone into business in the City and had been quite successful. If Bob could succeed, he reasoned, he might also prosper, better yet, perhaps he could partner with Bob in a family venture? A family firm might assuage his father's probable disappointment at his leaving the Army. All these thoughts rattled around in his head during his lone excursions into the hills and valleys around the Regiment's camp.

His brother officers rarely ventured far from camp, perhaps to the races at a nearby town or to another regiment's mess night. They certainly showed little curiosity about the locals, black or white, British or Dutch. Some of the older majors seemed to positively revel in their ignorance, which was on full display by the time the port was passed on mess nights. on the occasions that Brown overheard some of the more ignorant opinions being paraded, he found himself becoming irritated and on occasion came close to challenging the speaker when he heard something unusually foolish but his better sense prevailed and he kept his counsel.

There was one spectacularly pretty day that had him thinking that the world was in general a fine place and to be a young army officer in Natal might be not such a bad job after all. During the course of that day's excursion, he had chanced upon a local farmer who unusually, at least in that area, was of Dutch/German extraction. Despite that background, he not only spoke excellent English but was a pleasant and generous host who invited Brown to his table. Here he dispensed some simple but excellent food and home brewed ale. More interestingly, he was a font of information on the Boer people, their backgrounds and history and added immeasurably to the framework of knowledge that Brown had begun to construct in Maidstone.

Bidding his host a cheerful farewell, he mounted up and began the ride back to camp. Inexplicably for he was not a musical person, he found himself humming a tune from an operetta he had seen in Maidstone. But this was far from Kent in every respect. Much as he loved his native land, he could see why Englishmen would come here to farm. Aside from abundant and cheap land, the weather was reliable and pleasant, there was fresh water a plenty and the air didn't have the tang of coal smoke and sulphur.

Enjoying the ride with the sun on his back, he felt happier than he had for some time and even the prospect of the mess failed to dampen his spirits, in fact as he approached a piece of flat ground near the camp, he urged his horse into a gallop, for the sheer joy of the wind blowing past his face, the noise of the horse's hooves on the hard ground and feeling at one with his mount. He slowed as he neared the gate, returned the salute of the sentry and took the horse to the makeshift stable area where his servant was waiting to rub her down and clean his tack.

Walking from stable to his quarter, his head was full of the conversation he had enjoyed earlier but also of various other aspects of Africa not obviously interconnected except in his mind. As he went over the events of the day he pondered about the observation of his host who had told him in all seriousness that the Boers regarded themselves as God's chosen race and that they believed that the Black Africans had been created by God to be like the Gibeonites, hewers of wood and drawers of water for God's chosen. It amounted to slavery but sounded better in a biblical guise. The farmer, whose name was de Wet, was of the view that the blacks who worked on white farms whether British or Dutch were little better than slaves anyway. They could walk away it was true but to where? The farmers provided accommodation and food. Some were kind, some were brutal but the blacks recognised their strength and superiority. Well, that's what de Wet believed. For himself, Brown couldn't help but think that might be true of what might be termed 'domesticated' blacks who had lived around the white man for some time. The impis of the Zulus and the Matabele might have other ideas.

He remained lost in thought but cheery as he changed for dinner even continuing to hum as he made ready. His servant saw that all was in order and he smiled at the irony that he was effectively being inspected by a private soldier. Entering the mess, he noted the silver gleaming and the candles providing illumination and even a sense of gaiety. Maybe the Army was not so bad after all. The meal was reasonable and he was hungry despite the hospitality he had enjoyed earlier. The wine was tolerable and flowed freely and he made conversation with some of his fellows who had been to the races in Ladysmith and were full of conceit, having won some money and met some ladies. They asked him what he had been up to and he began to tell them a little about de Wet and their conversation. Seated across the table was one of the older Majors.

He was a purple faced old walrus with gooseberry eyes and rather threadbare attire. A man with few distinctions other than the ability to look and feel angry on any occasion. It might have been intimidating once although Brown doubted it. Now he just looked like a man who life had passed by. As he spoke, Brown felt the eyes upon him and wondered what might be coming. Whatever it was, it was unlikely to be interest or approval. Suddenly, there came a rumble from opposite and Brown found his discourse interrupted.

'What the devil are the bloody Dutch doing here anyway? They're nowhere else in Africa and these people seem barely civilised. They say that Kruger can neither read nor write and believes the world is flat. Why are you wasting your time talking to one of them?'

As he looked back with an anger that he had nurtured for almost two decades, he wondered what had finally broken his usual reticence that night. While typically, he would not be intimidated by this sort of rudeness and breach of etiquette. In the past, he had always sought a diplomatic response that would allow him to retire from any potential fray without embarrassment. Tonight, he found that the sheer pig-headed ignorance was too much but even so he paused to consider his response before returning fire.

'Strictly sir, as you say, the Boers are not pure Dutch. Take Kruger for instance, the family name is German – his Father was from Berlin. Most of 'em are a mix of Continental Protestants, Dutch, French Huguenot, German Calvinist. They arrived here in the 1600's and established the Cape as their colony but mostly as a provisioning station for Dutch ships headed to the Indies.' There was a brief pause but no interrupting voices. He had his audience's attention and decided to plough on.

'Kruger may have limited education but they say he killed his first lion at fourteen. Something probably more helpful than an ability to construe Latin. He actually reads and writes well but the only book he has ever read is the Bible.'

Feeling the eyes of the mess from the Colonel down upon him, perhaps incautiously, he said what he had been thinking earlier:

'Given our history with the Dutch, it wouldn't surprise me a bit to find a few Ulstermen amongst them.'

This met with some smiles but any laughs died in the glare of the Colonel. From being confident and irritated Brown was beginning to feel some apprehension. Relief arrived from an unexpected quarter as the silence was broken by Captain Peter Fitzherbert.

'I say Billy, that's some good stuff. Wherever did you find out all that?'

With his flank protected, Brown continued his advance: 'I have been exploring the country wherever I can and have talked to a number of the local farmers both British and loyal Boer, just to try and get some knowledge of the country. I remember reading that the old Duke of Wellington had said that all the business of war was finding out what you don't know from what you do. I thought the more I knew, the more helpful it might be.'

Quoting the Duke of Wellington in an Army mess at any point after Waterloo was sure to get you some attention, if done well it might even garner some respect. In this case, it halted the purple Major's percolating outburst and he confined himself to a loud 'harrumph' which was generally ignored. Rather than keeping his head down however, he proceeded to make himself look an ass by knocking his port over while lighting a cheroot.

'Well the old Duke was an Irishman himself, as you know and an Etonian' observed Fitzherbert. Keeping the conversation going while neatly underlining his own education and re-establishing a social distance between himself and the herd. 'but I'm interested in what you say' he continued. 'In all this reconnaissance, if I may call it that, did you find out how many of the Boers there are in case we have to come back again for another bout?'

Brown considered: 'As best I can tell, they might be able to field an army of about 40,000, but not an army in the way that we understand it.'

'No question of that' mutters the Major from across a spreading stain of spilled port on the white cloth.

Paying the Major no more attention he warmed to his theme: 'The Boers don't think of themselves as soldiers but merely citizens with an obligation to the state. There is no age limit on service so the entire male population including boys and old men may take to the field.'

'What's the point of boys and young men being out there?' Asked another of Fitz's set, a lieutenant called Joe Heslop.

'Boys can look after horses and cattle, load rifles carry out general camp duties, old men much the same and can also aid in cooking. The boys make good scouts having been taught to hunt from an early age and they are all damn good shots.'

'Good Lord!' says Heslop, 'don't say they all fight – you'll be telling me the women too next.'

'Well Joe, there are rumours on that score, don't forget that not that long ago, groups of Boer families fought the Zulus and other tribes. The point is, when you fight the Boers, you fight an entire people, not just their army.'

The Colonel's contribution was no more enlightened than the port juggling Major's had been but as it came from the Colonel it exploded like an artillery round.

'I fail to see how a knowledge of Paul Kruger's reading habits may be of any assistance in operations against the Boer.'

It fell again to Fitzherbert to rally the troops:

'Quite right Colonel, what he reads don't signify much but the size of the army now and how it's organised, sure that's good information to have wouldn't you say sir?'

It was a shocking put down but Fitzherbert spoke with his customary self-confidence smiling all the time and remarkably the Colonel said nothing. If it was thought that Fitzherbert could charm birds from trees, he certainly seemed to have this old buzzard under control. It was not long after that he rose from his perch at the head of the mess, bade the assembled company a curt 'good night gentlemen' and left them to their port and cigars and to pepper the regimental fundi[1] with questions on all matters Boer into the night.

Recalling that evening made him angry at the foolishness of people who prized social status above knowledge. Sipping his beer in London eighteen years later he could still recall awakening the following day to bright sun, strong tea, courtesy of his servant and a thick head courtesy of his brother officers, He reflected on his brief time as the centre of attention. It had been highly flattering to be indulged

---

[1] *'fundi'* from Zulu - an expert or teacher

by Fitz and his cronies but he knew in his heart that such attention was transitory and he would be of no more interest at breakfast than any other young subaltern, so about as fascinating as last night's cigar butts. Nevertheless, he had gone to breakfast and aside from a baleful look and a snort from the old major over the kippers and toast all was as usual.

He had regimental duties to attend to which kept him occupied for much of the day. After dismissing his men in the afternoon, he repaired to his quarter to write a letter to his Father. The old man liked to be kept up to date with the regiment's doings and his son's adventures. The letter he would receive had some of the former, little or nothing of the latter but many descriptions of the country and gossip about the diamond mines. It was a perfectly pleasant and well written epistle but not what he had come to expect from his younger son. When he finally read it at the breakfast table in Kent, the older Brown knew something but not what was up. He didn't worry overmuch, just wondered when he would learn more.

The younger man had a torrent of ideas washing around his head like sea washing around a shore. Sometimes the waves would deposit matter of use, sometimes it was just foam but slowly something was beginning to take shape in his mind which he then began to transfer to paper in note form whenever he could. He carried a notebook with him for the purpose. Many a nervous soldier saw their officer taking a note and prayed that it did not contain their name. They need not have worried, beyond the call of immediate military necessity. They were far from his mind. eventually, plans were complete, now he needed to test their viability and to this end, he made an appointment to see the Colonel.

That worthy received the request in his office and wondered what it might portend. Brown was likeable and a good young officer but seemed to waste his time talking to local farmers some of whom were Dutchmen. He hadn't been keen on having the son of a ranker join the mess but the older Brown had enjoyed a long and successful time with the regiment and he could not deny the son. The business in the mess the other night had confirmed his worries. The old Major, Venables was his name, was a fairly useless officer who had no right to get anywhere near a battlefield but deserved more respect than Brown had shown him. It was interesting that Captain Fitzherbert seemed to like him though. Now he wanted a conversation, what could he want? Leave probably, it was too much to hope that he wished to apologise. Whatever it might be the Colonel would be prepared.

The knock came, entrance was invited and in came the tanned young officer looking fit and confident but not a bit contrite. The Colonel concealed his disappointment and invited his junior officer to take a seat and explain himself. When it came, he found himself less prepared than he expected. He had been right about the leave element but not in the way he anticipated. He had expected a request for a few days in Ladysmith or Dundee but this young man wanted a leave of absence from the regiment to explore Africa if you please. He considered for a moment and a dimly remembered piece of the classics came back to him: *Tempora mutantur, nos et mutamur in illis*. Times change and we are changed with them. He had accepted the army reforms including the abolition of the purchase of commission, calmly if not enthusiastically. he feared the rise of some sort of meritocracy and young Brown here seemed to be an example of why his concern was justified. On the other hand he reflected, the peace seemed likely to hold so Brown wouldn't be missed and if he was going to give any further lectures it would be preferable for them not to take place in his mess. He would make it uncomfortable though.

'If you take a leave of absence, it will be unpaid, you do appreciate that and you will have to see to your own transport home?'

'Yes sir, I had assumed that.'

'Very well, I have no objections. Do you have a date in mind?'

'As soon as possible sir, if that's acceptable?'

'Perfectly but please discuss with the adjutant who will define 'as soon as possible' to you, oh and good luck I suppose.'

As the young man departed, he thought of his own young days in India. He had taken local leave but to hunt tigers or go pig sticking, not to gossip with local farmers. Shaking his head, he wondered if at the end of this foolishness Brown might transfer to a more suitable organisation, map making or intelligence perhaps, where his brand of inquisitiveness might be better thought of. Platoon commanders that knew who Paul Kruger's antecedents were, were a nuisance he could do without.

What his young subaltern was thinking he wouldn't have considered but had he troubled to enter the office of the adjutant, who happened to be Captain Fitzherbert, he would have heard all of Brown's plans, at least as regards travel, laid bare.

'So that's my thought Fitz. I'll ride up through the passes and then swing West across the Orange Free State to Bloemfontein and then just as far as the diggings at Kimberley.'

Fitz had been listening with his usual half smile but his eyes widened just slightly at the mention of the diggings.

'You're not thinking of trying your luck as a prospector surely?'

It was Brown's turn to react and he coloured slightly before brushing the notion aside.

'I'm sure that all the opportunities are played out, I just wanted to see it for myself, out of curiosity. I don't think I'm cut out to be a miner.' Nevertheless, Fitzherbert had touched a nerve and he knew it but made no further comment but asked Brown if he would then head down to the Cape and home.

'I rather thought I would make the most of the trip and turn North then East to follow the Vaal river for a time then ride towards Pretoria, Portuguese territory and then home via Delagoa Bay.'

Fitz gazed at him in silence just a little more intently than was quite canny and then the lazy smile returned and he dusted invisible specks of dirt from his immaculate uniform while saying:

'We'll miss you, you know, particularly the cricket team.' Brown was about to say something self-deprecatory, both men knew he was an average cricketer at best but kept his counsel. Fitz filled the pause by making envious noises but also enjoining Brown to make notes of his journey.

'The army got you here Billy, the least you can do is take notes in case we have to fight these fellows again.'

Brown gave suitable assurances that he knew to be untrue or at least unlikely to be fulfilled and the two shook hands and parted.

Two days later, just before dawn, he returned the salute of the sentry and rode out of camp for the last time. He was reasonably certain that whatever he may have told Fitz, he would not be re-joining the regiment. He had been truthful in saying he didn't think he was cut out for mining but he had other plans that did involve the diggings. He would certainly be adding to the notes in his book but it was unlikely to be anything of any military value. Looking back, he regretted being disingenuous with Fitz, who was a good soldier and had stood up for him. The Colonel, on the other hand he couldn't have cared less about. On that happy memory he turned to Joe for another drink but before he could order he was startled by a stranger seating himself at his table. He was well dressed, handsome and confident with a lazy smile.

Brown was about to protest at having his military memories intruded upon by some smooth looking stranger but there was something in the manner of the man that rang faint memories. Before he could pinpoint the recollection, his new companion spoke and with the slightest of Ulster brogues enquired:

'Now Billy, what about a drink for an old comrade? Jamesons I think.'

Brown's Ride 1881

CHAPTER TWO

A surprise meeting

A watching policeman in the tavern would have seen a well-dressed man seemingly lost in thought as he enjoyed a lunchtime drink. His clothes and bearing made him look a little out of place in such an establishment but our policeman might have been forgiven for thinking that the Jamaica's clientele was moving upmarket as a second elegantly dressed man of military bearing appeared and sat at the first man's table. He might have felt surprise at the reaction to the new arrival which seemed to be of astonished shock. Had he strained his ears a little, he might have detected a brief blasphemy and the name 'Fitz' uttered by the first man.

The unexpected translation of Captain Fitzherbert from his memories of South Africa to the Major Fitzherbert invading his present had indeed surprised Brown. While he was not displeased at the reunion, it unsettled him, as Fitzherbert had intended, for in his experience the unsettled had a tendency to say more than was cautious. Fitz was the same old smooth, confident charmer, deflecting Brown's enquiries as to what he was doing now and focusing all his attention on Brown's post military story as if it was the most fascinating tale he had ever heard. Physically, time had been kind to him, he was fit looking with no hint of grey in hair or moustache and Brown self-consciously looked past Fitz at his own reflection in a mirror for reassurance as to his own appearance. He was not ashamed of what he saw but it didn't relax him. Never comfortable talking about himself, he was also a little embarrassed at the recollection of the story he had spun back in Natal and he wasn't enthusiastic about telling that or his recent life history. Fitz was a hard man to refuse however. People naturally liked him and wanted to be liked by him. Brown was no exception and before he realised what was happening, his story spilled out. He waffled around the issue of his intention of leaving the army but Fitz showed little or no interest in that detail anyway.

It was close enough to what he had suggested was his plan all those years ago. True, he had failed to mention that he intended to leave the army all along and go into business but geographically it was as he had told Fitz it would be. He had travelled to Kimberley via Van Reenan's pass and Bloemfontein. There he had realised that his chances of striking it rich as a prospector were minimal, however, he also noted the vast amount of equipment and supplies that the diggings consumed each day and the few existing sources of supply. Armed with that information and a notebook full of names and addresses he turned himself around and followed the Orange River North East and then crossed into the Transvaal and thence to Delagoa Bay, pausing in Pretoria on the way. Fitz mostly let him talk, occasionally prodding for more details on points that interested him, particularly concerning the geography and conversations with the folk he had met along his journey.

As he talked, Brown began to wonder what this was all about. There was no chance that Fitz just happened to stroll into a pub near the Bank of

England and encounter an old brother officer, no question. He had come looking for Brown and had found him but why? Each time he attempted to find out what Fitz was doing with himself; he was elegantly rebuffed and found himself back in Africa talking about himself and how he and his brother had started their business exporting to the diggers of South Africa. How lucky they were in their timing by establishing their initial links and supply chain to the Cape just as gold was discovered in the Transvaal. Despite his usual reticence, he couldn't resist mentioning his acquaintance with the Bantjes family on whose farm he had stayed and where the gold rush was to start in 1884. In those days, the city of Johannesburg was just open veld. He had ridden right across it on his way to Pretoria bearing a letter of introduction from Bantjes the farmer to his Father, a member of the Transvaal government.

This piece of information interested Fitz greatly and he pressed Brown for more details of his conversations. Had he met any other members of the government? He enquired, Kruger even? No said Brown although he had seen Kruger from a distance, sitting on his stoep, drinking coffee and dispensing wisdom to his countrymen as they sought him out.

'That's remarkable Billy, it really is. So you came back to Britain, sent in your papers and began this business empire with your brother trading to South Africa?'

Well, thought Brown, I suppose you could look at it that way. It sounded so simple and while it was as good a summary of what had happened as any, it ignored the sleepless nights, worry over suppliers and shippers and all the other myriad concerns that any fledgling business might have. It had been successful however and had made the two brothers relatively wealthy. Now the current war had slowed business to a trickle and brought back all the memories of worrying over where the next deal was coming from. Maybe that explained Fitz's presence, if he was still in the army, perhaps he was seeking suppliers who could help the army's huge appetite for gear of all descriptions. As the thought crossed his mind his spirits rose and emboldened, he asked Fitz directly:

'Are you still in the army?'

'I am indeed.'

'Well then, you must be at least a half Colonel by now. Have they given you a command? Are you going to the Cape?'

The smile grew a little wider:

'I'm just a humble Major Billy working in Whitehall for now but who knows what the future holds?'

Whitehall, thought Brown and despite his knowledge of the man, wondered if he might be something to do with procurement and was looking to Brown to augment the army's supplies. His spirits lifted at the thought and mentally he began preparing a general sales pitch as he pressed Fitz for information.

'Here is some distance from Whitehall Fitz, what brings you to the City?'

'Well, I was looking for you actually.'

'And how did you know where to find me for heaven's sake?'

'We have our sources and ways and you weren't that hard to track down. I recollect that you were a man of habit and routine.

'My boss and I were talking about you a few days ago, and he would like to meet you. I have told him that I think you may be the right man to help us with a logistical problem we have been having. I just wanted to run you to earth first in order to sound you out.'

At any other time, alarm bells would have been ringing in Brown's head at the phrase 'we have our sources and our ways.' Today, his mind was more concerned with the likely improvement in profits that an army contract might bring. They had agents out across the world just to find the tens of thousands of horses needed for the campaign and the sudden influx of yeomanry would create a need for all manner of materiel. Brown was doing his best to remain calm and objective but his mind had begun to run with the possibilities and how to negotiate any potential obstacles. For now he expressed his happiness to give any help that he could and asked when he should plan on a meeting with Fitz's superior.

Fitz expressed his pleasure at the response and after a few more questions he stood and shook hands with his old friend and left the Jamaica to return to Whitehall. Before he left, he assured Brown that 'they' - the War Office? The Army? - would be in touch. Beyond that he would disclose nothing of substance. He left Brown happier than he had been for some days, albeit with a bill for three whiskies. Brown grinned at that and reflected that some things never changed, Fitz had never been noted for his generosity, despite his apparent wealth. Ah well, thought Brown, the cost of doing business. He treated himself to another beer and planned how he would announce this company saving coup to his brother. An observer outside the Jamaica might have remarked on the different departures of the two unusual customers. Major Peter Fitzherbert hailed a passing hansom cab and after he had settled in and the driver had whipped up, he pulled a slim, leather-bound notebook from his pocket into which he made some entries with an expensive looking pen. By contrast, his former companion made his way on foot, possibly a little unsteadily, back to an office building in Leadenhall Street.

Brown Brothers' office was in a nondescript building fairly typical of the area. It was not a huge office because it was not a huge firm. The two active directors, the brothers, each had pleasant offices full of dark wood and leather furniture. In turn, each had a secretary outside and beyond them stretched the main office where the clerks and typists worked. At busy times, the typewriters clattered with a furious noise. Today, when Brown returned, there was only sporadic typing and the rustling of paper. His secretary Beatrice, known only as 'Miss B' relieved him of hat and coat and then entered his office to update him on any significant matters that required his attention. She was a middle-aged spinster, in some ways quite formidable, particularly in her concern for William Brown. Few knew her real name within the company and she had little interest in the world beyond her work. In her eyes, her primary purpose in life was to keep her employer free of unwanted intrusion and to protect him from all unnecessary distraction. That she was infatuated with him was obvious to all of her colleagues except of course Brown, to the general but guarded amusement of the rest of the staff.

Thanking Miss B for her assistance he sought out his brother in his own, almost identical office and told his story. His brother and co-director listened attentively and posed a few questions about the reappearance of Fitz and his failure to identify what army department he worked for or even the identity of his boss. His enthusiasm slightly dampened by his brother's questions, the younger man agreed that they couldn't count on anything and must contain their enthusiasm until it became clear exactly what the army's interest might be, nevertheless, they agreed it could be a hopeful sign.

Time hung heavy on the Browns as orders slowed and it became harder to keep the staff happy and interested. One morning not many days after his encounter in the Jamaica, Brown was in his office fretting over the company's diminishing reserves at the bank and wondering if a business saving summons was yet to come from Fitz. Deciding that he had to carry on with business as it was rather than as he wished it could be, he resolved to pursue some of the cold leads that they had received from places other than South Africa. he recalled in particular, an old school friend who worked for a company involved in Indian coal mining. Resolving to issue a luncheon invitation, he opened his office door to give instruction to Miss B and was surprised to find her in conversation with a very large man clutching a bowler hat in an outsize paw. His demeanour did not encourage argument neither did the broken nose above the iron grey moustache or the scar tissue over one eye. Nevertheless, when confronted by Miss B, he found himself dealing with an opponent as implacable as he was. Despite the lady's steely eyed rebuffs, he remained both polite and patient but firm in his demand to see Mr. William Brown.

'I'm Brown, what can I do for you?'

'I'm sorry Mr. William, he says he has a message and he refuses to leave it with me.' Miss B seemed outraged at the man's intransigence but before she could go on, he spoke in a surprisingly gentle voice with a touch of Ulster about it. No question thought Brown, we Paddies get everywhere.

'My apologies sir but my orders are very clear. My message must be delivered in person and in private.' This last said with a look towards Miss B who simply sniffed although as she did so, she seemed to relax slightly. Such office noise as there had been had ceased altogether as the employees watched events play out.

'Very well Mr. er?'

'Wheatley sir'

'Very well Wheatley, you'd better come in.'

Wheatley entered after Brown and politely declined the offer of a chair. Brown ran an eye over him and decided that while he looked like a plain clothes policeman, ill fitting suit and brown shoes, he might also have been military at some time in the past. Despite that thought, he did not immediately connect the fellow with the summons he had been awaiting but rather wondered what on earth the staff were thinking about him entertaining such an intimidating guest.

'I have come from Sir John Ardagh sir'

Brown looked quizzical but was inwardly impressed and excited, emotions he strove to conceal. 'Ah, I'm sorry but that name is not familiar to me.'

Raising an eyebrow involuntarily, his visitor went on:

'The meeting you had with Major Fitzherbert sir?'

'So Sir John is?'

'The head of our department.'

'Which is?'

'I think it best that Sir John explain to you sir.'

'Very well then, you had better deliver your message.'

'Sir John presents his compliments and asks if you could meet with him the War Office next Monday morning at ten.' he didn't say 'sharp' but it was implied. Brown made a show of consulting his diary but as both men could see, the entries were sparse.

'Monday at ten you say? I will be there with pleasure. Is there any additional information you might have for me. The subject matter of the meeting for example?'

'I'm sorry sir, so I am but I was told nothing beyond time and place. Oh and to ask you to keep this confidential.'

It was Brown's turn to raise an eyebrow but while curious, he gave the only possible answer:

'Very well Mr. Wheatley kindly convey my compliments and acceptance to Sir John and I will see him on Monday at ten.'

He rose to show the fellow out but he had turned on his heel and was out of the door before Brown could round his desk. Without being asked, he had closed the door behind him which allowed Brown to sink back into his chair and wonder what it all meant. Today being a Friday, there was not long to speculate and frankly it was rather pointless anyway. He decided that he would have a conversation with his brother and perhaps take an early train down to his place in Kent.

Sitting quietly in his office, the room seemed a safe and comfortable place. One that he had no desire to leave. Even in winter it was warm and it was quiet. He knew that beyond the door his staff were gossiping about what the messenger's visit might portend. Sometimes he wished civilian life could be more like the Army. He could yell at soldiers to be silent but civilians were more sensitive, or so he was told. He couldn't blame people for speculating, if the outer office were curious, it was nothing to the nervous anxiety he was experiencing. When he finally decided to leave his refuge, he was happy to find few of his staff even looked up. Miss B, like any good NCO had silenced whispers and giggles and restored order. All in the office were calm except him but he knew better than to show it. He might not have had the temperament to conceal emotion easily but the Army had taught him to exude calm confidence in front of the troops.

Thanking Miss B for her earlier assistance, he requested she place a copy of 'Who's Who' on his desk. She looked at him expectantly but he just thanked her again and knocked on the door of his brother's office and entered. Leaving Miss B to carry out her tasks and speculate as to what seemed to be affecting her employer. As she retrieved the requested volume and placed it on his desk, she wondered if this was some family matter but could not square that with the request for 'Who's Who.' The big fellow with his mysterious message had disturbed her a little but he had been courteous enough and she was secretly a little excited at the air of intrigue he had exuded, just so long as Mr William was alright.

Mr. William at that moment was discussing the visit with his brother Bob or Mr. Robert as the staff knew him. Both agreed that the army were moving uncharacteristically quickly and that the request for confidentiality was odd but they could wait until the Monday meeting to establish what was wanted from them. In the meantime the younger Brown would do a little research on Sir John Ardagh to see who they would be dealing with and maybe to gain a hint of what he might want. 'Who's Who' not being the sort of easy volume to read on the train, he elected to do his research prior to his departure for London Bridge station, and the journey home.

He would have been better off waiting for his Monday meeting for what he found didn't seem to indicate any reason for the famed Sir John to have a reason to call on William Brown. Major General Sir John Ardagh KCIE CB was an Irishman as was Brown and like him had attended the Woolwich academy. At this point, any similarities in their career paths came to an end. Sir John had enjoyed an outstanding military career, rising to the rank of Major General before he was 60. He had begun his career as an engineer and had constructed fortifications in England and in North America. He saw extended and distinguished service in Egypt and the Sudan and had been secretary to the Viceroy of India until returning to England to head the school of military engineering in Chatham. None of this seemed to have much relevance to Brown's commercial activities and neither did his current post as head of military intelligence[2].

Intelligence, Brown pondered the possible implications. Certainly, not a department he would normally connect with the purchase of equipment and supplies but the army moved in mysterious ways. He put the thought on hold as he prepared to leave the office for a weekend in the country. Taking his leave of Miss B and buttoned against the cold damp air, he made his way through the increasing crowds

[2] Sir John Ardagh (1840 - 1907) had a distinguished career, including attachment to the intelligence branch of the War Office. In addition to the experience mentioned by Brown, He saw extensive service in Turkey as well as the Sudan and Egypt and in 1895 was commandant of the School of Military Engineering. As tensions in South Africa rose, he became Director of Military Intelligence in 1896 producing a detailed review of Boer forces and resources prior to the outbreak of war. He was unfairly blamed for providing poor intelligence but his name was cleared by a royal commission after the war.

towards London Bridge. Crossing the brown river where the barges and accompanying tugs fussed and the clusters of masts were visible to the east through the square frame of the new Tower Bridge. He allowed himself a moment of patriotic pride as he contemplated the new triumph of British engineering set alongside the ancient Tower of London. A thousand years of British civilisation he thought, conveniently forgetting the influence of the Normans and others. It was however, illustrative of the power of Great Britain, the busiest port, the oldest castle, the most astonishing feat of civil engineering in the world. As he paused to peer through the drizzle and the smoke he wondered what on earth the Boers had been thinking of by picking a fight with Britain. Kruger had been to Britain; he had seen all of these wonders surely he would wish to be a part of this great empire of learning and commerce? Then he thought back to his encounters with friendly Boers and remembered their expressed desire to be left alone. Resuming his walk he mused on what odd and contradictory people they were. They couldn't do their own mining much less build anything like Tower Bridge, on the other hand, doubtless they would say that they had no need of mines or drawbridges but just wanted to till their farms in peace. Not that that had prevented them from heavily taxing the miners and using the proceeds to fund weapons purchases for the current war. On that thought he arrived at the station and his mind turned from world affairs and history to the practicalities of ticket purchase and the location of platforms and trains.

Once seated in the first-class section of the train, he again mused on the Boer mind and their almost primitive old testament view of the world. He recalled Fitz's interest in his conversations with Bantjes and others and decided with a sudden pang of disappointment that this was almost certainly the source of interest for Sir John, his supposed knowledge of the Boers. He could be wrong he thought but if Sir John was head of intelligence, he was most likely interested in acquiring information, not purchasing supplies. Looking on the bright side, he reflected that if he made a suitably helpful impression, maybe there could be an introduction to the procurement side and he might yet turn the situation to one that might profit the firm and of course, aid the war effort.

He anticipated a pleasant weekend among family and friends and an opportunity to forge the travails of the business. He dined with his parents on the Friday night and all was well but by Saturday morning he had begun to feel an unspecified anxiety. He had taken the position that his meeting with Sir John would probably be a waste of his time but was of no great significance. At the back of his mind however was the question of why the head of intelligence would want to meet with him. It went back to Fitz of course but he was pretty level-headed and unlikely to exaggerate what knowledge he might possess. Ah well, it would all become clear on Monday and he told himself he really had no cause for concern.

After a pleasant Sunday lunch with friends, he reflected on his previous experience with senior officers in particular and authority in general. This had not been without difficulty during his brief years of service but since leaving the Army matters had, if anything, gone downhill. He wasn't unnecessarily rude or difficult but he didn't take easily to authority figures, whether they were ticket inspectors on the railway or the directors of companies wanting him to do their bidding. Sir John Ardagh, however, was on a very different level and he sensed he would have to be careful. Of what, he wasn't entirely certain but the uncertainty did nothing to improve his anxiety. In the end, he indulged himself on Sunday night by taking solace in more ale than was good for him in the village pub. The following morning saw him on the early train to London with a slight headache and a mounting resentment towards all authority and Sir John Ardagh in particular.

He went first to his own office, where the indefatigable Miss B fussed over him, bringing him the morning's post and tea. The tea partially improved his headache and the post, most of it bills and notices of orders cancelled due to the war, made it worse. Eventually, the time came and in a mixture of anticipation and anxiety he took a hackney carriage across London to the War Office. The capital was cold and wet and the smell and taste of coal smoke was everywhere as the city tried to keep warm. Brown barely noticed the sulphur in the air as he tried to calm his anxiety by looking at the passing scenery. The cab trotted by the Jamaica and he found himself wishing he had followed his Mother's advice and stayed out of pubs. Too late now as suddenly they were in the Strand then Trafalgar Square and then he was paying off the cab and entering the War Office.

Once inside, he had to compete with various other men in and out of uniform who were navigating the chaos of the reception area. Pushing his way to the desk of the commissionaire he stated his business and was asked to wait. The commissionaire was a fifty something old soldier with a patch over one eye and a row of medal ribbons on his jacket. he should have been harassed at all the activity but fielded all enquiries in a calm, world weary manner, occasionally tinged with some sardonic humour. He was assisted by a younger man who limped badly and had his own, smaller number of decorations. In the best traditions of the Army, the more mobile man sat at a desk and the man with the limp delivered his messages. Brown watched in wonder as the fellow went off, to announce his arrival.

After a surprisingly brief interlude, the messenger returned accompanied by a male secretary who took charge and showed him into the great man's office. It was much as he had anticipated: a high-ceilinged room with dark panelling decorated by gloomy portraits of long dead military men. There was a heavy desk at one wall behind which sat a slim, active looking man that he took to be Ardagh. He was flanked by two men, one of whom was Fitz, who moved forward to greet him and make the introductions.

The formalities over, Ardagh rang for tea and made light conversation until this had been served and the maid departed. Brown was then asked to reprise his company's activities and history and Sir John listened attentively making the occasional note as Brown spoke. When he had finished, he looked at Sir John expecting some sort of reaction or questions but there was a silence that was uncomfortable as the great man stared at the ceiling apparently lost in thought.

'Sharp of you to recognise the potential of Lourenço Marques.'

'No sharper than many sir' Brown responded. 'The Boers were never going to be happy having to rely on British ports like Durban and the Cape and the Portuguese naturally wanted to exploit it too. Of course, what really made the difference was the gold rush in the Transvaal. I couldn't have predicted that but it was very welcome.'

Ardagh leaned back a little and clasped his hands lightly together as if in prayer and thought for a moment.

'How well do you know Lourenço Marques?'

'Well, it's been a few years since I was there but of course we have contacts there and use the facilities for trans-shipping cargo to the goldfields, or at least we used to until the war. Good, natural anchorage with plenty of deep-water space. One steel and stone jetty capable of accepting ships, which is the property of the South African railway company, four steam cranes and everything else trans-shipped by lighter. Port officials are all corrupt of course but as long as you don't mind that, they are fairly compliant and helpful and they don't generally ask for an unreasonable level of bribe. At least, that's generally been my company's experience.'

'I see' said Ardagh not looking particularly concerned at Brown's admission of having bribed Portuguese government officials. 'And the railway to Johannesburg?'

'Opened 1895, well built with South African tax money mostly taken from our miners in the Transvaal. Designed by European engineers aided by a huge black labour force. Goes all the way from Johannesburg to the docks at LM. I haven't seen it but understand there is now a particularly fine stone and steel bridge at the border town of Komatipoort, which crosses the river there. Last time I was out that way you had to ford the river as best you could while dodging the crocodiles and hippos in the water.'

Brown was happier answering specific questions particularly on a subject which he knew well. He noticed an exchange of glances between Ardagh and the others when he volunteered his information regarding the Komatipoort railway bridge and wondered what it might signify but he held his tongue and waited for further questions. The wait was brief: did he maintain contacts among the Portuguese port officials? had he wider commercial contacts in Lourenço Marques? Finally, he had Boer friends, so did he have any doubts about Britain's position in the war? This final question surprised him and he simply observed that. British territory had been invaded and in his view every country had a right to defend itself and an obligation to defend its citizens. This brought a first intervention from Fitz who asked in light of his answer, how would he feel if Britain invaded the Boer Republics.

'My view would be that firstly they brought it on themselves, secondly, we are the dominant power in the region and lastly, in the case of the Transvaal, the majority of the inhabitants are British subjects.' It was a reasonable answer and certainly reflected the government's views of the conflict.

Judging from the smiles that followed his response, it also reflected the views of his audience, but after all this chatter, he was no clearer about the reasons for his presence in the centre of British military might. Uncharacteristically, he decided to be blunt and asked Ardagh just how he could be of assistance to the war effort. [3]

Ardagh resumed his not quite at prayer position before responding:

[3] It was an oddity of the period that the foreign-born population of the Transvaal referred to by the Boers as *Uitlanders* were probably double that of the Dutch and were nearly all British. Fear of being overwhelmed led to the Boers denying the right of citizenship to the uitlanders while heavily taxing them. Outrage on behalf of the British miners and their families was seen as a justification for subsequent hostilities in Britain.

'You are familiar with the current war situation?'

'Ladysmith, Mafeking and Kimberley all under siege, relief efforts in trouble but presumably the Boers will have to disperse eventually once we have had a chance to build up strength and concentrate our forces.'

'it's a fair summary and we have to hope that the outcome will be as you suggest.' Was that a suggestion of doubt? Thought Brown. Senior officers did not admit to even the possibility of an adverse outcome for British arms. Was Ardagh different or was he being admitted to a more serious council where facts were weighed carefully rather than being brushed aside by unrealistic patriotism. Busy with that thought, he realised that Ardagh was continuing:

'Typically with citizen armies like the Boers, they have limited ability where supply lines and logistics are concerned. We would naturally move to strangle their sources of supply wherever we can but we have two issues to overcome here. Firstly, the Boers made good use of the taxes levied from the Johannesburg miners. Prior to the outbreak of war they imported significant quantities of arms and ammunition from Germany and France and these are being used against our forces currently. Most of what they now have ironically came via our ports but of course these are now closed to them.'

Brown nodded as Ardagh went on: 'Secondly, they are able to use the rail link with Delagoa Bay port and railway to bring in supplies of all sorts - munitions, boots, bully beef indeed supplies of every sort. Also foreign mercenaries wishing to fight with them and against us.' He paused reflectively, 'I sometimes feel that antagonism towards Great Britain is a greater motivator than sympathy for the Boers.'

'Where do these volunteers come from?'

'Holland naturally and Germany but also Scandinavia, Russia and regrettably even from Ireland.'

'I can see the appeal if you're a Fenian Irishman but what have we done to upset the rest of them?'

'We are the most powerful country in the world, possessed of the greatest empire in history and they are envious and would like to see us humbled.'

While Brown could see a kernel of truth in this it seemed like a rather flip and even rehearsed response. Now was not the time and the War Office not the place for a discussion on Britain's place in world affairs however so Ardagh resumed his observations on the war situation.

'Having a neutral port as near to Pretoria as is Lourenco Marques with a good rail link means that the Boers have internal supply lines that we cannot control. While there is no doubt that our forces will be victorious, victory will come much more quickly and with the loss of far fewer British lives if we could cut off their access to supplies from overseas.'

'Well, the world's most powerful country and empire also has the world's largest navy, why not just blockade the port?'

Fitz intervened with a smile: 'You cannot blockade a neutral port without risking war. As I am sure you know, Portugal is our oldest ally and has been since Charles I married Catherine of Braganza in 1661. Breaking a two-hundred-and-fifty-year alliance might raise some eyebrows don't you think? We are quite unpopular enough in Europe over this war as it is. Only last week our Ambassador in Germany was carpeted over our stopping and searching some of their ships. The situation wasn't improved when we found nothing untoward on board. We know that the Boers are using German rifles and ammunition and much of their artillery comes from Krupp so stopping and searching was a reasonable thing to do but the cabbage heads don't see it that way and the Dutch and French are faking outrage about our stopping neutral shipping.'

Ardagh shifted uncomfortably as he listened to Fitz's light-hearted history lesson and frowned,

'A naval blockade would be logical but as Major Fitzherbert indicates, the diplomatic situation and relations with the European powers make this too delicate so we have to seek alternative means of disrupting the Boer supply lines. We have a very active consular staff in Lourenço Marques who have done their best to disrupt Boer shipments using a variety of methods but unfortunately they have only a limited knowledge of international trade and are hampered by the activities of Boer agents and some rogue Britons prepared to sell out their country for thirty pieces of silver.'

Brown was interested in the conversation and could quite believe that there were plenty of unscrupulous people looking to make money from the war, even at the expense of their own countrymen. He'd encountered them in the course of business over the years and was fairly certain that there were companies a few miles East in the City who were using European front companies to organise very profitable transfers of all manner of goods to the South African Republics. Times may have been hard for his company but that wasn't a game they would attempt. It should be noted that the restraint being exercised wasn't simple patriotism but patriotism reinforced by the certain ruin that would follow if discovered. Ruin that would be not merely professional but social too.

All things considered, had his curiosity not been temporarily dulled by his interest in the subject matter, Brown might have phrased his question differently or just kept quiet altogether. However, he asked what he was thinking:

'What you tell me doesn't surprise me but what are you going to do about it?'

Again, he caught just the flicker of a look between Ardagh and his two companions and then Fitz was supplying an answer. 'We have had some success in chartering all the lighters so that cargo cannot be easily landed and we have also occasionally outbid the competition for the stuff that does get ashore but we need more reliable information from the waterfront. The local officials occasionally can be bribed into offering tidbits but, of course, they play both sides and can't be absolutely relied upon. We need a permanent presence that can be aware of contraband coming in destined for Pretoria. A man that has some local knowledge, understands the workings of the port and the railway and can establish his own network of informants.'

'You mean a spy?'

'That's exactly what I mean Billy.'

Brown heard the words and caught the implication but dismissed the idea that he was being recruited as a spy as absurd. He had no training in such work beyond the subtleties of business life that occasionally required you to be someone you weren't or to like someone you didn't. He did have the requisite local knowledge and some contacts but so presumably did the staff at the consulate. The idea of him going to LM to play cloak and dagger games on the waterfront was patently ridiculous, they could only be looking for some exterior advice on the escapade but then Sir John looked directly at him and began to speak.

'You're clearly a man with drive and initiative as we've seen from your commercial success. You know Southern Africa and the difficulties of moving cargo from port of entry to destination. Furthermore' and he looked at Fitz while speaking, 'Major Fitzherbert attests to your officer like qualities and your ability to absorb and hold facts and detail. Most importantly, you are known as a trader, you have contacts and are unlikely to be doubted as being exactly what you are, a British trader doing his job.'

Brown felt rather as a man might who was walking along a scree strewn ridge when the scree began to slide under his feet. Suddenly control was not so much slipping away from him as sprinting. He kept his wits about him and his mouth shut allowing Sir John to lay out his many sterling qualities and appeal to his patriotism and sense of right and wrong, all of which happened as if he was being subjected to a sales pitch, which of course he was. Sir John concluded his peroration by asking Brown if, in principle, he could offer assistance subject to all details being addressed to his satisfaction.

There was silence as Brown considered his answer. His experience of the business world told him that 'in principle' agreements opened the door to all manner of departures from the original pitch because, as the lawyers might say: the devil is in the detail. Sir John Ardagh did not look particularly saturnine and Fitz was seemingly as jovial a fellow as you might find but Brown was in no doubt that a commitment on his part would be open ended. He was also aware that he could be socially and financially ruined by a refusal. Nobody would say anything of course. Gentlemen didn't threaten one another but centre of the world's mightiest empire or not, London could be a very small town and gossip moved swiftly increasing in size and malice with each exchange. Word would somehow slip out that he had refused to help his country in time of need, he would be shunned by friends and customers as would his brother and the company. By the time the story had done the rounds, he would be suspected of the crime that he was being recruited to stop, trading with the enemy.

Certain that there were no options, he did his best to nail down Fitz and Ardagh to the exact scope and length of the task. Their plan, which he was reasonably certain was Fitz's baby, was for him to travel to Lourenço Marques where he would meet with the consular staff responsible for intelligence operations and then assume the role of rogue British trader prepared to deal with the highest bidder irrespective of allegiance. This would hopefully enable him to identify Boer agents operating on the docks and enable any contraband shipments to be intercepted in one way or another. When he protested gently that he had no background or training in such work Fitz demurred:

'But you have Billy all you have to do is be yourself and go after the deals, making mental notes as you go along of people and places for the benefit of Captain Crowe and his people. Crowe's our consul in LM but also oversees the intelligence gathering effort from there. You just have to forget that you have scruples about who you do business with. You won't be alone; we'll have people watching for you in case that was bothering you.'

It had been bothering him quite a lot as he thought about the consequences of being unmasked. Not unreasonably, he had no desire to finish his days face down in an African harbour, which he surmised might be his fate if the Boers got hold of him. While contemplating that happy thought, he saw Fitz whisper something to the other officer in the room who nodded assent and slipped out of a side door.

'Sir John, would you be prepared to give me a letter explaining that I am an agent of Her Majesty's Government acting on instructions from London?'

'Whatever for?' Asked Ardagh.

'Because if anything were to become known about this, there would be no shortage of business competitors to insinuate that I am a traitor.'

'But you couldn't carry that with you.'

'Indeed no but I could lodge it in my brother's safe for use in the event of my demise and any subsequent adverse commentary.'

'It would be most unusual.'

'And so is what you are asking me to do.' Brown was firm and while he registered the offence on Ardagh's face, he knew it was the right thing to do. He loved his country but he was alive to the ease with which governments, even British governments, could use their citizens and then conveniently forget them if matters went wrong. Only four years ago, Jameson had been disowned and imprisoned by Britain. Would that have happened had he succeeded? [4]

---

[4] Doctor Leander Starr Jameson was a British born doctor and surgeon who moved to South Africa for health reasons, establishing a medical practice in Kimberley where he became close friends with Cecil Rhodes. By all accounts a remarkable man in many ways, he is generally remembered for the 1895 attempt to incite a revolt by the Transvaal miners. Jameson led 500 armed men hoping to spark open revolt among the foreign (Uitlander) residents of the Transvaal, thus providing an excuse for Britain to annex the Transvaal Republic. Both London and Pretoria knew of the plan and it ended in farce and Jameson's

Ardagh made a show of reluctance but realising that he now had effectively secured agreement from Brown to carry out the job, he acquiesced and told Brown that an appropriate letter would be drafted. Before any details could be offered, the office door opened and a large, vaguely familiar looking man was ushered in by the officer who had left minutes before.

'Now Billy' said Fitz 'you'll remember William here?' Brown's face was blank until realisation dawned. Here was the messenger that had delivered Ardagh's invitation looking no less imposing than when he had been trading points with Miss B in the office. Brown rose and proffered a hand which was taken firmly but not with the bone crushing grip one might have anticipated.

'Yes indeed Wheatley, how are you?'

'I'm well sir thank you.'

'Now that you've agreed to assist Billy, you'll be glad to know that Wheatley here will be going with you.'

Try as he might, Brown could not recollect giving actual agreement to join what looked like a highly dangerous venture but if he was going, Fitz was right, he would be glad to have someone like Wheatley alongside him. He knew there was little point in arguing now and so he kept fairly quiet, bar the odd question, as Fitz began to fill in some of the missing

arrest. Tried in Britain under the Foreign Enlistment Act he was found guilty and sentenced to fifteen months in prison. Brown obviously suspected that the UK government was far from innocent in all of this but were quite happy to see Jameson take the blame. Suspicions born out by subsequent history. After his release from jail, he returned to South Africa becoming Prime Minister of Cape Colony in 1904 and a Privy Counsellor in 1907.

63

details. He would be travelling and paid as a Major in the Ordnance, Wheatley as a Sergeant. In that guise, they would be unremarkable among all the other troops travelling to the Cape. Asking Wheatley about his prior service, he was glad to learn that his future companion had seen service in the Zulu war of 1879 as a cavalry sergeant. After that war, bored with garrison duties in India, he had joined the Irish Constabulary and had spent some time chasing Fenian agents before being joining the Intelligence. If he had to put his head in the lion's mouth, a man like Wheatley might be able to stop the jaws closing.

Finding himself outmanoeuvred and entrapped, he tried to look at the positives. He liked the idea of being a Major even if only a wartime Major. He would be doing something that, while underhand, appealed to his sense of patriotism and despite any doubts he may have had, he was sure that he could do what was required. He wasn't absolutely certain it could be done safely but now he has Wheatley along, maybe there was nothing to worry about. Looking out of the window at the grime and the rain of London, he reflected that there might be worse things than a couple of months in Africa at the Queen's expense. Then Fitz asked him:

'Tell me Billy, have you ever had any explosives training?'

CHAPTER THREE

An explosive beginning

Whether or not Major Fitzherbert felt he had gone too far too fast was impossible to tell. His face betrayed no emotional change, indeed, he looked mildly amused at proceedings unlike everyone else in the room. The newly arrived Wheatley feigned interest in a painting behind Ardagh while he and his brother officer contrived to hide their surprise. For his part, Brown looked at Fitz blankly as if he had spoken in some oriental tongue. Finally he broke the silence.

'Explosives Fitz? As a matter of fact no but what's the relevance?'

A brief pause and exchange of glances followed before Ardagh intervened:

'My apologies Mr. Brown or should I say Major. What I am about to tell you is extremely sensitive information that had to be kept secret until we were sure of your commitment. I think it was you that made reference to the new bridge at Komatipoort carrying the railway over the river?'

'Yes, what of it?'

'As you know it is just over the Transvaal border from Portuguese territory but it is also not far from Swaziland. Crowe, the consul in Lourenço Marques, has established a network of native informants in Swaziland and the Transvaal. He also has at his disposal what I might term an irregular force operating from Northern Swaziland.'

'Isn't Swaziland a neutral Boer protectorate?'

'In theory, yes but for the most part, the natives hate the Boers and there is a sizeable British population. The Boers tried to kick them out when the war started and even tried to enlist our people into their Commandos but it's a wild place and they have limited resources. Our forces there will be few in number but laden with military experience and more importantly, excellent bush skills.'

'These troops will rely on mobility and their field craft to operate effectively; their supplies and command will come from the Consulate in Lourenço Marques but of necessity they will be lightly equipped. Their objective is to do all they are able to cut the Boer supply line from the coast. A significant part of this effort will involve the destruction of the railway bridge at Komatipoort.'

Brown could see the military logic here, although he questioned the legality. He was neither diplomat nor lawyer but it seemed to him that supplying a military unit from a consulate was hardly in keeping with diplomatic convention. That the unit in question was operating in the territory of a friendly African King also struck him as of questionable legality. However, he was not required to worry about such matters and as he had read somewhere, we have the Maxim Gun and they do not. Or to put it another way, the Swazis if offended, were not in a position to do much about it. What was of far greater import was how the antics of these bush warriors were connected with his future efforts in LM.

Ardagh had paused and was looking directly at him now as was the rest of the room.

'We will want you, in company with Sergeant Wheatley to take a quantity of explosives from LM to Von Steinaecker - that's the fellow leading the Swazi force - and then help them to blow up the Komatipoort bridge.'

Unlike Fitz, Brown was no card player and his emotions, principally surprise followed by apprehension were plain for all to see. If anyone else in the room was wondering if they had the wrong man for the job, it wasn't apparent but that didn't mean that those questions weren't crossing the minds behind the impassive faces.

'Surely the men in Swaziland can plant explosives?' It was a fair question and one Fitz was quick to answer.

'That they can stick a fuze in dynamite and light it I have no doubt. Bringing down a bridge so that it stays down is a more demanding job and requires some specialist training and that they don't have.'

'Neither do I so is Wheatley here the expert?'

Wheatley's expression never changed as Fitz brightly announced: 'you're both going to be experts after a short course at Woolwich. Now we know you're on board we will make all the necessary arrangements with the instructors there.'

'But you must have dozens of experts already in South Africa?'

'Yes we do but they're busy doing their own jobs and none of them to my knowledge, have any knowledge of Lourenço Marques and the workings of its port.' Fitz paused and looked at Brown. He was still smiling but he knew he had to be sure of his man.

'No second thoughts I hope Billy?'

Dozens thought Brown but responded as confidently as he could: 'none, just making sure I understand.'

His face told a different story but Fitz was unconcerned. As he would point out to Ardagh later, if you pluck a man from a comfortable civilian life and ask him to do something potentially deadly and certainly dangerous for his country, a degree of apprehension was to be expected. A man without questions or concerns was probably also a man without judgment. He might well get himself and those with him killed because he charged on without thinking first. Fitz knew his man and had confidence in him. He was intelligent and resourceful and would follow orders but not unthinkingly. He might be a little naive about elements of the job but he would have Wheatley there to cover him if necessary. As Fitz discussed with Ardagh later, what was of greater concern was that as yet, the commander of the Swaziland force had no troops no supplies and was nowhere near Swaziland.

All that could be managed however together with the ambitions of a local miner named Forbes who expected to be given command of a unit of horse to do the job that would be entrusted to Von Steinaecker. In theory, Forbes was well qualified for the job having been born and raised in Swaziland and successfully used his local knowledge to evade the Boer authorities. The plan for Komatipoort was originally his although given time, the staff would have got there. Forbes unfortunately had run afoul of the military establishment who dismissed him as an amateur soldier. Nevertheless, they saw the value of the bridge's destruction and resolved to attempt it using their own picked men.

Sir John Ardagh excused himself and left Fitz to wrap up the meeting. Brown would be confirmed as a Major in the Ordnance with immediate effect. He would tell none of the true nature of his job except his brother who would have to be given some details but limited to the Lourenço Marques part of the plan. As far as other family and friends were concerned, he was rejoining the colours as a patriotic Briton who wished to serve his country. Arrangements for explosives training would be made for him and Wheatley and he agreed to make himself available when the call came. A uniform and equipment would be found and after all of that, berths would be booked, probably in January, for two more gentlemen in Khaki going South.

Once he finally extracted himself from the meeting and the bowels of the War Office, Brown stepped out into the bustle of Whitehall. It was cold but he decided to walk a little to reflect on what had just happened and where it might lead. He crossed Whitehall and walked past the mounted guard onto the Horse Guards Parade. He was heading towards the relative calm of the park but as he crossed the empty parade ground, his mind became clogged with military trivialities such as the correct way to dress ranks or if drill had changed much over the last eighteen years. Deciding that these were the least of his worries, he made a plan for what exactly he was going to tell his brother. Knowing that he could count on his discretion, he decided to tell the story the way it had been told to him. The difference would be that he would leave out the part about the bridge and Swaziland altogether, rather than just slip them in at the end as had happened to him.

He walked through a section of the park enjoying the relative quiet and some slightly cleaner air as he planned his meeting with his brother and certain subsequent discussions with his parents and Elizabeth Lloyd, a young lady from his village that he had been seeing for some time. To none of them could he mention Fitz or Ardagh or their meetings, even the one in the Jamaica. The less he said, the less there was to argue about and he resolved to tell them that in the aftermath of the Black Week defeats, the army would be short of experienced officers and he had felt it was his duty to volunteer to help plug the gap. He had no doubt of his parents' support but was unsure how Elizabeth might react. He had recently entertained thoughts of a proposal but had held off for fear of rejection. He considered combining a proposal with an announcement that he would be leaving for South Africa but doubted it would help matters. Finding himself at the Embankment, he hailed a cab to return him to the City. Once inside, he continued to wrestle with the best way to handle the matter but drew no conclusions. He liked women a lot but in common with many of his contemporaries, found them incomprehensible. Possibly why he continued to enjoy a bachelor life as he approached forty.

While Brown was planning his future meetings, in a room at the War Office, Fitz and Sir John Ardagh were discussing his future. Ardagh was impressed with his insight and intelligence but wondered if he had the enthusiasm and nerve for the job. Fitz reassured him on these points, saying what he had previously thought that the failure to leap at the task was a sign of maturity and intelligence rather than an indication of a lack of courage.

'With respect Sir John, we don't need another dead hero, we need a live source of information who knows what he's looking for. If he can attend to that bridge as well, then so much the better.'

'If? You have doubts?'

'Things can go wrong sir. I have every confidence in Brown for the LM job. If anything goes wrong, well, that's unfortunate but we still have the ability to feed weapons and explosives to Von Steinaecker's gang of roughnecks. Even if they can't blow that bridge properly, their presence will distract the Boers and keep them busy. I'd hate to lose Brown, he's a good man but he wouldn't be the first good man we've lost in this war.'

'Very well Major. I will rely on your judgment. Please arrange to get the pair of them to Woolwich as soon as possible and take care of the other details we discussed. Will you be going with them?'

'To Woolwich? No but I will sail with them to LM and make the introductions to Crowe etc. I won't have time for fooling around in the bush with a half mad Prussian and some colonial cutthroats.'

'Will they be colonials?'

'Yes, Australians I fancy. Many of them already have first class field skills and can ride and shoot as well as any damn Boer. By all accounts, if kept away from liquor, they're good soldiers. Von Steinaecker is reportedly the sort of man who can deal with their type and while they're in Swaziland, they can only cause trouble for the Boers, not for our army or civilians.'

This was a detail yet to be given to Brown. He had left the meeting believing that it would be just he and Wheatley going to LM alone. Nobody had mentioned Fitz accompanying them. That officer had sold Ardagh on the idea that he would be intelligence liaison between London, LM and the army in South Africa. He would also be able to keep an eye on Brown and Wheatley to help their mission get underway safely but also with the power to cancel it if circumstances required or just if it looked as if his confidence in Brown was misplaced. His comments about 'fooling around in the bush' were disingenuous.

Major Fitzherbert was frustrated that his career so far had been marked by a lack of actual fighting. he had been cheated by the quick peace in 1881, had failed in attempts to be sent to the North West Frontier and was determined to make the most of the opportunities presented by the current war. He might be operating in civilian dress from one of Her Majesty's diplomatic establishments but he would be close to the action and who knew what might happen once he was there? Despite his comfortable background and education, Fitzherbert came from a long line of warriors. In that sense, he and Brown were similar. The difference was that Fitzherbert's antecedents' careers and identities were well documented and they had bought their commissions. Brown knew that his Father and Grandfather had been soldiers but further back than that was uncertain. What was not in doubt was that he was the first of the Browns to enter the officers' mess as of right.

Fitzherbert felt the pressure of the past upon him. He had a keen need to equal or do better than all who had gone before. The Boers had offered him a chance once that had been scuppered by a pusillanimous government. He wasn't going to let the current opportunity slip away and if that meant piggybacking onto Brown's trip to LM and perhaps into Swaziland as well, then so be it.

Ardagh left him to tie up what loose ends remained and he swiftly issued instructions to the various bodies that would be required to assist in the despatch of this strange little Imperial expedition. As he completed the last form needed to set wheels in motion, he reflected that even if he was not destined for the glory of Waterloo or the Heights of Abraham, away from the constraints of the main army, then perhaps he could distinguish himself by fighting war in a new way.

Unlike Fitz, Brown did not feel the weight of family history on his shoulders. He did, however, feel the weight of obligation to family and to employees, friends and, of course, Elizabeth. Recognising that wrestling with all of this at once would get him nowhere, he planned each conversation in turn beginning with his Brother.

On his return to the City, he sought out his brother and told him of his discussions with Fitz and Ardagh and his agreement to travel to South Africa. He explained what was expected from him in LM and that he would be commissioned into the Ordnance to give an official veneer to some of his anticipated activities. He stopped at that and waited for a response. His brother was a jovial, hardworking man with a strong wife and young children. He was dedicated to the company that he and his brother had created and however noble the cause, did not want to jeopardise all of their work. Accordingly, he first expressed concern as to the potential danger to the company's reputation should his Brother's work come to light and be misunderstood actually or maliciously. His worries were only partly mollified by the assurance of an exculpatory letter from Ardagh.

'If the stories start circulating, the damage will be done long before anyone looks at a letter.'

'If I didn't agree to go, the stories about that would be circulating next week.'

His brother looked suitably shocked but thinking the matter over, he knew the risk to their reputation was far greater if William declined to assist than any gossip that might arise from his doing so. Besides, there was the added cover of his commission to deflect any such talk. The physical risk to William was another matter but whatever his brother felt about that there was little he could do.

'Any idea of when you might be leaving?'

'I suspect quite soon but there's some details to take care of.' Like learning the most effective way to blow up a railway bridge he thought but kept it to himself as he had planned.

'We'll have to tell the staff beforehand and some of our suppliers and clients. I suppose we'd better organise a send-off party too.'

'Must we?'

'It would look odd if we didn't. What will you tell Mother and Father?'

'As far as everyone but you is concerned, I'm volunteering to help make up for those officers lost in the last battles. Because of my age and experience they won't let me go back to the infantry but to the Ordnance to assist with logistics.'

His brother nodded, it was a fairly reasonable tale, not that anyone likely to hear it would think twice anyway. They agreed that William would give as much notice as the army would allow and then turned to the more mundane affairs of Brown Brothers. Concluding their discussion, William Brown turned to leave his brother's office. As his hand touched the door handle, his brother asked:

'What will you tell Elizabeth?'

'The same as everyone else.'

'Yes, I suppose you will have to. Ever thought of marrying the poor girl?'

He paused, turned and sighed.

'Thought about it often but never seemed to find the right moment to ask.'

'You might consider looking a bit harder. She's not going to wait forever.'

The younger man sighed again: 'you may be right, let me think about it.'

'Think hard and quickly Bill, you won't be here for much longer.'

He knew the thought was meant kindly and was not intended to reference any danger that he might encounter. He hadn't really given any personal risk that much consideration himself, rather he had focused on the possible effects on his business and social standing. Now that his brother had unwittingly planted the thought, he was determined not to allow it to grow and flower. For one thing, it did no good to dwell on such possibilities, for another it was a distraction that could interfere with the job and had the potential to become a self-fulfilling prophecy. Nevertheless, it was there.

There it remained, at the back of his mind mostly but every once in awhile sneaking forward to interrupt meetings, meals and simple, quiet moments. He pushed it away by applying himself to whatever task was in hand, be it work or just reading the newspapers. What was harder to suppress was what he would say to Elizabeth. They had met years before in the village where he had grown up and her Father had taken over as the parish priest. Some years younger than he was, he had barely noticed her until they danced together at a local event some two years ago. She was tall, dark haired and in a quiet way, a beauty. As one might expect from a vicar's daughter, she was blissfully unaware of her effect on men in much the same way that Brown had failed to notice her following him about the place for years before they had danced together. She had been a young girl then of course, now she was a young woman and Brown was pleased to have her on his arm whether strolling in the park or attending her Father's church. They both anticipated a marriage but progress was slowed by their failure to communicate that idea to each other. Her Father and his parents had tried dropping hints to each of them but to no avail. Her Mother might have been able to move matters along but she had sadly died some years before, her Father was an admirable priest but was just as confused around his daughter as he was around all other women. Left to themselves, this state might have lasted for years but Fitz and Sir John Ardagh had provided an unexpected catalyst to the course of love. Faced with his imminent departure to Africa, Brown resolved to put the question when next they were together which was to be this coming weekend. It made him uncomfortable and nervous but it had to be done and would serve to keep her other admirers at bay. He decided against purchasing a ring in favour of letting her choose something for herself and the thought crossed his mind that she might not say yes.

On the Friday morning the two brothers announced to their staff that Mr. William would soon be putting on uniform once more and heading for Cape Town. There was cheering from the junior clerks made louder by the promise of a leaving party and the typists and female staff looked proud and made patriotic noises. Only Miss B appeared distracted and snapped at one of the typists that caught her dabbing at her eye with a handkerchief. William was embarrassed at the attention and declined the invitation to say a few words beyond stating that he felt it was his duty to do something. In the intervening days, he had received his invitation to attend at the great arsenal of Woolwich the following Tuesday, which gave him something to take his mind off Elizabeth and suggested that matters were now moving quickly.

This thought stayed with him as he made his excuses and left for the railway station for the train that would take him to his home in Kent. His parents had settled there when his Father had retired from the army. His father had augmented his savings by taking the post of school attendance officer and having grown up there William Brown had decided that it was as good a place as any, buying a property for his weekend use while maintaining a small flat in London for the working week. It was a small village composed mostly of farmers and those who made their living from the land. Aside from the church, there was a school and a thriving inn that had been a coaching stop on the way to London. Nowadays the coaches were pulled by steam locomotives rather than horses and a few hardy souls took the train to London each day. Not far from the county seat of Maidstone, it was as good an English village as one might wish for. Pretty in the summer, on this winter evening it was dark and just a little bleak. He walked past the cemetery and was reminded of his father's recitations of Grey's Elegy when he was a boy. Seeing the lights of the rectory nearby, he was reminded of a more difficult conversation he would have with Elizabeth tomorrow? Sunday after church? He was not by nature a procrastinator, but he wasn't sure when would be a good time. Thinking on his brother's words, he resolved to call on her the following day.

Full of resolution, he made his way to his own residence in order to leave his bags and to clean away the soot and smell of London. A brief toilet completed, he arrived at his parents for supper. His Mother fussed and his Father joshed her gently while enjoying a pipe before the drawing room fire. When his Mother returned to the kitchen, to put the last touches to dinner, he told his Father that he would be rejoining the Army. The old man was surprised and a little concerned but his life had been soldiering and so he was mostly proud. He asked some questions that were obvious and natural but which his son had not prepared for. His Father raised a bushy eyebrow at the news that his son was now a Major and looked askance when he told him he would be a part of the Ordnance.

'What? Infantry not good enough for you?'

Brown blushed and explained that there was a need for officers who understood modern logistics and his commercial knowledge would be valuable for getting supplies to where they were needed. His Father knocked his pipe out by the fireplace and refilled it while giving his son a look that suggested he found his story a little odd.

'Have they told you when you will be leaving?'

'I have to do a course at Woolwich next week but probably within the next few weeks.'

'Refresher at the academy?'

'Er, no at the arsenal.'

'What in heavens' name are you going to do there?'

'Oh well, just getting acquainted with the new rifles, packing of ammunition, that sort of thing.'

He was feeling uncomfortable now as he could see the doubts racing across his Father's face. Why hadn't he just been vague about the details as he had intended. His Father, of all the people would realise how unusual his situation was compared to the way the army normally operated. On the other hand, he could be relied upon to keep his thoughts to himself and if he had to practice a story, this was as good a place as any.

Mother asked less difficult questions but had a more difficult reaction. Why was he putting himself in harm's way? Wasn't it the turn of younger men? The sort of questions even military mothers ask of their sons, particularly ones long retired from service who are proposing to rush towards a war. His Father hushed her and they talked of other matters over the meal. When it came time for William to leave, he did so with a vague feeling of guilt at the details he had omitted from his announcement. His Mother was clearly distressed and his Father knew that he had not been given the full story. Nevertheless, they were all children of the Empire and whatever doubts and concerns any of them might have, they knew he had made a commitment to do a job and he would soon be on his way to do it.

However uncomfortable the evening had been, in some ways, it had been helpful in showing him which aspects of his story should be highlighted and which downplayed or glossed over. He rehearsed the changes in his head as he waited for sleep. He had plenty of time as sleep was very slow arriving. When he awoke, the editorialising of the previous night was fresh in his mind but seemed less convincing when exposed to daylight. He rationalised that he had only so much material to work with and there weren't too many changes possible without outright lying which he would not do, partly for moral reasons and partly because of the difficulty in maintaining a convincing pretence. Fortunately, Elizabeth knew little or nothing of military matters so she would not be prey to the same doubts as his Father. If all went well, she would be overwhelmed at the romantic proposal of her hero as he prepared to depart for the cannon's mouth. Well, that was how the heroines of the popular novels she read would react he thought, so hopefully she would follow suit. The question he had was whether to announce his departure first and then ask for her hand or to ask for her hand and then let slip the news that he would be leaving for the Cape.

In the end, events dictated the course of their conversation.

He found her at her Father's rectory, drinking tea with a young farmer from the locality by the name of White. He possessed a face as pale as his name, which was unusual even in gentlemen farmers. Brown suspected he was a lot more gentleman than farmer, unlike his father who was a ruddy faced carouser well known on various hunting fields and in local society but who took farming seriously and could be found out with his labourers at all hours and in all weathers. The son seemed to spend little time about the farm and far too much time in Elizabeth's company for Brown's liking. While the son lacked his father's obvious coarseness, he also lacked his hardiness and diligence except in the pursuit of women. He fancied himself as an elegant and learned romantic, prone to quoting poetry over the teacups like an Oscar Wilde hero. The father by contrast was pure Fielding, the boozy Squire as ever was, pinching the bottoms of the wenches in the pub while his farmer chums roared with laughter. Brown found them both highly unpleasant and his dislike was deepened by White's presence disturbing his planned moments with Elizabeth.

He was polite if indifferent to White while he waited for the man to leave. Despite increasingly pointed hints, he showed no sign of quitting the field. Brown had come on a mission of great seriousness and was becoming increasingly irritated at the triviality of the conversation and White's unspoken refusal to give way. Following a discussion about the lack of flowers in the church and the quality of this year's harvest and its likely effect on jam production, he could contain himself no longer.

He thought of Elizabeth as absolutely the best sort of Englishwoman. Cream complexion with hints of pink about the cheeks and head of light brown curls that seemed to fall effortlessly into place whatever the circumstances. A gentle personality who was kindly and attentive to all, which was probably why the odious White kept turning up at inopportune moments. As Brown looked at the innocent and sympathetic face, he came within a whisker of shirking the first of his announcements. Duty required him to proceed however, so he explained that he would be rejoining the army with the rank of Major and would almost certainly be departing to the Cape of Good Hope immediately after Christmas. He anticipated some sort of congratulation if not admiration, which would lay the ground for his second announcement, hopefully after shaming White into departure. He was surprised then that Elizabeth began to cry. Not being too sure what to do he handed her a handkerchief and patted her hand rather helplessly. Although he was doing his best to ignore White's presence, he was secretly pleased that White appeared put out by her distress.

The awkward silence that was unbroken save for Elizabeth's sniffling was broken by White saying what he thought was appropriate:

'Gad I envy you, I wish I could go myself'

'What's stopping you?' Responded Brown, perhaps a little too curtly.

'Ah well, you know there's the farm' he said vaguely 'and Father's none too well.'

This was not Brown's recollection of the Father who had looked in rude health chasing women and foxes about the place with the enthusiasm of a much younger man. Naturally, Brown said nothing to contradict the younger White but instead offered his sympathies:

'Yes of course' he said, 'you have so many concerns, it must be very frustrating as a man like yourself at your age, would almost be guaranteed a position in the Imperial Yeomanry.' White caught the irony in the tone, and reddened but made no sign of leaving. Exasperated and confused by his intended's condition, Brown ignored him and turned to Elizabeth who had begun to compose herself. Feeling himself ignored by both of his companions, White finally began to appreciate that his presence was unwelcome and rose preparatory to leaving. Elizabeth dabbed at her eye and bade him a subdued farewell that was barely audible. Brown, feeling that matters were beginning to go his way, gave him a firmer handshake than was absolutely necessary and couldn't help but tell him:

'Should you change your mind about serving your country, I could have a word to help you with the Yeomanry.'

'Thank you, I shall remember that if the opportunity arises but the farm, you know?'

They both knew that White would never consider the army and Brown took undue satisfaction from his discomfiture. As the door closed behind him, Brown offered up a silent thanks that the bloody man had finally gone. He now turned back to Elizabeth to pursue the second part of his mission to find that his objective was once more in tears and sobbing quietly.

'You are so mean and selfish' she said between the tears.

'Mean and selfish? Was I too harsh on White? I was just doing my best to help him on his way.'

Before he could continue she erupted with a fury he had not thought her capable of and words that he would never have expected to hear from such a delicate creature.

'Damn Peter White and damn you too. I could understand if he was running off to the colours but what are you thinking about?'

Her anger was like a runaway train and he decided to allow it to pass unhindered.

'You're almost forty years old and you have responsibilities here in England but you want to rush off to South Africa and play soldiers?'

As the train slowed he saw an opportunity and began to say something about Queen and country and then wished he had kept quiet.

'The Queen and the country can manage quite well without you but there are many others depending on you.'

'My Brother will take care of the business and my other interests in my absence. I shall be back before you know it and I thought perhaps then?...'

'Perhaps what?'

'Perhaps we might marry.'

He had originally thought of this as a moment of high romance. Putting aside his fears of rejection, he had anticipated cries of joy and excitement. Now he could see that perhaps the circumstances might not be quite right for that. Surely however, he might take the unexpected heat from the conversation by this suggestion. Any interested observer, had there been one, would have seen that this understated proposal was more likely to make matters worse rather than better. Brown was committed, retreat was unthinkable, he had only one choice and that was to go forward, which he did, by suggesting dates and an appropriate jeweller in which to seek a ring, all the time overlooking the absence of any reply, positive or negative.

Elizabeth Lloyd, demure parson's daughter or not, was not about to be harried by anyone, not even the object of all the affection not reserved for her Father or her horse.

'I haven't said yes and why should I volunteer to be a grass widow or even an actual widow? You announce that you have rejoined the army and are off to fight a war in Africa and then casually suggest that we marry? No! I'll not marry you. If you prefer soldiering to me then marry a blasted soldier.'

Another man would have recognised this as a preliminary skirmish and found ways to keep the battle going until the lovely parson's daughter came round to the idea. Brown though, began to think the unthinkable and looked for ways of making his escape. He made some mention of how duty and service must come first and seeing that the heat was once more rising began to apologise for misunderstanding where matters had stood between them. In military terms, he was attempting to retreat under the cover of a smokescreen of words, which were now spilling out of him like wine from a punctured barrel. Years of business meetings had honed a natural verbal dexterity but now he found himself struggling and eventually fell silent.

Elizabeth was watching him through eyes that though red, were now dry. The anger that had so shocked and surprised him had not entirely departed but he sensed the worst had passed.

'You're asking me to become engaged to you when you may be dead before the summer.'

'If you agree to marry me, I won't die, you can tell the Boers that you forbid it.' He said with a relieved grin, realising that as he was still in her presence and she was talking, he might not have lost the battle. Confidence returned as he pointed out that the flow of troops into South Africa would soon overwhelm the Boers and noting that as an officer of the Ordnance he would be well out of harm's way. This was a lie but he justified it to himself as being for the greater good.

'So will you reconsider?'

'Will you reconsider the army?'

'I can't do that I'm afraid. I have given my word.'

Again she looked at him and he began to have doubts. Wondering what would happen if he sent word to Fitz that he would not serve. It was impossible, he might live but at what cost and wonderful as she might be, Elizabeth might have second thoughts about hitching her wagon to a recipient of the white feather, particularly if he was also penniless. So he was firm that he had to go and told her as much.

Again he was taken aback as she seemed to soften and there was the hint of a smile as she expressed her understanding and suggested that they talk with her Father after tomorrow morning's service. He looked confused until light began to dawn.

'You mean?'

'Yes, Papa will have to approve.'

'But you said...'

'Never mind what I said before. I was angry and irritated because Peter wouldn't go and your proposal, such as it was, might have been confused with a suggestion for a cup of tea. I can't stop you going to Africa but I hope you understand my misgivings.'

He nodded assent and tried to add some words of his own but she was unstoppable and began to talk about arrangements and plans that must be made with or without his presence. She went on at some length and he let her, not that interruption appeared to be an option. She finished by giving him instructions for tomorrow's church parade and then dismissing him. As he walked home, he was as confused as he had been by Pythagorean theorem at school. That could be taught, understanding of the fairer sex seemed to be something you either possessed or you didn't. Reflecting that if nothing else he knew what he didn't know, he continued on his way.

CHAPTER FOUR

RMS Goorkha

The meeting with the Reverend Lloyd went better than Brown might have expected given the drama of the previous day. The parson could barely contain his excitement and had to be calmed by his daughter. She seemed to have forgotten the anger and doubts of the preceding day and beamed happily as she took Brown's arm. Because they lived in a village, every person of consequence was quickly aware of the engagement and his impending departure to South Africa. The men of the village, led by his Father, stood in line to shake his hand and the ladies dabbed at their eyes. Their emotions fuelled by the presence of young love and strengthened by patriotic thoughts at the imagined heroics of the groom to be. His Mother had seen her own husband off to war and had lived on too many posts to shed tears. She was pleased at the engagement but unhappy at her son's return to the army. She understood duty as well as any man though and no one watching would imagine she had any concerns as she fussed over the happy couple and laughed with the Reverend Lloyd as any proud parent might.

The resolution of his domestic affairs complete for the present, it was understandable that William Brown relaxed a little and enjoyed being the man of the moment. That evening in the inn, the older White clapped him on the back with a thunderous blow and congratulated him on his two engagements: to the fair Elizabeth and to the army. He made disparaging reference to his own son and a vulgar remark about married life that only served to increase Brown's detestation of the pair of them. Despite this, he returned home happy, optimistic and full of beer. Something he was to regret the following morning as he took the railway back to London.

The sun had yet to rise when he boarded his train the following morning. His head was throbbing and the noise of the train and the smell of the smoke did nothing to improve things. Entering his office early, he was fussed over by Miss B who ministered to him with strong, sweet tea. The routine correspondence she brought him was dull and now seemed not merely unimportant but also irrelevant. Looking at the office walls and listening to Miss B chivying latecomers, he began to look forward to getting away. Then he felt guilty about those he would leave behind, Elizabeth principally but also his Brother and parents and then he began to worry about what might lie in store on the Lourenço Marques waterfront and perhaps elsewhere. Tomorrow he and his new companion Wheatley were to report to Woolwich arsenal for their instruction in the use and handling of explosives. His unfamiliarity with the subject and his absence from military matters for so long concerned him but he contented himself with the thought that army instructors were generally first class and they were unlikely to let him kill himself and deny the Boers that opportunity. Being pulled in several directions at once might have been expected to make the day pass quickly but in fact it did the opposite and he accomplished little. He briefly toyed with the idea of having a restorative pint in the

Jamaica but decided it would be tempting fate and made do with a light and unsatisfying meal in a nearby cafe. Eventually, he gave up and went home to read and worry until the next day.

Tuesday dawned cold but dry and he made his way to the great arsenal at Woolwich[5] and his date with Wheatley and the explosives experts. The two instructors assigned to them were briskly efficient and possessed of that dark sense of humour common to the army. The first item that they took care of was to issue their pupils with gloves and brown overalls to go over their civilian clothes.

The gloves piqued Brown's curiosity and he asked why they were of importance. One of the instructors explained that they would be handling dynamite. 'If you don't wear gloves when you handle this stuff you'll soon develop a headache like a sailor's second morning in port. It's caused by an exudation from the explosives. Normally it's kept wrapped in waxed paper but when you come to use it always wear gloves.'

His colleague then chimed in with his own warning: 'Despite the work of the Noble Swede[6] in

---

[5] The arsenal covered 1,200 acres south of the Thames and employed tens of thousands in the manufacture of armaments. It was also home to the Ordnance Corps who kept the army supplied with weapons and explosives and had among their number many experts in their development and use.

[6] Alfred Nobel (1833-1896) was a Swedish chemist, engineer, inventor and businessman. Most famous for the invention of dynamite which incorporated nitro glycerin into an absorbent inert substance, making it safer and easier to handle. Further experimentation led to the

developing dynamite, it must still be treated with respect. Engineers around the world use it to blow holes in solid rock. If it goes off near you, you won't be troubling the gravediggers cos there'll be nothing left.'

He paused to regard his pupils and to gauge their reaction. Brown and Wheatley glanced at one another and then returned his gaze without speaking. Seemingly satisfied, he continued:

'Now we have you togged up appropriately, let's take you into the next room and you can see what you'll be working with.'

They moved into a cold, dank room lined with wooden shelves and crates bearing the familiar War Department stamps. The second instructor was searching through some items on a shelf and having found and retrieved what he wanted, turned and faced them. He was holding a small device in one hand and what Brown presumed to be a stick of explosive in the other.

'Now, if you drop this stuff it shouldn't go off, but no experiments please.' he held up the smaller object. 'This is a detonator which we affix to a primer which is then fixed to the main charge. We connect the whole lot to a fuze, which is used to transmit ignition to the detonator which then causes the charge to explode. What you might call a chain reaction hopefully ending with a loud bang and the destruction of the target once you are at a safe distance. Right, we'll show you how to rig a charge

---

invention of gelignite in 1876 which was a more powerful variant of dynamite. In addition to his invention of dynamite and gelignite, Nobel also had a thriving business in military explosives. Shocked by a reference to him in a French newspaper as 'The merchant of death,' Nobel left the bulk of his estate to establish the five prizes that bear his name.

ready to blow. 'Here, catch' and he threw the stick of explosive towards Brown. Taken unawares, he let out a yelp of fear but managed a clumsy one handed catch.

Reddening furiously but relieved he asked the instructor none too gently: 'what kind of bloody respect was that?'

The instructor grinned back at him: 'It's just a dummy sir. We'll try you out on this first then let you loose on the real thing when we think you're ready.'

As good as his word, Brown and Wheatley were soon seated at wooden benches attaching fuses to detonators and detonators to imitation explosives with varying degrees of success. Wheatley swore that he had never attempted such a thing before but worked with an ease and dexterity that left Brown flailing in his wake and cursing his own clumsiness. Once the instructors were satisfied that both men could assemble a charge safely, they decided to allow them exposure to the real thing. In order to achieve this, they moved outside to a patch of rough land enclosed by high walls and strewn with bits of debris.

In the interests of safety and giving Brown the chance to observe, Wheatley went first. The task was to assemble a charge with its detonator then a length of fuze, which had to be cut to an appropriate length depending on how long it would take the operator to get safely into cover. They had been told the speed at which the fuze would burn and from that they could calculate a safe length to use. Wheatley excelled at first attempt, cutting a fuze deftly and twisting it into a detonator before placing it at a distance and running the fuze material through his hand until the instructor stopped him. As he had been shown Wheatley struck a match, guarded the flame with his hand and lit the fuze. They took cover quickly and watched as the charge exploded, spraying pieces of earth around but otherwise doing no harm.

The instructor consulted the stopwatch he had in his hands and pronounced: 'twenty seconds Mr. Wheatley very good. Right Sir, your go.'

Brown attempted to replicate Wheatley's effortless example but quickly ran into difficulties. He struggled to insert the detonator and had to be helped by the instructor. It took him three attempts to get the fuze into the detonator but once successful he measured and cut his fuze and struck a match to light it but failed to guard the flame, which promptly went out. Cursing, he tried again and this time the fuze took. Not unnaturally, he turned to run but didn't get far before the explosion sent him flying.

As they brushed debris from their overalls and hair, Brown's instructor grinned at him over his stop watch: 'fifteen seconds, a bit lively there sir. Try not to run once the fuze is lit, it smacks of panic and what's worse increases the chance of your falling. As a general rule, hurrying things with high explosive is a bad idea. Let's try again but this time let's be a little more careful about the length of fuze.'

So they went at it again and again until both men could perform the task with grim efficiency. It was almost dark before the instructors pronounced themselves satisfied and outlined the programme for the following day. Brown recalled Fitz's words as their instructors explained that there were techniques for maximising the force of any explosion and they would be introduced to these mysteries the following day.

The next day saw them sweating in their overalls and gloves despite the winter temperatures but by the end of the day they were both confident that they had mastered the course and travelling back over the river for his London home, Brown caught himself mentally plotting the destruction of Blackfriars railway bridge. There was something else though, he began to feel a sense of purpose and commitment and realised that he was enjoying a return to soldiering, particularly as he didn't have to deal with the parades or the mess nights or any of the other irritations that accompanied military life. Had he been able to operate like this, detached not from authority altogether but from the petty rules and snobbery, he might have stayed and enjoyed it but then, he thought, however enjoyable that might have been, he would be relatively poor and Elizabeth would be out of reach.

After that, rather like a railway truck on a steep incline, matters took on a momentum of their own. He had a brief meeting with Fitz at the War Office, took possession of his new uniform and signed a number of forms acknowledging his return to the army in the rank of Major. Then, as is the army way, he waited. Civilian life went on around him, Elizabeth came to London to choose a ring and to talk about the wedding arrangements, which he thought a trifle premature but wisely didn't say so. They dined the following Saturday with his parents and the Reverend Lloyd and there was much excitement from all but less from Father and Son. They were both happy at the engagement and associated festivities but were also conscious of the small matter of the South African War, which even the Jingo press had to concede was far from going all Britain's way. Christmas had come and gone and so he entered the New Year as a Major with a doting fiancé making plans for a wedding but unable to set a date and waited for the army to call.

His summons finally arrived in the form of movement instructions including travel documents that required him to travel from Waterloo to Southampton and there to board the RMS 'Goorkha' which would carry him to the Cape of Good Hope. A handwritten note in Fitz's hand informed him that Sergeant Wheatley would be accompanying him. It did not mention that the writer too anticipated being aboard the 'Goorkha' when she sailed. Fitz had considered the matter and decided that there was little point in unsettling Brown in advance of his departure. Far better to present a fait accompli and he could then smooth matters over during the voyage.

Curiously, Brown was much happier having some certainty about his departure. He busied himself with preparations of baggage and such campaign necessities as he thought might come in useful. He was careful to include sufficient civilian clothes in a tropical weight which would facilitate his role as the rogue British trader of Lourenço Marques. These were easy enough matters to arrange. Giving the news to others, beginning with his fiancé, was rather harder and he had a difficult conversation with her before he could advise others including his brother who agreed to be his executor if he failed to return. Suddenly the brakes were off and there followed a whirlwind of farewells and parties including at his London office.

Aside from Brown Brothers staff and the brothers themselves, there were a number of business associates on the guest list. Champagne flowed and fuelled the unctuous speeches that were made, not to mention Miss B's tears and the post boy's martial ardour. Brown was obliged to politely decline the boy's offer to be his servant while disentangling himself from a distraught Miss B. Whatever the true purpose of the party, even if Elizabeth was still on his mind, it had the unintended consequence of making him look forward to Southampton and the company of honest soldiers. Of course, he was not aware that he would be accompanied by the opaque Major Fitzherbert.

On the other side of London, that worthy was making his own preparations for his departure. Unlike Brown, he was in uniform although that would have to be put aside once he was in LM. His position there would be to perform a liaison role, preparing reports for Sir John in London and Field Marshal Roberts in South Africa and attempting to keep the different intelligence operations from tripping over one another. He had his own ideas of how that might turn out however. Placing a carefully selected bottle of Irish Whiskey in his trunk, he discarded his sword in favour of extra revolver ammunition. If he was going to be involved in any fighting and he was determined that he would, a sword would be little use against the Boers' Mausers. A revolver would do for close work and he would get his hands on a rifle when he reached Africa. He had a genuine confidence in Brown's ability to manage the tasks assigned to him but in the unlikely event that his confidence was misplaced, he would be on hand to see matters to a conclusion. Preparations complete, he dressed for dinner and immaculately turned out, he left his apartments for dinner at the Café Royale with the beautiful Lady Arabella, his fancy of the moment. Despite the winter cold, he eschewed a cab and walked down Piccadilly humming the regimental march, his mind focussed far from the fair Lady but rather on a bridge in Southern Africa.

The day of departure came and the two majors bade their individual, final farewells. In Brown's case to his parents and then to Elizabeth and her Father.

Chastely kissing her cheek and shaking the hand of the Parson as he had that of his own Father. Fitzherbert's farewell to Lady Arabella was more robust in nature and to his parents he simply sent a note. Accustomed as they were to the demands of his job they took no offence and besides, there was an estate to run and foxes to hunt. Each man made his way to Waterloo Station by hansom cab or the Southern Railway. Being the London terminus that served Southampton from whence the troopships departed, the station was bedlam. Uniformed porters hurried hither and yon moving mountains of baggage. Whistles shrieked and the air was rank from smoke and soot. By the time Brown found his correct platform he was overheated in his army serge and sweating from the exertion. He had hoped to travel with Wheatley so that he could find out more about his companion for the foreseeable future but then remembered that whatever operational advantage that might convey was overshadowed by the class divisions of the army. Officers travelled first class, NCOs and other ranks in third. He didn't even catch a glimpse of his man on the platform, which, in view of his size was surprising. Just as he was straining to see if he could find his man among the crowds of troops he was startled and then irritated by the sudden appearance of Fitz.

'What the devil are you doing here? Worried that I wouldn't come?'

Fitz smiled serenely at the rudeness.

'Not at all Billy, I thought you would like some company for the journey.'

'To Southampton?'

'Oh no, all the way to Lourenço Marques.'

'Christ! Are you replacing me? Or Wheatley? You said you were staying in London.'

'Well the plans of the great change and Sir John has decided he needs an intelligence liaison officer in LM to coordinate the efforts of the army and the consulate with London. I'll not be interfering in your shenanigans but I shall be looking forward to hearing how you get on. Shall we board?'

And with that, he indicated an empty first class compartment, the door of which was immediately opposite where they were standing. Other, less fortunate officers were on their flanks and were forced to follow in their wake. Fitz stowed his hat and bag in the rack and was seated comfortably while Brown fumbled with his kit and bumped into a red faced Colonel who glared angrily the more Brown apologised. With all finally seated the wait for the train to depart began. All the occupants of the compartment were uniformed, Fitz wearing the badges of the Queen's Own, the rubicund Colonel those of the 60th Rifles. There were several other regiments of greater or lesser distinction represented but only Brown wore the insignia of the Ordnance. His travelling companions nodded but otherwise ignored him. Irritated by his collision with the senior officer and Wheatley's absence and caught off balance by Fitz's surprise appearance and announcement, as any other British gentleman would do, he took cover behind that day's edition of The Times.

If the officers' compartment was physically comfortable but atmospherically unpleasant, further down the train in third class was akin to hell on wheels. If the windows worked properly, the air was fetid with the smell of sweat, stale alcohol and tobacco. The glass was covered in condensation and soot rendering anything outside invisible. In carriages where the windows had failed and there were plenty of them, the air was slightly cleaner but the men in them would be half frozen and covered in smuts by the time they reached their destination. They may as well have travelled in open trucks as indeed they would when they reached South Africa. Sergeant Wheatley found himself squeezed into a space in one such that might have accommodated a smaller man but was not ideal for one of his size. The men around him were all NCO's and like Brown's companions, of varying units. Unlike their commissioned brethren, they soon had a lively banter going born of shared discomfort and experience. On the whole, they probably had a more pleasant journey.

If Waterloo had been bedlam, Southampton dockside was worse. It was cold, dark and extraordinarily noisy. Trains arrived with piercing whistles and disgorged their cargoes of yelling soldiery. Ships' hooters howled in the dark and the whole chaotic scene was wreathed in smoke and fog. Brown was appalled. It was many years since he had experienced anything like it and he was beginning to wonder if social and financial ruin might be a small price to pay to escape. Fitz wasn't a mind reader but he could see the lack of enthusiasm on Brown's face and took control, steering him towards the relevant ship. Before he had time to think further, Fitz had propelled him up the gangplank and after a swift consultation with a harassed naval officer they were installed in the berth they were to share all the way to the Cape. It was cramped and hot and in no way like the last ocean voyage Brown had taken. On the other hand, it was a considerable improvement on HMS 'Tamar', the troopship that they had sailed on in 1881. Had he had the opportunity, he would have noticed that the 'Goorkha' was a modern, good looking ship that was barely three years old. The

'Tamar' had accomplished the voyage at a leisurely five knots whereas the 'Goorkha' would cruise at more than double that. She was owned by the Union Castle line and, all being well, would have them at the Cape in fifteen days. Brown's mind was not on the ship however, even if he was.

Fitz's presence rattled him, which gave Fitz some quiet, unexpressed amusement. What was he Brown doing there? Ardagh had recruited him to do his patriotic duty but now he felt enmeshed in what might be not only a dirty but a dangerous game, the rules and objectives of which kept changing. Now he thought that Fitz might not trust him to get on with his part in it in his own way and it rankled. Had he known that what Fitz had told him about the Lourenço Marques intelligence operation was true but that he hoped for an opportunity to do more, it might have settled him but probably not. Whatever the truth, he was stuck with it now and must just play the bowling as it came down.

When their kit for the voyage arrived courtesy of some burly and tired looking sailors, they stowed what they could and then they were at a loss. The ship had not moved and even Fitz seemed to have little idea of when they might sail. The heat in the cabin was oppressive but the alternative was to be cold and wet on deck. If only for variety, they opted for the deck and leaning against the port rail, they had a fine view of the smoke and fog obscuring Southampton. The wind blown drizzle was an additional attraction that would have sent them below had the ship's engines not begun to throb signalling their imminent departure. They watched, damp and cold as the mooring lines were retrieved and tugs began to shepherd the vessel out of the harbour towards the Solent.

'Well, Billy, we're off' grinned Fitz, 'I'm cold and wet. Let's find the mess and see if they're serving whiskey or even better dinner.' They left the chill and the spray on deck and sought refuge among their brother officers in the dining room that served as a mess. Brown wondered about Sergeant Wheatley as he accepted a glass of Jamesons to assuage the chill. The Sergeant was on deck at the after end of the vessel retching and shaking with seasickness. He would eat little for the first few days of the voyage and keep little of that down. He was not alone among the soldiers and in truth, while 'Goorkha' was a good, modern vessel, the weather in the Channel was rough and once they entered the Bay of Biscay would be foul. Fortunately the time spent in the sunnier waters off the African coast would allow the men afflicted to recuperate and regain some strength. Had they put into Gibraltar and been asked to fight they would have been hard pressed to overcome a party of washerwomen.

The 'Goorkha' ploughed on with the men entertaining themselves with games to pass the time and by the time they sighted the flat top of Table Mountain above the port of Cape Town, for the most part they were happy and well fed but keen to put their feet on dry land again. For some too, there was the excitement at the prospect of action. The details of how they came to be at war didn't trouble them. They knew that British territory had been invaded by the Boers and they knew that they were the men who were going to send these half breed Dutchman back to their farms. The sad truth was that many of them would die of enteric fever or dysentery without ever firing a shot. Those that survived the disease and poor food would also discover that the Boer was a good irregular soldier who was fighting for what he regarded as his home and family. Officers like Brown and Fitz knew this but they were the exceptions among the officers. Most of them had absorbed the same diet of jingoistic rhetoric as their men and led them accordingly. Brown had recognised with some regret that the army had changed little since he had last worn uniform. The old scarlet tunics had gone thankfully and the more practical khaki first used in India had now been universally adopted. The weaponry had also improved and during the voyage, he had enjoyed a discreet refresher on the new Lee Metford rifle from Sergeant Wheatley. What troubled him though, was the lack of any knowledge or even curiosity about why they were there and why they were fighting. It was as if the descendants of his old Colonel and the port stained Major had taken over and perpetuated the blind ignorance of the previous war but on a far grander scale. He was now of an age when he might have taken issue with some of the ignorant prejudice that was aired in the mess most evenings but he knew better than to draw attention to himself and kept quiet. It was too tiring to be bothered with and the clowns doing most of the talking would find out the error of their ways soon enough. He just hoped they didn't get too many of their men killed in the process.

In the meantime, there was the prospect of Cape Town the port at the tip of Africa nestling at the foot of the mountain. This was where the troops would entrain for the journey towards the front and Fitzherbert, Brown and Wheatley would trans-ship for their onward voyage to Delagoa Bay. The star shaped castle originally built by the Dutch was the headquarters of the British in South Africa and the three of them would be lodging there for a few days prior to their departure.

They were greeted on the dockside by a tight lipped Sergeant of Artillery who had transport to take them and their baggage to the castle. The three of them waited on the dockside blinking in the sun and soaking up the sounds and smells of Africa. A couple of sweating blacks saw their luggage aboard a carriage and they set off through the streets to the old Dutch fort. Clattering over the cobbles of the courtyard, they were deposited by a high doorway which the Sergeant indicated they should enter. More blacks in the service of the army appeared and hauled away their cases to the interior of the castle. If it had been roasting hot and blindingly bright outside, inside the stone structure was blessedly cool if not calm. The war was being run from here and Lord Roberts had only recently taken over as army commander from the unfortunate Redvers Buller. Changes in administration generally raise the levels of activity in any organisation and an army fighting a difficult war far from home was no exception. Having entered as bidden, they were escorted through a number of dark corridors until they reached an ante room occupied by a flustered looking staff officer who was busily engaged in leafing through the files of papers on his desk to no apparent purpose.

Looking up, he peered at the three before him and asked their names. On being given the answer, he recommenced his paper shuffling until satisfied that they were on one of his various lists.

'Ah yes, Majors Brown and Fitzherbert and er, Sergeant Wheatley is it?'

Fitz took the lead and confirmed their identities and that they were expected by a Mr. Evans. The staff officer nodded and shuffled and checked his lists and finally asked them to take a seat until Mr. Evans was ready for them. Brown and Wheatley sat while Fitz paced gently around the room making the man behind the desk uncomfortable. Eventually his anxiety was relieved by the opening of a yellowwood door and the appearance of a well sunburned Captain of some colonial corps who bade the three enter. In the cool, stone flagged office beyond sat a bearded civilian who rose and greeted the trio, introducing himself as Samuel Evans on the staff of Field Marshal Roberts. In turn, he introduced the Captain whose name was Forbes and Brown recognised the name as the man Ardagh had indicated was the first to suggest the destruction of the Komatipoort Bridge.

Brown had been briefed about both men by Fitz on the journey to the Cape. Of the two, Forbes had the shorter biography, his family-owned coal mines in Swaziland and he had great familiarity with the country and the people including, it was said, the Swazi King. He had served against the Zulus and had also been on commando with the local Boer forces against renegade bands of natives. He gave the impression of being overactive and perhaps a little arrogant. In Brown's estimation, these qualities and him being a colonial led to him being dismissed as an 'amateur' by the High Command. The fact that he knew the country inside and out and had the wit and intelligence to propose the plan to down the bridge counted for little. He was a bumptious outsider, so the task would fall to an officer and Sergeant brought out of retirement, and some mixed troops led by a former German aristocrat.

Evans himself had a story that would have been hard to believe had it not been made at the height of the British Empire's reach and influence. He had started life as a Welsh journalist, had somehow found his way to Egypt where he served in the coastguard and later migrated South and set up in finance in Johannesburg as a member of the House of Eckstein and a Director of the South African National Bank. When Milner[7] had arrived in the Cape, he had drafted Evans into the civil administration and had sent him off to Delagoa Bay to report on the importation of contraband and what could be done to stop it. There he had encountered Forbes and listened to his experience and his plans and had brought him back to Cape Town to explain himself to Roberts. And from there thought Brown, the genius and snobbery of the British High Command conspired to take a good idea from Forbes, promote it as their own and find some other poor dupe to put his head in the lion's mouth to see it through. However, an hour or so in the company of Forbes began to make him believe that the High Command might have been more astute than he originally thought.

Despite his being a shameless self-promoter of the worst kind and somewhat uncouth, Brown was interested by what Forbes had to say about the interaction of the Boers with the black population in Swaziland. From his description, if they were not actually enslaving blacks, they were using them for forced labour and treating harshly any that dissented, taking whips to them or even employing summary executions on occasion. Cattle were removed at gunpoint and the Boers generally made free with the blacks' property. He didn't say it but Brown suspected that would include the black women. The Boers seemed to have a rather unusual view of what

---

[7] Alfred (later Viscount) Milner was appointed by Britain's Colonial Secretary Joseph Chamberlain to go to South Africa in the aftermath of the Jameson Raid to attempt to uphold British interests in the region while dealing with the two Boer Republics of the Orange Free State and Transvaal. It was an almost Sisyphean task given the Imperial ambitions of the British and the intransigence of the Boers. That he failed was not for want of effort.

constituted a protectorate and having started a war on their own doorstep, their behaviour towards the natives did not improve.

As soon as hostilities began, the Boer administration had issued orders for all whites to leave Swaziland with the exception of their burghers who were expected to report for Commando duty. Apparently they viewed this as including Forbes who had fought with a Boer Commando against the Zulus. They did not take his declaration that he was a British subject and damned if he was going to turn traitor kindly and he and his family were forced to leave their home and flee. As he was relating the story Brown found his outrage almost amusing (after all he was born there and had fought with them once) but he kept his thoughts to himself and heard the man out. When he had finished Brown began to question him about conditions in the Swazi Kingdom, in particular, the number of Boers, the ease or difficulty of movement and the attitudes of the natives to the British. Fitz said nothing but he and Wheatley listened intently. In fact, Fitzherbert was impressed by Brown's line of inquiry and happy to let him get on with it while he attempted to absorb the information for future use.

Being a good administrator and a busy fellow, Evans knew how to run a meeting with maximum efficiency. Recognising the point at which Forbes had disgorged everything of value he stopped the flow by thanking him courteously but with unmistakable firmness.

'Well gentlemen, we know the problem and we have a plan to intercede in Lourenço Marques with the aid of Major Brown and our network of corrupt Portuguese officials. Ultimately, however, there seems no doubt that blowing up the railway bridge at

Komatipoort will be the most effective way of reducing the flow of contraband to the Boer forces. Von Steinaecker has begun to recruit his band of ruffians and he will be moving into Swaziland as soon as possible. he will reconnoitre the bridge and surrounding countryside and provide Crowe at the LM consulate with details of what he discovers. Major Brown, we are going to forward you and Sergeant Wheatley to LM by the next available fast steamer, along with Major Fitzherbert here. In the meantime, we will accommodate you all in the castle. Cape Town is a British city but we are aware of Boer spies operating here. If you must go out of the castle, be discreet and be careful.'

With that the meeting would have ended but Forbes failed to recognise the reality and attempted to insert himself into ongoing operations with offers to guide Von S through the Swazi bush or even join his command. Evans brushed him aside easily enough and smoothly exited the room leaving Forbes to complain to the remaining three about his treatment by the fools of the staff. Given that he was talking to two superior officers and in the presence of a Sergeant, he was pushing his luck. Fitz made sympathetic noises and assured him that his advice and intelligence was most welcome but suggested that his undoubted talents were being considered for other, perhaps more vital tasks.

This appeared to mollify him, although why he imagined that a Major newly arrived from London could know such things was a mystery. Fitz's charm, as Brown ruefully reflected was most persuasive. Making the obvious excuse that they needed to find their temporary accommodation, the three decamped, leaving the colonial gnashing his teeth in frustration. Brown suggested mildly to Fitz afterwards that perhaps they were squandering a useful talent in not having Forbes along.

'The man has no subtlety' said Fitz dismissively. 'If we had him in LM, he'd pick a fight with a Boer and give the game away. Besides, did you not notice the ego on the fellow? Did you know that he expected to be given command of a squadron of cavalry and have them called 'Forbes Horse'? No, I've no doubt he'd be good in a scrap but we've no shortage of chaps like that. We need your cleverness for LM and you and Wheatley with Von Steinaecker's roughnecks will do the business where the bridge is concerned. Forget about him and spend some time with Wheatley. He's a good man with some talents of his own that may serve you well in LM'. With that, he left Brown to his own devices as he wandered off to an unspecified meeting humming cheerfully.

Brown looked at the ceiling and sighed. While Forbes was undoubtedly bumptious and irritating, he couldn't help wondering if his omission was wise. He wondered if he could insist on his inclusion then remembered that Fitz had said that it was Buller himself who had taken against him. Reluctantly, he resigned himself to following orders and went in search of Sergeant Wheatley. He ran him to earth outside the Sergeant's mess as he was about to enter.

'Would you care to come in as my guest sir?' Enquired the Sergeant gravely.

'That's jolly kind of you Sergeant and ordinarily I would jump at the invitation but I would also value some time alone with you. Perhaps a turn around the town?'

The big man looked briefly dubious. Whether he was disappointed at missing the conviviality of the mess and the stout it contained or mindful of Evans' warning about discretion was unclear. Like the clouds scudding over the top of the mountain, the moment passed and with a smile he said: 'I'd be glad to sir.'

The two turned and walked across the courtyard to the gate, giving way to the carts arriving from the docks and Brown acknowledging the salute of the sentry as they passed under the gate and walked towards the centre of the town. Safely outside the castle walls, Brown asked Wheatley to remind him of his personal history. From Belfast and a staunchly Protestant family, descendants of Scottish Presbyterians planted in the province as a bulwark against Catholicism, Wheatley had decided that following his father into the shipyard was not for him in the same way that previous generations of Browns had eschewed the weaving mills of Tyrone. He had briefly apprenticed as a carpenter but had then chosen the army. After a number of years with the Inniskillings, including active service against the Zulus in 1879, he found himself on garrison duty in India which was both boring and unhealthy. After a bout of cholera laid him low, he secured his discharge and returned to Ulster where he joined the Police. His natural intelligence and toughness had been spotted and he had stalked Fenian agents who were seeking an independent, Catholic Ireland undercover through the back streets of Belfast and Londonderry at considerable personal risk. Spotted once more by army intelligence he crossed the water to London before his luck ran out in Ulster.

'Quite a story there Sergeant' said Brown admiringly. 'But tell me again your first name. We can't go around the warehouses and go downs of LM calling each other by rank.'

The Sergeant was happily surprised and quickly responded: 'William sir, same as yourself and I see you've some instinct for this kind of thing if you'll forgive me.'

'No forgiveness required William.'

'Ah, not in uniform sir.'

'Queen's regulations?' Brown asked with raised eyebrow.

'No sir. It would sound odd to anyone listening and they might take a closer interest.'

Chastened by his naivety, Brown said nothing for some moments as they continued their perambulation around one of Britain's finer colonial cities. Uncharacteristically, it was William Wheatley that spoke next.

'Do you have any experience of this sort of thing sir?'

Brown thought for a few paces before responding:

'Well, I can read upside down, which is helpful in a competitor's office. I'm quite good at pretending to like people I don't and affecting ignorance of a subject on which I am well informed. Whether or not these are skills that are transferable from the City to your world I don't know.'

I was Wheatley's turn to raise an eyebrow and Brown wondered briefly if he had shocked him. He was, after all, still an officer and gentleman even if engaged to perform ungentlemanly tasks. But Wheatley was thinking before responding.

'I think it's a start sir, the rest we can work on.'

'Oh and I have little experience of fighting but I used to be accounted a fair boxer and fencer, not to mention a good shot.'

'Well let's hope it doesn't come to that sir. Now see those two fellers on the corner? Don't react sir, just keep walking and look casual like over towards that tavern. Do you see the two outside with the beards and corduroy trousers?'

Brown let his eyes move without turning his head and spotted a villainous looking pair leaning against a tavern wall smoking pipes. In his part of London the police would have moved them on for loitering but they were far from the Jamaica now.

'Do you think?'

Wheatley cut him short: 'who knows sir? Maybe, maybe not; if they are, there's nothing we can do and they don't seem that interested in us and why would they be? There's Lord knows how many soldiers in uniform strolling round Cape Town so there are. We're just two more in the crowd. The trick sir, is to look without people seeing that you're looking.'

'Here beginneth the lesson' said Brown.

'Indeed sir, indeed it does.'

CHAPTER FIVE

Lourenço Marques

If Cape Town had been hot, Lourenço Marques was miserably so. The trio of British soldiers had shipped out of Table Bay after a few days of rest on a mail ship that deposited troops in Durban, loaded new passengers and cargo and then sailed North up the East coast to Delagoa Bay. Brown remembered Lourenco Marques with little affection from his initial visit in 1881 and a subsequent trip made in the course of business. The port was just as he remembered, it was hot, sweaty and it stank. It was bigger and busier now than on his previous visits and every sort of sharp and adventurer thronged the port area and the wharves. Brown was uncomfortable in the heat even in his tropical weight civilian togs. His plight was as nought compared to that of poor Wheatley who had once again suffered the miseries of seasickness and was now a mass of pale faced sweating muscle crammed into a suit of clothes that seemed to exacerbate his plight. He and Brown had enjoyed some useful conversations in Cape Town but the education of William Brown in the black arts of covert police work had been cut short by the voyage and Wheatley's sickness.

The three stood on the wharf looking about them at the forest of masts in the port and the noisy crowds of various nations going about their business on the dockside. Even Fitz was glistening in the fetid heat, as he joined them in contemplating the chaos. The water of the Indian Ocean that should have been a tropical blue was foul with oil and tar and the rubbish from passing ships. The air was heavy with the heat and the discharge from funnels of steam ships, trains and steam cranes. Insects buzzed and swarmed over the filthy water carrying the genesis of fever that would be far more deadly than any Boer bullet. Out of all this desolation appeared a vision. A pink cheeked, fresh faced vision dressed in a tropical suit and speaking English in the tones of the young and privileged. Inevitably, the vision addressed his remarks to Fitz.

'Major Fitzherbert? And you must be Major Brown and Sergeant Wheatley?' The vision turned slightly to the more dishevelled pair.

'No call for ranks laddie. We're just three Britons in need of consular assistance.' Fitz delivered his admonishment gently smiling serenely all the while.

The vision turned from pink to scarlet and waved on a couple of black porters to handle the luggage on to the back of a horse carriage. Beckoning his visitors to mount the carriage with the bare minimum of 'sirs' that he could deploy even including the hapless Wheatley, who neither noticed nor cared, the young tribune of empire whisked his charges away from the unsavoury atmosphere and dangers of the port to the relative safety and comfort of the British Consulate. Here in a low white building with manicured gardens, the Union Flag hung limp in the humid air and all was tranquillity and civilisation at least on the surface.

Ushered into a cool room graced by dark wood furniture and a portrait of Queen Victoria by the young man who introduced himself as Lieutenant Campbell, the three took their ease and gratefully accepted glasses of iced lemonade. While they enjoyed their refreshments, Campbell went out and returned after a few moments with the Consul, a naval officer named Crowe. Theoretically a diplomat, Crowe had the direct manner of a blunt sailor. As Brown listened to his opening remarks, he found it hard to imagine the man using diplomatic niceties and smoothing the agitations of the representatives of foreign powers. He ran down the steps taken to deal with the Boer contraband since his arrival, which Brown had to concede were often original and listed the Portuguese officials on the consular payroll, one of whom at least Brown was familiar with.

'Pedro Nunes' said Brown thoughtfully, 'rather oily individual, thinks of himself as something of a ladies man?'

Crowe looked at Brown with surprise: 'Indeed, that's the fellow. You know him then?'

Brown sighed: 'Pedro is a necessary evil, a cog in the Portuguese machine that requires regular oiling with brandy and the occasional cigar. I imagine that he is quite senior in the administration now.'

Crowe frowned: 'frightful man but, as you say, necessary. He has risen through the ranks but not too high. Even the Portuguese recognise his limitations which mostly arise from his appetites and his corruption. As a consequence of his rise, he now believes himself sophisticated and a gentleman.'

'A Portuguese Lothario' interjected Fitz. 'How original and in a place like this. How far would we trust this Pedro fellow?'

'For myself, not at all, but then I have never had to do so' said Brown and turned to Crowe: 'how do you find him sir?'

Crowe thought for a moment: 'I shouldn't trust him further than I could throw Mr. Wheatley' he said, causing poor Wheatley to redden. 'But, he's taken our money and our single malt - he's a whisky man now by the way- and he knows we could have a word with his higher ups that might make his life difficult.'

A silence followed the character assessment of Mr Nunes. Everyone in the room was reaching the same conclusion that if he would take Her Majesty's money in return for information, would he hesitate to offer the same service to her enemies? Britain had more influence but Crowe had to answer to the Treasury, which probably meant the Boers had deeper pockets. Breaking the silence, Brown pointed out that as he would be portraying himself as a rogue prepared to betray his country, he had little to fear from Nunes unless he became aware of the truth, which was unlikely. Nunes would be a resource for Brown in his search for information about the Boer activities in and around LM, no more than that.

The issue of Nunes having been dealt with, they set to outlining the means, methods and opportunities to be employed in the process of information gathering. Fitz appeared little interested but, he was, of course, not to be directly involved other than to coordinate the dissemination of intelligence among the parties that needed it. For all that, he was listening carefully but discreetly. Crowe explained that he had arranged accommodation at a hotel for Brown and Wheatley, they would use that as their base and would be conveyed there by one of the Consul's black agents who would also be available to deliver messages if needed. A regular briefing meeting was set for twice a week with changes to be notified by coded note left at the hotel concierge, who was a supposedly trustworthy individual named Walter. Brown and Wheatley would arrive separately. Whatever Wheatley's undercover skills, no one would buy into him as a trader in contraband. His role would be to do what he was good at, stay in the shadows and keep an eye on Brown and those he dealt with.

As the discussion neared its end, Brown enquired into the methods of communication within LM and further afield with Von Steinaecker in far Swaziland. Crowe explained that he employed a network of black natives who could pass unnoticed in both territories. Curious, Brown asked what motivated them to perform such dangerous work for a white, colonial power.

A look of irritation crossed Crowe's face: 'You sound like my predecessor Casement. [8] Look, the blacks hate the Boers because they mistreat them and steal from them. We don't steal from them and we pay them for their work. Nobody notices one black more or less and they can't read any message they carry because they're all illiterate. It is a system that works well.'

In his army days, it was unlikely that he would have raised the question but times had changed:

'And if the Boers catch them?'

'Highly unlikely' snapped Crowe angrily.

'And if they do, we'll probably need another messenger but don't worry Billy, there's no shortage.'

---

[8] Sir Roger Casement had preceded Crowe in LM. He had worked in the Congo and due to that experience had become increasingly uncomfortable with the exploitation of native tribes by the Colonial powers. He was an early human rights campaigner who was knighted for his work among the Indian tribes of South America. An Irishman, he became embroiled in Irish Nationalism and foolishly attempted to supply the Republican movement with arms during the First World War, an act of treason that would lead to his arrest and execution.

Fitz seemed amused by the exchange but nevertheless, had brought it to an end.

Brown swallowed his indignation and decided silence was his best option. There followed a brief discussion of other operational details and the meeting concluded. Crowe sniffed as he bade them a cursory farewell and Campbell announced that Joseph, the horse and buggy driver was waiting outside to take Brown to his quarters. He would return for Wheatley later. As Brown watched Joseph load his luggage and then climb on board for the journey to the hotel, he couldn't help but feel that at the least Crowe and Fitz displayed a callousness and lack of gratitude for the risks taken by their native helpers. Maybe Britain did treat them better than the Boer but we didn't treat them overly well, even Crowe hadn't attempted to deny that. After all, he thought, we are British and we're expected to be better. Henceforth, he determined to do his best to treat Joseph and others he might encounter with a modicum of decency. They were uneducated and childlike even and certainly in no way equipped to govern themselves but they were human beings. If it was wrong to enslave them as Britain had been insisting for the best part of a century then it might be time to start helping them improve themselves. For one thing, the businessman in him thought, it was a shocking waste of a potential resource.

While Brown was engaged in such humanitarian musings, Crowe and Fitz were in a further discussion regarding intelligence gathering and the analysis and distribution of what had been gathered. A part of their deliberations naturally related to the role Brown would assume in LM.

'Do you think he's up to it?' asked Crowe with characteristic bluntness. 'He seems to have a bloody naive view of the blacks.'

'Billy Brown is a sound man,' replied Fitz. 'He knows Africa, and more importantly, he knows the import export game and the port of Lourenço Marques. If he has a fault, it's that he thinks too much but I need a thoughtful man in this job, not a blind follower of orders.'

Crowe looked doubtful but Fitz's confidence was clear and after all, if he was wrong the fault would lie with him and not Her Majesty's Consul. In fairness to that grand official, he was more concerned about the successful prosecution of the war than his own reputation. Part of that concern was for his network of black messengers and informants. Not from any fellow feeling or humanitarian instincts but for fear of any damage they might do if captured and the time and effort required in recruitment and instruction. In some ways, he and Brown shared a view of the black African as a resource. The difference was that Brown envisioned their potential; Crowe's view was much more short term.

Some distance away, Brown's thoughts were not on the future development of the native African but were rather focused on attempting to gain admission to his room at the hotel that had been arranged. Joseph had dropped him at one establishment from where he had made his way on foot to the correct hotel in order to confuse anyone taking too keen an interest in the comings and goings at the British Consulate. As a consequence, he was hot, sweating and irritable as he tried to explain who he was and what he wanted to the Portuguese clerk at the hotel desk. The clerk spoke no English, neither did he understand Brown's French. Finally, in desperation Brown attempted Afrikaans, having acquired a working knowledge of that language on his travels. With a certain amount of extravagant gesturing, communication was achieved and Brown was handed a key to his allotted room.

Turning towards the stair, he became aware of a young lady standing at the foot of the ornate wooden stair and smiling in his direction. He felt himself reddening as he tried not to stare but she was worth a stare. Slightly above middle height with a tanned face surrounded by chestnut curls, piercing green eyes and a smile that might have been mocking but was definitely infectious. Despite the initial blush, he smiled back and to his surprise, the lady spoke to him:

'An Englishman speaking the taal, now even if not done well, the wonder is that it is done at all.'

'Dr Johnson?' Said he, almost subconsciously, and the heat returned to his cheeks as she continued to regard him with amusement.

'An educated Englishman too, so clearly not a soldier?'

Her forwardness and the nature of the question made him not merely uncomfortable but concerned that this attractive but assertive young woman might know more or be more than just a casual bystander. Realising that he had halted in his tracks and might be looking unusually foolish, he put his concerns aside and became the travelling businessman he was supposed to be.

Smiling back at the tanned face before him, a face that would turn heads in West London, never mind in wartime Lourenço Marques, he shook his head and said with a grin he hoped as sincere:

'Not a soldier, no, just a humble businessman who happened to read some Johnson on a long journey. 'William Brown at your service ma'am.'

To his surprise, she stuck out her right hand and announced: 'Johanna Reilly Mr. Brown, what brings you to Portuguese Africa?' Now English ladies did not shake hands or start conversations with strange men. They waited to be spoken to and to have their hands kissed. This second vision of the day was quite outside of his experience but he took the proffered hand and before he could raise it to his lips, found his own hand gripped and shaken firmly.

Taken aback, he suddenly realised that she was waiting for a response to her question. Thinking quickly for a suitably vague answer, he said airily: 'business, just business. I am in the business of importing and exporting goods between Britain and Southern Africa.' this sort of obscure generality might have worked among the ladies that he was used to at home but Johanna Reilly was a different character.

'You must have some specialities surely? What sort of commodities are you bringing in or taking out?'

Despite the oddness of being asked very specific business questions by a woman and a most attractive one at that, it touched some inner instinct and suddenly he was in character. Discussing mining supplies and requirements for the mining fields, hinting at tents, tinned food, and maybe even explosives or similar commodities. It sounded good and it gave him much needed confidence that he could perform the allotted task and perform it well. In his impromptu presentation to his new acquaintance he may have indulged in some innocent flirtation too, subdued but the lady noticed it even if he failed to. They were both intrigued but only one knew it. Eventually, the tide of words ebbed and Brown was forced to excuse himself with some reluctance.

in his room, he checked his luggage for any signs of interference as Wheatley had shown him and found none. Thus elated by arriving at the hotel apparently undetected and by his successful and enjoyable exercise of his cover story he unpacked his traps, less his uniform which had been left at the consulate and began to feel a certain exhilaration about the job in hand and how matters might develop. In this cheerful frame of mind he sought refreshment at the bar of the hotel in the form of some imported gin with the tonic water[9] accompaniment that may or may not have been proof against malaria.

Seated contentedly nursing his drink, Brown began to rough out a plan of campaign in his head, a plan that seemed doomed to interruption by thoughts of Johanna Reilly. However, he persevered and after two drinks had the basis of a loose plan that might be adapted should conditions change. Satisfied with his efforts he considered imbibing a further gin but decided that food was a better option and was able to secure a plate of shellfish and rice washed down with a white wine that was chilled to a surprising degree. Thus fortified, he stayed a little longer in the hopes of a further encounter with Miss Reilly but when she failed to appear, he took the sensible course and repaired for the night the better to face the following day.

The following morning saw Brown in a slightly rumpled and sweat stained linen suit walking through the port area. It was not an idle stroll but a walk that knew where it was going and had a sense of purpose. That sense of purpose took it to the office of the superintendent of the port and one of his

---

[9] Originally the quinine in the tonic was flavoured with gin and often lime to hide the bitterness of the quinine. By the mid 19th Century Schweppes had developed their carbonated tonic water or more specifically: 'Indian Tonic Water.'

deputies, Captain Pedro Nunes. Brown had sent his card over in advance and the Captain made himself available after a short period of waiting as befitted a man of his stature and importance.

Brown had last seen the Portuguese that was grinning at him from behind a desk covered in papers some years before. He had been thinner then, not thin but thinner than he was now. The moustache had flecks of grey and the teeth were even more tobacco stained but he was recognisable as the same repulsive individual as before, simply grown more expansive on the fruits of his corruption. His grin grew ever wider as Brown proffered a bottle of malt whisky from the consular stores and he could not have been more effusive in his welcome. He waved Brown to a chair and the two exchanged details of changes in their lives like the old friends that they had never been. Nunes scented a new and potentially rich income stream in the reappearance of Brown. His appearance indicated that he was hungry for business and Nunes felt certain that he could make the Englishman sweat gold and whisky as he strung him along. For his part, Brown scented that Nunes' ego would make him an admirable source of information, for he loved to be first with the news and that trait would also mean that he would publicise William Brown's presence in the port possibly to their mutual advantage.

After an hour or so of Brown polishing Nunes' ego and fending off questions that were too intrusive while dropping hints about the lengths to which he would go to secure a deal, he could take no more and pled a meeting at his hotel. Unfortunately this set off Nunes' lascivious side and he made various grotesque and prurient remarks about who Brown might be meeting displaying clearly what was on his own mind if not on Brown's. Extracting himself as cleanly as he could with the minimum necessary winking and suggestive remarks, Brown set out for his hotel room and a hot bath to wash away all traces of eau de Nunes. Despite his distaste for the man, he nevertheless felt that the meeting had been useful and through Nunes, he had put down a marker as a potential player on the LM waterfront and one who might well crossover lines of loyalty if the price was appropriate.

Walking away from the muck and bedlam of the port, he passed a rather grand park and was pleased to see the avenues and streets broaden as the noise and stink diminished. Thinking about his discussions with Nunes, he idly wondered what Wheatley was up to and if he had covertly followed him or for that matter was he following him now? He paused and looked across the street and behind him without seeing the big fellow. He wasn't unduly concerned, just curious as to how his Sergeant operated. With this on his mind, he began scrutinising passers by and the loafers on the street corners. LM was enjoying a war time boom, so there was plenty of material for him to contemplate but for all he looked, he never saw Wheatley. Mostly, it was just blacks, going about their business of wandering the streets apparently aimlessly or just squatting in the shadows. Among the natives were local Portuguese of varying degrees of prosperity, chivvying the blacks out of their way and greeting each other for all the world as if they were in Lisbon and in between the Portuguese and the blacks were others, others of European origin who were harder to classify. Some perhaps were Boers, none of them looked English and some of them looked positively hostile. Suddenly wary, Brown pressed on to the hotel.

Approaching his accommodation, he was looking forward to a bath and change of clothing. For all of his distaste for Pedro Nunes and his appalling suggestions, he did find himself secretly hoping for a further encounter with Johanna Reilly. He told himself that this was no disloyalty to his fiancé, just an enjoyment of an interesting woman's company and possibly even something that would assist his job for his country. There was, he conceded, no evidence for that second consideration but he could not rule it out either. All moral dilemmas thus swept aside; he entered the hotel. He did not encounter Johanna, which may have been a blessing for both of them as he carried the reek of the port with him from his morning's exertions. This he dealt with by bathing and changing his clothes and only then returning downstairs in search of luncheon. In doing so, he came face to face with the lady that was on his mind. Whether it was the heat or the success of his meeting with Nunes or some other factor such as the pretty face that was smiling at him, he found himself inviting her to lunch; something he would not have done in London. Surprising himself by his boldness, he was yet more surprised when the lady accepted.

Having extended the invitation, he was them forced to put himself in Johanna's hands regarding an appropriate venue. She guided him to a nearby tavern and had the waiters dancing attendance on them in no time. Without ceremony, she ordered wine for them both and suggested that he leave food choices to her as well, which, once he was over the novelty, he was happy to do.

Seated, alone and with wine, the two had much to learn about each other. Though both notionally British, they came from wildly different backgrounds. Brown being strictly of the patriotic, military side of the Empire by upbringing if not always nature, he was quite taken aback by some of the views espoused by his companion. If his family was as much the British Army as anyone else, her background was quite different. It seemed she was the daughter of an Irishman, one Patrick Reilly, who had seen service with the Dublin Fusiliers but had little love for England. He had drifted down to South Africa to try his hand at the diggings but had married a local Afrikaans woman named Frieda Naude and opened a shop in Pretoria where Johanna had been brought up. Her upbringing had swung confusedly between the Calvinist traditions of her Mother's family and the more relaxed occasional Catholicism of her Father. A common thread however on both sides was a deep dislike of the English grown and nurtured over years of nationalist grievances both real and imagined. Despite twenty or more years of tales of English cruelties, he assumed she kept an open mind on the matter or she wouldn't be lunching with him. He had mostly let her make all the running since she had taken over the ordering of the meal but now began to ask her more details about herself, in particular what was she doing in LM?

    She began some tale about her Father sending her away for fear of what British troops might do if they entered Pretoria but he had the feeling that she wasn't being honest with him or at least, not completely honest. For one thing British troops were months away from Pretoria with thousands of Boers between them and the city. Equally, her Father would know that whatever old blarney he had grown up on, British troops were highly disciplined and were not allowed to let their base instincts get the better of them whether at home or in an enemy country. The days of soldiers like his Father looting what they could as opportunity presented itself were long gone, at least officially. He wasn't about to contradict her but instead asked how she passed her time, the cultural amenities of Lourenco Marques being somewhat limited. It seemed she performed some secretarial and translation service for a South African enterprise located in the town. Instantly, he wondered if she might be a spy but dismissed the thought due to her age and gender. He then considered if the enterprise that she was involved in might be in the contraband business and he pushed for a little more detail as to what they did. Receiving only bland responses regarding a trade in clothing, in fact, she insisted that European fashions were particularly in demand, he began to convince himself that delightful as Johanna might be, she was mixed up in something that was not quite right.

Both of them were being disingenuous but in Miss Reilly's view, Brown's vague responses were generated by a fear of the consequences of being caught by his fellow Britons. Brown's interpretation of Johanna's deceptions was less certain. That she was being less than honest was not in doubt but her motivation was more of a mystery. Brown made no complaint about the various sallies she made concerning British behaviour, he was, after all, implying a lack of patriotism on his part. He listened carefully and only commented intermittently. In doing so, he realised that her self-confidence had limits and having seen the gaps in her story, he could tip her off balance quite easily by asking awkward questions. Because he liked her and he didn't wish to have any concerns confirmed, he kept any questions benign but of course, he wondered.

Eventually, the wine began to dry up and with it some of the conversation. He paid the bill and she thanked him and they strolled back towards the hotel each wondering about the other in a number of ways not always related to their purpose in Lourenço Marques. When they parted, they agreed they should meet again but were uncertain as to when as both had unspecified matters making demands on their time. In the end, they agreed to aim for a further lunch towards the end of the week. Johanna repaired to her room to write her diary and Brown to his in order to make notes of their conversation. He was to meet with Crowe and Fitz the following day and wished to give a full account of their discussions. As he wrote, he considered whether he had anything of substance to disclose. It was true that her family background suggested she might not be friendly but she had made few directly hostile remarks about Britain and her questioning had not been particularly incisive or difficult. All that seemed innocent enough, but he was sure the story about her employment was a fiction. The only European fashion in vogue in that part of the world was khaki battle dress and Mauser bullets. Possibly that was her interest. He considered tearing up his notes but decided that Fitz and Crowe could make a determination of whether Miss Reilly was worthy of investigation or not. If he was starting at shadows, that would be better than missing something of substance.

It proved to be a wise decision, Fitz and Crowe had listened to his account of his talk with Nunes politely but without any obvious excitement. When he moved on to Johanna, he had their full attention, which was both gratifying and slightly uncomfortable as he attempted to be as objective as possible.

Wheatley was unusually demonstrative in his attention. Typically he would listen to discussions of this nature with impassive features that Brown decided were the result of hours spent listening to Irish subversives in the smoke filled bars of

Londonderry or Belfast. The reason for his overt interest became apparent when he mentioned his acquaintance in the course of business with a Reilly who had been accused of spreading false rumours among the Dublin Fusiliers some years previously. However, as Wheatley himself said, that would have been well after Johanna's Father had left the army. Possibly a relative but given how many Reillys were in the Dublin Fusiliers, more likely coincidence. A reminder, however that the Boers were not the only people to resent British rule.

Brown concluded by proposing that he continue to walk the wharves of LM and to cultivate both Nunes and Reilly as potential sources of information. As he referred to Miss Reilly again, Fitz looked up and asked innocently if she was pretty.

'Very' responded Brown and then wished he hadn't, adding quickly: 'why do you ask?'

'Just idle curiosity Billy and making sure you have your priorities straight.'

Crowe looked quizzical at this and Wheatley found a point on the ceiling of acute fascination to occupy him.

'Are you suggesting that I am neglecting my duties?' Asked Brown with a flash of anger.

'Not at all, not at all just satisfying my curiosity.' Genial old Fitz once more but Brown had glimpsed the steel and would not forget it. Crowe too, had taken the point and began to wonder about their man in the rumpled suit. He said nothing but Brown caught the look on his face which kept his anger at Fitz smouldering.

To prevent a conflagration, Brown changed the subject and asked Wheatley how he was finding the hotel and the town. He wasn't just being diplomatic; he hadn't seen anything of Wheatley and wanted to be reassured about his security. What he heard was that Wheatley was very comfortable thank you, the town was lively and too hot for his taste but he had been able to track Brown's movements quite well and proceeded to give chapter and verse on the subject including the two or more hours spent with Miss Reilly. The response might have given him reassurance had it not been the cause of a hard look from Crowe and a knowing grin from Fitz. Embarrassed, he thanked the Sergeant for his attention and asked for any other questions, which nobody had. Wheatley had not been dishonest but neither had he told all of the story. Despite the Sergeant's skill at merging into his background, this was more difficult in a tropical port with a predominantly black population than it might be in London or even Cape Town. Wheatley had taken advice and was utilising a brace of Crowe's local blacks to follow Brown and report on his movements to Wheatley. He in turn, armed with this information, could ensure that he was close by but unseen, ready to respond to any threat to Brown reported by the watching blacks.

Aware that he was watched over but ignorant of the methodology, Brown left via consular buggy for his hotel. His colleagues went about their own business after a brief further conversation between Crowe, Fitz and Wheatley. Their talk was much about the Reilly woman and her potential to distract Brown from the job in hand. Wheatley's opinion was sought and he confirmed that she was indeed a stunner. Crowe looked ever more concerned and Fitz assured him that Brown would be fine.

'Look here Captain, I've known Billy a long time and he's no skirt chaser. He's just become engaged as well, to a nice girl, a parson's daughter in Kent. This Irish girl may be a looker and he may look but he won't let her get in the way of his job.' Both Elizabeth and Miss B could have vouched for the truth of that last statement but Crowe had to take Fitz's word without corroboration. Fitz knew his man and his business. However, he had put down a marker that had got under Brown's skin. That was unfortunate but it would make him additionally cautious in his dealings with Johanna.

For the next few days, Brown wandered the waterfront keeping his eyes and ears open. He plied Nunes with more whisky and laughed at his vulgar jokes but without learning anything of significance. He failed to see Johanna anywhere which added to his frustration although, mindful of Fitz's questioning, he wondered if that might be to the good. At the end of the week in sheer desperation, he began an afternoon's drinking with Nunes in the hope that the boastful fellow might let slip something of interest. It took several lewd stories regarding Nunes' recent amorous adventures and the best part of a bottle of malt, most of which Brown made sure went into his companion but finally, patience brought forth a reward.

Nunes had paused in his retelling of his night with some local lady and Brown took the opportunity to bemoan his difficulties in attracting business. Nunes smirked and told him he was wasting his time if he was hoping to sell anything to the Boers. Brown waited and Nunes ploughed on as to how their contraband passed through the port on a daily basis. Occasionally, the Portuguese would confiscate something for form's sake and to placate the British but otherwise, they took the Boers' money and looked the other way.

Brown trod carefully, he had to cloak his interest as being purely a search for a business opportunity and suggested that he would be able to supply clothing, boots, tents etc. at reasonable prices. Nunes agreed that he would be sure to make that known to his friends but given the sort of supplies they were receiving, he doubted that such non lethal goods would hold much excitement. Inwardly appalled but unsurprised, Brown professed not to understand what the Portuguese meant. Perhaps sensing that he had gone too far Nunes would not be drawn further on detail although he foolishly said something about 'German engineering' with a knowing wink.

'No doubt from that German ship that offloaded on Tuesday?' Suggested Brown and Nunes just giggled stupidly.

'I could not say Senor, but it is possible.' Brown was now trying to speak in banalities while his brain was analysing how to make the most of the information provided by the now intoxicated Nunes. As he uttered just enough words to convince Nunes that he was paying attention, he was thinking that whatever cargo had been landed would be highly unlikely to have left the port for its final destination. It should not be that difficult to find out where the cargo would have been taken prior to trans-shipment to Pretoria, if it was indeed weapons bound for the South Africans. He prodded Nunes as far as he dared but without discovering much more of use. Recognising that he had obtained everything he was likely to from the Portuguese and having rendered him a sweating, giggling wreck in the process, he made his farewells and began a return to the hotel.

As he walked, he considered what, if anything, he had learned. A drunken and corrupt port official had hinted that a German ship had landed cargo that might have been weapons destined for the Boer forces. Even that was to put his own interpretation on what he had been told. It all sounded damned thin but despite this, he was certain that he was onto something of greater or lesser significance and something that should be passed on to Crowe and Fitz but only after he had distilled the information into a coherent form. The German vessel 'Elbe' had docked on Tuesday but had not been able to get alongside the wharf. instead, the cargo she had landed had been trans-shipped by lighter. This would have slowed further onward movement, and he was as certain as he could be that whatever had been brought ashore would still be in a warehouse. Between his own contacts and Crowe's, it would not be too hard to trace the lighterage company and from there, they could establish the location where the lighter had delivered. After that, diplomacy had to take over and Crowe could decide what should happen next.

In his room, he wrote a note in the schoolboy code that Crowe had devised for emergencies, inviting a Mr. Bird for tea at his convenience. 'Tea' indicated a request for a meeting, 'convenience,' urgent and as any halfway intelligent Boer would probably have discerned, 'Mr. Bird' was Crowe. Far from enthusiastically, he sealed the note and asked Walter, Crowe's man at the hotel, to arrange delivery. That task completed, he made some notes of what he knew and what he suspected, tucked them into a pocket and then waited for Crowe's response.

The response arrived in the form of Joseph driving the consular horse and buggy and a summons to the consulate that he accepted with alacrity.

While waiting, he had become more certain in his own mind that he was on to something of significance and any concerns he may have had about the dangers attendant upon interfering with illicit arms shipments had given way to a feeling of satisfaction at being able to deliver some solid information in the face of the previous embarrassment he had suffered at the hands of Fitz and Crowe. To his satisfaction, his story found an interested audience, less sceptical than he had anticipated. Crowe and Wheatley listened intently and while Fitz initially displayed only polite interest, when he explained the link between the lightering and the cargo's location, Fitz raised an eyebrow and observed:

'Finding out what you don't know from what you do eh?'

'Let's hope so' Brown responded with a smile at the quotation and named the lighter company he believed might have been the most likely recipient of the 'Elbe's' cargo. Crowe nodded and said that he would make enquiries in that direction as they had been well disposed to Britain in the past. Busy and strategically important as it was, LM was not Southampton or Liverpool, it was a small port and secrets were hard to keep in such a close society. People and companies had established relationships and rarely departed from these. Whatever had been discharged, it would not be long before they discovered it's probable location. What to do after that was more delicate and a matter for the consul to consider.

Even though it seemed that the game was now afoot, there was little to be done until further information could be developed. As this might take some hours at a minimum, Brown departed the consulate to await developments. As he was leaving Fitz enquired if he had plans to see Miss Reilly that evening. It sounded innocent enough, a conversation among friends but it irritated Brown. What irritated him more was that he let it show as he denied the suggestion.

'Just curious Billy, I'm sure she's charming and innocent. Just be careful what you say.'

Gathering his emotion, Brown thanked Fitz for his concern and assured him that he would, of course, be careful. He then left with a fury boiling inside him that he found hard to explain. On the face of it, a reasonable suggestion, particularly given the dangers surrounding him but it felt as though he was being warned off and he resented it.

He had been honest with Fitz. He had no arrangement to meet Johanna but he desired one. In making his enquiry, Fitz had touched a nerve. He felt guilty about his interest in Johanna but he resented Fitz intruding and the implication that he did not know what he was doing. He dwelt on his irritation which of course increased it. By the time he had regained his hotel room he was angry and uncomfortable.

He had a bath drawn and washed the stink of the port and Pedro Nunes away, and then changed into fresh clothing before taking a seat in the bar of the hotel. Nursing a gin and his anger, he wondered what the outcome of Crowe's enquiries might be. In the meantime he must wait for confirmation and where better to wait than a hotel bar he thought, particularly when there was a chance of bumping into Miss Reilly, an act that would be a pleasure for its own sake and with the added bonus of cocking a snook at Fitz.

Time and drink passed and he began to feel more relaxed but his wish to see Johanna had only increased. Then as if summoned by some psychic phenomenon, he glimpsed her passing the open door of the bar. He stood and strode through the door calling her name. Turning, she greeted him with dazzling smile and a mock curtsy. Finding himself grinning like a fool and with no idea what to say after the initial 'hello,' with gin fuelled confidence, he enquired whether the lady might be available for dinner that night and once again, to his confusion, she assented. Sending him into the same crisis of uncertainty that had marked their first encounter of any length. Recovering quickly, he proposed a return to the previous tavern and to his great relief, the lovely Johanna agreed.

Confidence restored, he ordered drinks and then food and he and Miss Reilly talked, expanding on their first discussions, occasionally finding that they had missed details from before and correcting each other gently as they moved the conversation on and into new areas. Like the Walrus and the Carpenter, they talked of many things but Johanna was particularly interested in Ireland. Like many members of that island's diaspora, she had conceived some romantic notions about heroic struggles against the brutal English. Brown, despite his role as a man more interested in profit than patriotism, patiently refuted many of her preconceptions and being Irish himself, albeit from the Protestant North, he spoke with some authority.

In particular, he spoke authoritatively and passionately against any form of armed insurrection:

'For one thing it would be doomed to failure, amateurs against trained professionals will only have one outcome but what is worse, all the people killed and maimed and all the homes and businesses destroyed will be Irish. The Irish are represented in the Westminster Parliament, home rule has sympathetic ears, the second Home Rule Bill passed the Commons for heavens' sake. Any attempt to push home rule by violence will set that cause back and potentially cause the devastation of Ireland in the process. If there's truly a majority for home rule it will come in time.' He was passionate because he believed in what he said, and his passion gave the lie to any supposed lack of patriotism.

'The Boers are amateurs and they seem to be doing quite well against your professionals.' Observed Miss Reilly.

'Our army in South Africa is only just assembling' he responded. 'When it begins the march towards the Free State and Pretoria, the soldiers will suffer all the usual privations of a campaign, wounds, illness, short rations etc. but they expect that it's what they're paid for, but who will bear the brunt of their resentment? The Boer, because in their minds he caused them to be here, he may have killed their friends and he's the enemy. The soldiers will suffer but nowhere near as much as the Boer Republics because they're a citizen army and the fighting will all be on their land.' She shuddered quietly as he spoke but did not argue.

Her silence cooled his enthusiasm for the subject and they turned away from politics to happier subjects but she couldn't help wondering about what Brown had said and the conviction with which he had said it. It was a far cry from the cynical businessman that had hinted that he would trade with anyone. Just who was she talking to?

CHAPTER SIX

Breaking and entering

While Brown and Johanna Reilly were discussing the future of Ireland and confusing each other, another discussion was underway at the consulate between Crowe, Fitz and William Wheatley. Wheatley spoke only when spoken to unless he had some particular knowledge to impart that was relevant to the subject. For the first part of the conversation he remained silent.

Crowe had reluctantly conceded that Brown had potentially contributed valuable information that might enable them to interfere with some supplies intended for the Boer armies. The question now was what, if anything might be done. Crowe was sensitive to his diplomatic responsibilities up to a point. There had been serious incidents when French and German vessels had been stopped and searched by the Royal Navy in the past but in the present matter, the contraband, if it was contraband, was ashore. Any action that Britain took might be plausibly denied if carried out with care. Crowe was for taking a look once the location had been determined and both he and Fitz turned to Wheatley for his thoughts.

'Will there be guards sir?'
'They can be bribed to look the other way.'
'What about locks and fences?'
'We can send you in the front gate once the guards have been turned the other way. Most of the godowns

are secured with heavy chains and padlocks. We can supply some bolt cutters. You'll have to make it look like a robbery gone wrong.'

An uncharacteristic smile crossed the face of the big man. 'Trust a policeman sir' he grinned and reached into his pocket from whence he withdrew a large bunch of lock picks. For most people, picking a lock would be a slow if not impossible task but for an experienced hand like Wheatley it was child's play.

'It will be a highly unusual lock that I can't open so it will.'

'Very good Wheatley' said Crowe, feeling much more comfortable now that any criminality would be hard to track back to Her Britannic Majesty's Consul. 'So when we have confirmation, we can send you in to take a look?'

'If you can take care of the guards sir it should be easy enough for me to slip in and open a box or two.'

Fitz looked across the table and said quietly: 'safer with two of us I think.'

Wheatley looked uncertain. He wasn't too sure what housebreaking skills the Major might have developed at Eton or in the officers' mess.

'Don't worry Wheatley' smiled Fitz. 'I'll be as quiet as a mouse and can keep *Cave*[10] while you're picking locks and opening boxes.'

Wheatley had no idea what keeping Cave was but assumed it meant lookout in some form or other. He looked at the Major with a sense of concern. This was serious business and Wheatley understood that and the risks involved. Major Fitzherbert appeared to be treating it as some sort of skylark but as Wheatley reflected, the Major appeared to find life itself little more than a source of amusement. He had no choice, he was a Sergeant, Fitzherbert was a Major.

---

[10] *Cave* from the Latin to beware.

'Glad to have your company sir' was all he said.

The following morning, Brown woke with something of a headache and cursed his foolishness in pouring gin and wine on top of the whisky he had drunk with Nunes. He planned to stay close by the hotel all day, not in the hope of seeing Johanna but in the expectation of a summons from the consulate when they had located the cargo from the 'Elbe.' In this, he was to be disappointed. The information came into the possession of Crowe, who shared it with Fitz and Wheatley but they, that is Crowe and Fitz, decided that they would conduct an initial examination without involving or advising Brown. Their reasoning was that he did not need to be involved, he had no known skills in that direction and what he didn't know, he couldn't tell anyone about.

So while Brown kicked his heels in his hotel, reading aged copies of the Times while keeping an eye out for a sight of Miss Reilly, Fitz and Wheatley planned their excursion into the docks for later that night. Wheatley cautioned Fitz against bringing his revolver on the grounds that it was too noisy and too military for what they were doing. Seeing the sense of what the Sergeant had told him, Fitz decided to rely on a small cosh and his fists. His best weapon was usually his charm but that would be of limited value against non-English speakers. Word came back to Crowe late that afternoon that Portuguese port officials were most grateful for the gifts they had received and would be sure to allow the two English gentlemen to stroll the port that evening without interference.

When the time came, the two English gentlemen, who were both Irish, made their way on foot to the port. The streets were dark and almost deserted bar the odd native shuffling his way home. The sun may have long gone down but the night could not have been described as cool in any way. The heat and humidity hung heavy on the town and mosquitoes and other insects troubled them on their journey. Fitz joked to Wheatley that the blood suckers were attracted by the Guinness flowing through his veins. Wheatley, who was valiantly swatting insects while mopping perspiration from his brow didn't exactly fail to see the amusing side of things but did suggest that the mosquitoes must enjoy a good imagination, it being some time since he had last enjoyed any stout of any description. Then, to Wheatley's consternation, Fitz guffawed loud enough to turn the head of a late street dawdler. He couldn't shush his officer but he did engage him in a quiet conversation about how they would effect their break in once on scene. They had gone over the details a dozen times before setting out but Wheatley wanted to keep Fitzherbert focused on the task and to dull his exuberance. Bribed guards or not, the last thing they needed was to attract attention.

As they entered the vicinity of the port area, the darkness seemed to deepen and while attempting to project confidence, their pace slowed as they made certain of their direction and kept wary eyes open for any untoward movement. Now that they were close to their objective, Fitzherbert had his previous exuberance in hand and his hand on his cosh. It would be unfair to say that he was hoping to use it but it was fair to say that he wouldn't regret the opportunity.

The smell of the port was now pungent and as they turned a corner they both spied two people apparently lurking by the side of a small office building. They proceeded without pause, neither hurrying nor ambling and ignored the figures on the other side of the street while praying Crowe's people had done their job with the authorities. They passed the men who barely glanced in their direction but their nerves were tingling as they walked with their backs to what might be danger. It was only when they heard the scrape of a match behind them and smelled the tobacco smoke in the distance that they relaxed a little. It seemed that Crowe had successfully neutered any official guards but Fitz and Wheatley knew that the British were not the only power in LM and kept their wits about them for guards who might have accepted gifts from a different quarter.

After a couple of missed turns they found the godown they wanted and Wheatley examined the padlock on the heavy chain securing the door. Fitz wanted to observe his man at work but maintained a discreet foot patrol of the immediate block of buildings to spot any unwanted company while Wheatley worked. It took a few minutes but then Wheatley gave a slight grunt of satisfaction, followed by the sound of a chain being gently slid away from the doors that it was securing. Fitz allowed Wheatley to open the door undisturbed but then backed up and entered behind his Sergeant, having ensured they were unwatched. Inside was pitch black, hot and damp. They closed the doors gently behind them to hide their entry but having done that, it was impossible to see until Wheatley produced a candle and some matches and provided just sufficient light for a swift search.

They looked at the various piles of boxes and sacks and began their search. Sacks they ignored as being unlikely to contain weapons. There were any number of crates and boxes and they began to move down the various ranks, inspecting the markings as they went until they found what they were looking for: crates with German markings recently landed.

Each one they looked at was marked as '*Werkzeug*' or tools. There were three in total lying side by side and Wheatley looked at Fitz for instruction. He nodded to the middle of the three and Wheatley produced a small claw hammer and began to remove the nails holding the lid. The lid came up and was stacked gently to one side and they looked down at the contents of the crate, which proved to be, spades and pick axes. Their disappointment was palpable but Fitz looked harder at the crate and moved several of the spades in order to lift the light wood they rested on. Beneath this covering lay packages in waxed paper approximately rifle sized. Closer examination revealed the prize, a number of brand-new Mauser rifles with boxes of ammunition. The two men looked at one another and Wheatley whispered:

'Shall we do the other two sir?'

Fitz consulted his watch and nodded. The procedure was repeated twice more with the same results.

'Right Wheatley' said Fitz, 'Get these resealed as best you can so that they don't look as if they had been opened and we'll get out of here. I'll take a quiet look outside to make sure that you're not disturbed.'

'And the rifles sir?'

'Too much for you and I to move and we may not want to, depending on what the Consul thinks. Let's just ensure that we leave everything the way we found it and then report back.'

With that, he gently opened the door and slipped outside to scout around the building. Fitzherbert wasn't shirking manual labour and Wheatley knew it. He could work more quickly and efficiently than the Major and he would do so with greater confidence in the knowledge that he could do so undisturbed. So each man stuck to his task until Wheatley was done. The pair looked over their handiwork in the guttering light from the candle and hoped it would pass muster to the casual observer. Even if it didn't, for now, nothing had been removed and even the recipients, however great their curiosity, would be hard put to establish who had been at their goods and probably less interested in that than they would be in moving the weapons to where they were needed.

The boxes having been restored as close to their previous condition as was possible, the two exited the godown, Wheatley replacing lock and chain and as the padlock clicked into place once more, the two began to retire in the direction of the consulate. The streets remained silent and seemingly deserted but the darkness might shroud all manner of unseen watchers and followers. Neither man would have appeared concerned had there been light enough to discern their faces but each now carried a dangerous secret and it kept their senses sharp as they bore it back to the consulate and relative safety.

Back in that relative safety, the tension was replaced by exhaustion. By now it was the early hours of the morning and Fitzherbert decided that they would let Crowe sleep on. Any discussions on actions to be taken could wait until later. They had the location of the weapons and could infiltrate some of Crowe's native runners into the vicinity to report any attempt to remove them. In the meantime, Fitzherbert found a member of staff to make tea and produced a bottle of whisky to toast a successful reconnaissance. Given the late hour, Wheatley bedded down in the consulate. Brown would be safe enough under the watch of other members of Crowe's network. Safe also from any concerns about that night's work which was bringing them ever closer to the war. A movement that Wheatley would accept as part of his job, Fitzherbert would relish as an opportunity and Brown would accept but worry about.

Later in the day when Crowe, Fitzherbert and Wheatley convened to consider their available options, again, they met without Brown. The meeting quickly established that three courses of action were open to them. Firstly, they could do nothing other than report the landing of contraband from a German ship to London. Secondly, they could have the godown watched until someone came to remove the weapons and then spring an ambush or they could attempt to lift the weapons themselves. The first was quickly dismissed as pointless. The second would be difficult, to ambush anyone in the port would be to draw attention to themselves in a way even the Portuguese would find impossible to ignore. To trail any shipment out of town and then attempt some form of armed robbery would be riskier still as the party moving the weapons could be meeting an escort. The third option seemed to present the best opportunity. This was no simple matter however and the three men spent some time considering the best way to accomplish their theft. It was one thing for two men to sneak in under darkness and examine a couple of crates, it was quite another to remove heavy goods from a building in a busy port and then transport them across town and therein, as Wheatley suggested, lay their best course.

Crowe and Fitzherbert listened closely as Wheatley made the case for turning up with some mules and black labourers in daylight, picking the lock once more and then removing the goods. As Wheatley explained, people saw what they expected to see. A few mules and labourers being directed by two white men in the busy port was far from unusual. They could walk in, enter the godown and remove the cases in under thirty minutes and be back at the consulate in another forty five. If there was activity at the godown, they would either attempt to talk their way in or abandon the attempt. Once loaded up, there was little chance of anyone stopping them.

Crowe looked unconvinced and questioned Wheatley on some further details while Fitz smiled and congratulated him on the plan. Fitz was delighted at the audacity and simplicity of the plan and barring the unforeseen, like the owners of the rifles turning up at the wrong moment, it had every chance of success. Eventually, Crowe too was convinced and he set about organising a team of mules and a second team of blacks to do the lifting and carrying. Time was not on their side as the Boers were unlikely to keep their rifles idle in a warehouse for longer than they had to. Taking that into consideration, it was decided to go the following morning, meanwhile, Patience, Crowe's chief spy would ensure that word would be passed if it looked as though the goods were being moved.

Blissfully unaware of these developments, Bill Brown kicked his heels in and around the hotel, waiting for word from the consulate. He was bored and a little apprehensive as to what the lack of communication might portend. His boredom was accentuated by Miss Reilly proving somewhat elusive. In the absence of any company, male or female, he amused himself with Boswell's 'Life of Johnson' to give him material for further discussions with Johanna, who had proven a rather well-read shopkeeper's daughter.

He was thus engaged over a pre luncheon gin in the hotel bar when he became aware of a man standing over him. The fellow was above middle height and bulky. He wore a suit of corduroy that had seen better days and must have been hell in the heat of LM. His mouth was garnished with a prodigious set of unkempt whiskers set on a face the colour and texture of old, dark leather. When he finally spoke, it was in halting English with a heavy Dutch accent. There was nothing about the fellow to make Brown feel comfortable but he conquered his nerves by playing his part as the corrupt trader and listened to the man as he issued an invitation to a business meeting with his boss who was apparently nearby.

Brown tried a few probing questions such as 'how far away is nearby' and 'what is the nature of the business your boss wishes to discuss' but received nothing helpful in return. He didn't like the look of the messenger above half so heaven knows what the boss would be like. It was what he was there for however, and he was supposed to be desperate for business, so silently praying that Wheatley was nearby and watching, he tucked Boswell and Johnson into his jacket pocket and followed the man out of the building and into the heat.

Wheatley was not present, being at the consulate with Crowe and Fitzherbert but as Brown and his guide left, a dozing native across the street tipped back his straw hat and followed the pair with his eyes, only getting to his feet and moving when they were a little distance off but keeping a watch from a distance and pausing to remove his hat and spit into the gutter, an action that seemed to catch the attention of another black further down the street who rose to his feet with a yawn and then turned to walk in the same direction as Brown.

Brown's companion was not much of a conversationalist and responded to his comments and enquiries with monosyllabic grunts. He was, however, true to his word in one sense, the building he took Brown to was not far away from his hotel, which was a blessing in the heat and also enabled the young black who was watching them to get a message to Wheatley quickly. This he did by running up the street back to the position opposite the hotel where the first man was taking his ease. A swift exchange then took place in their own tongue and the man hurried away to deliver his message and the youngster retraced his steps to the building Brown had entered minutes earlier.

Inside, Brown had been shown into an office lined with bookcases and yellow wood panelling. It was a handsome room and judging by the titles of the books, the owner was Portuguese. The man facing him across a desk didn't look Portuguese and as he rose to greet Brown, his voice left no doubt that he was, in fact, Dutch. Brown surmised that the building was rented or borrowed which would suggest it was a temporary location for the Dutchman. He was now speaking slow, ponderous English, pausing to pick what he felt was an appropriate word of greeting and waving Brown to a chair.

Brown sat and allowed the chap to talk. He was older, perhaps sixty odd based on the grey beard and thinning grey hair. Unlike his messenger, this man was well dressed in comfortable linen and sported a silver watch chain across his waistcoat; a gold signet ring glittered on one finger. That he was a Boer was in no doubt but this was not some backward farmer who read nothing but the Bible, this man was sophisticated, perhaps a lawyer or a doctor and Brown wondered if the way he spoke was an act put on to mislead him. He introduced himself as Carel van Der Merwe and Brown instantly had his doubts as to the authenticity of the name which he knew to be common among the South Africans. On the other hand, he thought, this chap might feel the same way about Brown.

The customary small talk having been dispensed with; Brown waited for the fellow to get to the point. After a bit more waffling, Van Der Merwe duly obliged. He understood that Mr. Brown could supply a variety of goods and had some experience of assisting with mining operations. Brown nodded assent and wondered where the conversation was going. It seemed that Mr. Van Der Merwe was planning a hunting expedition into Rhodesia and he was looking for supplies of tinned food, khaki clothing, boots and tents.

'How many men?' Asked Brown, as any trader would.

'About fifty' replied Van Der Merwe, 'initially.'

Brown looked surprised:

'That's a very large hunting expedition and why do you say initially?'

'There is a lot of game and there may be future expeditions.'

The trader in Brown saw a substantial business opportunity with the promise of repeat orders. In other circumstances, he would have been excited and giving assurances of how he could deliver the best goods at the most reasonable terms but the soldier in him knew that the only creatures this man and his friends would be hunting were British soldiers. He knew that the Dutchman saw the recognition on his face but having put his toe into the water, he was bound to swim.

Shutting his mind to the reality of Van Der Merwe's needs, Brown let his natural business instincts have the stage. he asked all the relevant questions regarding delivery schedules and point of delivery, pricing expectations and how payment would be made always assuming he could deliver what was required. He had pulled a pencil from his pocket and in the absence of anything else, made notes on the blank page at the front of his book.

When he had down most of the details that he would need to attempt the transaction, he thanked Van Der Merwe for his time and told him that he would make enquiries among his business associates and advise on his ability to fill the requested order in a few days. His potential customer had been somewhat vague on some of the details, which confirmed Brown's view that he was being lied to but that was to be expected. As he was saying his goodbyes, he enquired casually as to how the Dutchman had known about him. It seemed that they had a mutual acquaintance in Pedro Nunes who had advised Van Der Merwe of his presence and current business interest.

Once out in the street, Brown actually felt a slight sense of well-being, he had touted for business and used his contacts and now had a second success to go with his discovery of possible contraband. Even Crowe would have to agree that he was producing the goods, whatever else he may think of him. On that happy thought he walked back to the hotel to prepare some notes for Captain Crowe. He didn't notice the black boy walking thirty paces behind him or the one that stood up in the shade across the street as he entered the hotel. The second boy hurried off and his place was taken by the follower who found a comfortable patch of shade and sat down to watch the hotel entrance.

At the consulate, Wheatley had been alerted to Brown's movements and the nature of his escort. He knew where he had gone and enquiries suggested that the building he had entered was the home of a prosperous Portuguese merchant. There was some excitement about what it all meant but most pressing would be the confirmation from the second runner that he had returned safely to his hotel. This duly arrived some time later and there was a debate about whether or not he should be summoned to explain what had taken place. Fitz squashed this idea, pointing out that a meeting was scheduled for tomorrow afternoon and Fitz and Wheatley had some breaking and entering to do in advance of that. Both Brown's meeting and the breaking and entering could be discussed at leisure tomorrow.

The morning arrived far too slowly for Brown. He had found sleep hard to come by as he went over the meeting with Van Der Merwe and associated matters in his head. He thought about the ghastly Pedro Nunes and how helpful he had been, although Nunes himself did not appreciate the full extent of that help. He was an important man to have on your side so long as you realised his support was only as good as your money. Naturally, in his position as an officer of the port, he would know everyone of consequence including the ladies of the town in whom he had a keen interest. Apparently he had attempted to take an interest in Johanna Reilly at one point, according to the lady herself, who quipped to Brown that he might be dangerous with a sword as he had such fast hands. Brown didn't see Nunes as a fencer, even when he was younger that would have been a stretch, neither did his attempted friendship with Johanna bother him much. After all, she was nothing to him but pleasant company and when all this was at an end, he would return to Kent and Elizabeth, always assuming Elizabeth had waited.

Fitz too had found sleep elusive as he contemplated the state sponsored thievery to come. It wasn't just a schoolboy excitement either. He recapped the plan and considered ways that it could go wrong and how he and Wheatley should react in different scenarios. The most important thing was not to draw attention and to act as though everything was as it should be. As far as he could see, unless they were surprised in the act of lifting the cases by people who would employ violence to stop them, very little could go seriously wrong. In the event of the worst happening, they could scatter their blacks and cut free. If it was just a challenge, they could bluff and even if he couldn't charm any challenger, Wheatley could intimidate them. Cheered by these thoughts of how he would bring home the goods and the early sunlight, he dressed and went in search of breakfast while he waited for Wheatley to arrive.

After his breakfast, Fitz found time dragging as he waited for Wheatley to arrive. Crowe's blacks were already fussing round a number of evil smelling and braying mules that would be doing the carrying assuming they had anything to carry. The blacks had arranged their harnesses and fed them and like Fitz, they were ready to go. Brown by contrast was busy transcribing his notes from book to more conventional stationery and combing his memory to ensure that he left nothing out including a nod to Nunes for his intervention. He had the whole morning to assemble his thoughts prior to the afternoon's meeting and took a leisurely but methodical approach to the task. In his opinion, the most important fact if Crowe wished to act on it was the location of Van Der Merwe's office. This was already known to Crowe thanks to the black boys keeping their eye on Brown but of course, Brown did not know that. Having time on his hands, he did wonder what could be done about Van Der Merwe. The British had no powers of arrest in LM and as far as anyone knew, he had committed no crime. That he was a Boer agent Brown was certain but he couldn't prove it. On the whole, he thought that the best course of action would be to have the place watched and Van Der Merwe and any associates followed to see where they went and to whom they spoke. Then again, his opinion had only limited worth. The decision would be Crowe's.

A little way from where Brown was musing about further action, at the consulate all was bustle. The mules were screeching on and off as the blacks fussed over their harnesses. Fitz and Wheatley discussed final details and checked their weapons. The officer had kept his cosh and discreetly added a dagger down the side of one of his boots. Sergeant Wheatley contented himself with a brass knuckleduster in his jacket pocket, his bunch of lock picks and his size. They both knew that the worst possible outcome would involve violence, not because of the danger of injury or death but because it would mean discovery with all the inconvenience to Britain that would accompany it. Fitz would do everything he could to make matters run smoothly but if matters were to go wrong in any way, he was prepared for the eventuality.

When the last strap had been checked and tested and the mules and the blacks were ready, the little cavalcade set off for the port. The streets were all a bustle and no one took any notice of a few mules led by black muleteers under the orders of two white men. It was a common sight in LM and particularly in the port area which they reached without hindrance. It took little time for them to locate the correct godown once more and any inquisitive eyes had turned away from the aggressive stares of the two white men. There were ample opportunities for a quick robbery in LM that didn't involve going up against a well found mule train led by two solid individuals such as these. Any would be bandits turned away in search of more helpless prey as did the merely curious when subjected to Wheatley's baleful stare.

The mule train masked the godown doors as Wheatley quickly picked the lock once more. Fitz stood on the other side of the mules keeping a weather eye on passers by and their blacks until Wheatley signalled to him that entry had been made. Swiftly, they moved inside, established that the particular cases remained in place and once again removed the lids and checked for the contents which were as they had left them. Discarding the spades and pick axes, the bundles of rifles and boxes of ammunition were loaded into the mules' panniers by the blacks and secured. The transfer was accomplished as quickly as possible and once the mules were loaded, Wheatley threw the various tools into the boxes once more and nailed down the lids then had them restored to their original positions. Fretting with impatience, Fitz questioned the purpose of tidying up behind themselves now that they had lifted the goods until Wheatley pointed out that while it would in no way fool the rightful owners, it would stop a casual observer from realising that a robbery had taken place. Thus educated, Fitz noted the point for future use and resumed his picket duties outside until Wheatley emerged and put padlock and chain back in place.

'Always make things look untouched sir' said Wheatley grimly 'if nothing else, it may buy some time and we can never have enough time.'

Fitz saw the logic and thanked the Sergeant before wheeling the now laden mules in a semi circle and beginning the short journey back to the consulate. Hopefully no one had taken any notice of them and they would unload in the consulate courtyard without notice of their journey or arrival having been taken. There was no outward sign of any interest in them as they walked through the streets, nor as they entered the consulate. Wheatley, ever the realist, reflected that however well Crowe treated his blacks, it was unlikely that the Boers had no LM spies on their payroll and unlikelier still that they didn't have the British consulate under surveillance. Whoever may or may not have been watching, they returned unmolested and had the weapons and ammunition unloaded and stored in a strong room. Then after the mules and the blacks had been dismissed, Fitz and Wheatley joined Crowe in some iced lemonade while they waited to give Brown their news.

Brown was delivered by Joseph in the usual way and when he was ushered in to the room where he was awaited, he noticed Crowe looking more cheerful than was customary. Fitz too seemed to share the mood of general bonhomie although as Fitz was perpetually cheerful, it was hard to judge, only Wheatley sat inscrutable as usual. Brown seated himself and announced that he had news only to be cut off by Crowe.

'This would be about the meeting you had yesterday?' Ostensibly it was a question but Brown recognised that it was in reality a boast that Crowe knew everything that was going on. Briefly, it threw Brown off balance as he had looked forward to telling his tale and hopefully impressing Crowe and Fitz.

Fitz the would be warrior, moved swiftly to become Fitz the peacemaker, as he caught the flash of anger darkening Brown's face. Before Brown could retort to Crowe, Fitz smilingly announced that they were keen to learn what new information Brown had discovered but it might be more logical for them to lay out all that had resulted from his first intelligence coup. Unaware that he had scored an intelligence coup, Brown looked blankly at Fitz and then suggested that he proceed. So Fitz told his story making certain to highlight the part that Brown had played in laying out how they might locate the German cargo. Of course, he was unable to emphasise Brown's role in subsequent events because he had had none and had not been told what was afoot. Fitz knew that the exclusion would cause annoyance and frustration, so he deployed his considerable gifts of charm and flattery to stop any protest erupting. Many people would have succumbed but Brown saw right through all of Fitz's blarney and remained angry but he couldn't sustain it. Fitz had bought just enough time to allow tempers to cool.

'So you just went in there in broad daylight and robbed a godown?'

'I think the expression you're looking for Billy is 'confiscated enemy weapons' rather than 'robbery'' Fitz grinned. Happy at both his memory of the deed and his verbal dexterity which he deployed again to give Brown the floor and to prevent further discussion of the removal of the weapons from the port to the consulate.

'But you too were busy yesterday, come, tell us what happened and what you learned.'

So Brown told them of the approach, the house where the meeting took place and his discussions with Mr. Van Der Merwe, which they all agreed was unlikely to be a real name. They also agreed that any hunting the Dutchman was planning would be a lot further south than Rhodesia, all of which was a concern but the most important question was, having identified Van Der Merwe as a Boer agent, what should be done about him?

When Brown thought about it afterwards, he realised that he should not have been so astonished when Fitz mooted the idea of assassination. The Dutchman was an enemy and was engaged in clandestine conduct that could contribute to the deaths of British soldiers, however, as Brown had pointed out, he was also a civilian and they had no absolute proof that he was supplying the Boer forces. Furthermore, they were in a friendly, neutral territory and had no authority there. Fitz gave a tolerant smile as he voiced his concerns but Crowe was less indulgent.

'We're not in a courtroom and neither is this some sort of game Major Brown' Crowe snapped when he raised his objections. 'If the boot was on the other foot and they knew that you were a British officer, do you think they would hesitate to kill you?'

It was a fair point and reminded him that what he had been doing was not without risk. Nevertheless, murder of a civilian went against his upbringing and his sense of right and wrong. Indeed, Crowe might have a point about what the Boers might do but they weren't British. In Brown's view, Britain was better than that, she stood for and upheld the rule of law. Hadn't she been a signatory to last year's Hague Convention on the rules of war which set out the limits on what belligerent powers might do? As a signatory, Britain's actions as a belligerent power were limited by international law. He had not in truth read all of the text but was tolerably certain that the murder of elderly civilians in neutral territory based upon the flimsiest of evidence would fall outside the law. While military exigencies might result in rules and norms being bent or broken, it was surely only in exceptional circumstances. In the past, there had even some rough play in Ireland and of course, in India during the Mutiny but these were either isolated incidents or retaliation for the crimes of the mutineers. He did not accept the argument that all was fair in war and whatever Crowe might think or say, he was not prepared to connive at any sort of extra judicial murder.

As it was, he wasn't called upon to compromise either his principles or his commission as assassination was decided against. There were several reasons but all of them practical rather than ethical. Firstly because there would be limited opportunities to do the deed, secondly because of the risks of embarrassing the Portuguese authorities and principally because Van Der Merwe potentially might provide an unwitting source of information alive. Dead he could contribute nothing. He had already confirmed what British intelligence suspected, that the Boers were short of clothing and food in the field. Boer prisoners that had been taken tended to be half starved and often dressed in rags or pieces of cast off British uniforms. Similarly, when British troops were captured by the Boers, they tended to be relieved of not only their weapons but also their boots and uniforms. As the Boers lacked facilities and proper organisation, such prisoners were then often released to find their way back to their army in undergarments and bare feet.

Having decided that Van Der Merwe might live, it was agreed that Brown would pursue and prolong his dialogue with the Boer with a view to obtaining more hints as to Boer supply weaknesses. At the same time, Wheatley and Crowe's spy network would watch the building Van Der Merwe had been operating from. Any one emerging would be followed and a note made of where they went and to whom they spoke, in the hope of building up a picture of whatever network that might be operating in the town.

At the meeting's end, all of the participants were dissatisfied. Fitz had relished the idea of striking a lethal blow but recognised the wisdom of not doing so. Crowe had been angered by Brown's objections that only served to confirm his initial opinion; the man was a naive and unqualified operative that should never have been engaged. Brown was shocked at the casual brutality proposed by Fitz and endorsed by Crowe and Wheatley, while outwardly unmoved, was inwardly worried by divisions amongst his officers. He was quite prepared to follow orders just so long as they were clear and the task was achievable. Morality was the province of the officers and their civilian masters.

Brown and Wheatley returned to their hotel by different means and routes. Crowe gave new instructions to the natives who spied for him and a watch was maintained on the building that housed Van Der Merwe and his associates. With these measures put in place, Crowe again voiced his doubts about Brown to Fitzherbert. Fitz knew that the complaint was coming and poured both of them generous whiskies to sooth the mood. He reminded Crowe that Brown had been engaged for his expertise and that had been used to good effect. He went on to reiterate his judgment about Brown being a thoughtful man who could form his own opinions and act on his own initiative. Crowe was forced to concede that Brown had indeed proved useful but grumbled about his foolishness over the blacks and questioned whether he would be up to the job if he was obliged to kill someone. Fitz reassured the consul on the second point and reminded him that as far as the Van Der Merwe matter was concerned, Brown had not said anything that wasn't accurate, even if it was inconvenient. Crowe grumbled a little further but eventually Fitz had him mollified if not happy.

All of the players had retired to their various corners, Fitz and Crowe sipped whisky in the consulate, Brown nursed a gin in the hotel bar and Wheatley perspired over a bottle of ale at a nearby tavern. Opposite Van Der Merwe's house, a young black squatted in the lengthening shadows watching for the comings and goings of the white men from the other side of the street. He had been recruited by a cousin already on Crowe's payroll and had only a hazy idea of the significance of what he was doing. He feared all whites, having had his share of beatings but the people paying him to watch while just as unapproachable seemed less inclined to casual brutality than the local Portuguese. He had no experience of the Boers but they were spoken of as cruel men who hated black people. He didn't know if that was true or just gossip but he knew better than to put it to the test. He sat quiet and watched for activity without result. The sun went down and no light appeared in the windows and he wondered if this lack of anything to report would affect his pay for the job, a concern he voiced to his cousin later when he came to relieve him. Having reassured his relative on the subject of payment, the new man settled in to maintain his own watch in turn. The white men had given him the name of Patience and he lived up to it, maintaining his vigil until the dawn and a new face appeared to take his place.

Brown concluded over breakfast that there would probably now be a period of inactivity while a note was made of the Boers' movements and meetings. He was surprised then to receive an urgent summons to the consulate to which he responded with more curiosity than alarm, at least until he discovered the reason for the meeting. A man's body had been pulled from the waters of the port by some local fishermen, no one could be sure whether he had drowned or the savage blow to the back of the head had killed him but, as Fitz remarked, either way Pedro Nunes was stone dead.

CHAPTER SEVEN

Incursion into Swaziland

Brown was last to the emergency meeting at the consulate. As he entered the room, he took stock of the faces of the other participants. Crowe had a face like thunder, Wheatley wore a look of quiet concern and young Campbell, who had been asked to join them, looked nervous, twisting his hands and occasionally scratching an ear. Fitz was his usual self although he seemed excited, which made the prospect of the meeting more intriguing. At least, these were Brown's initial thoughts until Crowe began speaking.

He announced the murder of Nunes while looking directly at Brown, in such a way that Brown felt he was being accused of doing the deed himself. Brown expressed his shock and regrets at the crime, observing that for all his faults, Nunes had not deserved such a fate. To his surprise, Crowe responded with considerable heat that as a man devoid of loyalty other than to himself, Nunes probably did deserve to die but it was a considerable waste of all the time and money that had been spent cultivating the man. Expanding on the cost to Her Majesty's Treasury, Crowe then made it clear that he believed Brown was in part to blame for Pedro's demise. Crowe attributed the murder to associates of Van Der Merwe who were most put out by the loss of their shipment of arms. In his view, the only reason

Brown had been summoned when he had, was to confirm their suspicions that Nunes had been talking to him and was probably responsible for giving him details of the weapon shipment. Crowe believed that Johanna Reilly was part of the Boer gang and had spotted Brown for what he was straight away, whatever Brown may have believed to the contrary. She had passed his details on to Van Der Merwe and when the loss of the shipment of rifles was discovered, the Boer gang elected to wreak vengeance on the closest and easiest of those they deemed responsible.

Brown was initially dumbstruck, then angry and ultimately furious at the charges laid by Crowe. He wasn't the one who thought it would be a good idea to steal weapons believed to be the Boers', dammit he hadn't even known about it until after the fact and now this ship's captain turned diplomat was making him the scapegoat for a murder that could have been the result of any number of things. Fortunately, Brown wore his emotions on his face and once again, Fitz jumped in to prevent his indignation exploding in the face of Her Majesty's Consul.

'Sure, it's an interesting theory Captain' Fitz said in soothing tones. 'But you know, there's no certainty that the young Reilly woman was caught up with the Boers and even less that she knew what Billy here was about.'

'There may be no evidence in a legal sense' snarled Crowe 'but it seems damned odd that Major Brown has a meeting with a Boer in a house that has been unoccupied for some weeks and is unoccupied again. Our watchers saw no one come or go and no lights in the house. We have asked around and the owner, one Goncalves has been absent from LM for weeks. Either the Boers borrowed or rented the property to give some authenticity to their pose as a legitimate business, or they simply broke in and used it for the one meeting. We're doing our best to find out but we may never know for sure.'

As he paused Fitz interceded and pointed out that Nunes had plenty of enemies from outraged husbands to scorned lovers and people from whom he had extorted money. He stated quite reasonably that any one of a number of people may have been responsible although, in his heart, he was sure that Crowe was probably right in some sense. He was not so sure that he was right about the woman's role but it didn't really matter now because as he said to Brown:

'Whatever may be the case Billy, this place is no longer safe for you. As soon as we have the men to form an escort assembled, we're going to have you and Wheatley here on your way to our friend Von Steinaecker in Swaziland. In the meantime, you can both move in here to keep you away from prying eyes or worse. We'll send a couple of the boys down to the hotel to pick up your kit and we'll arrange to settle the bills with our man Walter.'

Large as the consulate building was Brown had no desire to be confined there under Crowe's malevolent glare. He was angry at the intimation of incompetence and at the callousness with which Nunes' demise had been discussed. It was true that few people if anyone had liked Nunes, but he didn't deserve to be brutally murdered. Arguably, it was the high-handed theft of the contraband which Crowe and Fitz had instigated that got him killed, not any conversation Brown might have had with Johanna. Crowe's main concern now appeared to be that he had invested government funds in a resource that had now been denied to him and to pin responsibility on him. Regrettably, irrespective of any of that, moving to the consulate was the sensible thing to do and so he nodded his assent and asked the obvious question:

'How long will it take to assemble an escort? And how many men will there be?'

Fitz and Crowe exchanged glances before Fitz answered:

'There will be ten men in total, all with good bush skills and most with experience of Africa. Some are here already and waiting for orders the rest should be here in a matter of days. After that, it's just a matter of getting the men and the mules together and plotting a route to find Baron Von Steinaecker.'

'Mules?' Queried Brown, 'why do we need mules?'

'Von Steinaecker needs arms and ammunition, those rifles we lifted are doing no good here. You're going to take them to the Baron together with the explosives needed to blow that bridge.' He would also be taking a fair quantity of cash to pay Von Steinaecker's troopers but Fitz decided he would slip that information out at a later date. He had given Brown enough to worry about for now and he inwardly cursed Crowe for putting his man on edge. Even if there was something in what he said, throwing speculations about blame around would not bring Nunes back to life and what was one dead Portuguese more or less? Crowe would just have to cultivate his successor.

Brown absorbed the information and its implications and worried. Firstly, he worried about running guns and explosives across enemy territory. Even if Swaziland was neutral, it was under Boer protection and by all accounts they were quite active there. Secondly, even if he had a strong escort, they would be slow moving due to the cargo they would be carrying. Had he known about the money that he would also be carrying, he would have worried about that too. To his credit and that of his military training, he was most concerned at the obstacles to getting the job done rather than about any personal risk. He would worry about that when the time came but for now, he began to focus on the task in hand.

The meeting now was reduced to Brown, Fitz and Wheatley as it was one of purely military aspect. Where were they going? What was the safest route? How long would it take? There were also questions of supplies for men and horses, order of march and other details that had to be addressed before any movement could even be contemplated. Crowe had stayed for a time but could contribute little so to Brown's relief, excused himself. After an hour or two, they had roughed out a plan that seemed reasonable or at least within reasonable bounds, given the task at hand. When the escort was all in, they would then be able to brief them on the outline so that all of the party knew what to expect. Wheatley cautioned the two officers to allow the troops to have a say in the final plans. As he explained, some of these men would know the ground and the realities of moving through a hostile environment patrolled by hostile forces. Despite their experience as Victorian officers, the sense of Wheatley's advice was obvious and they agreed that once the men arrived they would be fully briefed on the plan and asked for their contributions. For Brown, who had been away from the army for some years, this was not a difficult adjustment, he was used to taking advice from experts in business but he wondered how Fitz might feel about listening to the views of ordinary soldiers. He needn't have worried, Fitz was quite the independent thinker and freed from the restraints of a regimental command structure, he was happy to work in different ways, so long as they showed a likelihood of success or offered him a chance of action.

Brown kicked his heels at the consulate, passing the time by reading and wondering what Johanna might be doing and if she had noticed his absence. He also thought about Elizabeth and the contrast between the two women. He felt guilty about the frequency with which Johanna popped into his head but consoled himself with the thought that it was just the unknown about her and how she may have played a part in the death of Nunes. For himself, he had no doubt that she had had no involvement. He did not believe for one moment that she was a Boer agent, although he conceded that she had little love for the English as a nation. Her notions about Irish home rule were naively romantic but that was unsurprising given her upbringing. He rather hoped he might see her again if only to discover the truth about her. For his own satisfaction, nothing more.

Fitz's estimate for the arrival of the escort party was fairly accurate. Four days after Brown and Wheatley moved into the consulate, word came in that all of their men had arrived in LM and were awaiting orders. A meeting was duly arranged to run over the outline plan and discuss any points the troopers might have. It would not do to have all ten arrive or leave together, so five parties of two were given different times to arrive during the course of the afternoon. However long their business took to conclude, no one would be leaving before dark to minimise the risk of arousing the curiosity of any Boer agent watching the comings and goings.

They were a hard looking group of men. Despite their relative youth, some of the faces were lined, all of them darkened by constant exposure to the sun. They wore khaki but not uniform and certainly no badges of rank or regiment. Brown looked at them and remembered Wellington's words: 'I don't know what they'll do to the enemy but by God they frighten me.' Happily, they seemed friendly enough if a bit more familiar with their officers than Fitz or Brown had been used to. This seemed to bother Wheatley rather than the officers, possibly because they expected it. Wheatley said nothing but his cringes at some lapse of etiquette were evidence of his discomfort.

As to the troop, a number were Australian, a couple Scots but all had a lot of African experience mostly military or police. They had arrived in LM by different routes, including in some cases overland. They listened carefully as Brown outlined the details of Von Steinaecker's unit and the planned march to join it. Every now and then one would ask a question or suggest an amendment but overall, to Brown's relief, they seemed content with what was being suggested, although one of the Australians, who had listened in silence wore a look that suggested he had doubts. Only when everyone else had spoken did he stand up and walk to the improvised map board on which Brown had outlined the proposed route in to Swaziland. He looked at the board carefully and then turned to Brown as the room fell silent.

'So as I understand you, you propose to march South to M'tini, cross the Swazi border there by the river and then follow the river in to the interior until we can find this Von Steinaecker character?'

Brown agreed that this was the proposed route, and wondering if there was an objection asked if the questioner might have an alternative suggestion.

'No Major, it's probably the best, particularly with us carrying cargo. In fact, I travelled here from Natal along some of the same paths.'

Brown's face relaxed into a smile: 'Well that's splendid news, so you know the country well?'

'I know it well enough. What's not so splendid is the smelling out and killing off that's going on. The whole country is in chaos since the king died.'

'Smelling out? Killing off? What the devil are you talking about?'

'Devilry is about right. It's an old native custom and damn deadly it is.' Seeing the blank look on Brown's face not to mention Wheatley, Fitz and even some of his companions, he attempted to explain.

'See, when the King dies[11], the blacks believe that evildoers may have caused the death. The witch doctors are brought in to sniff out the culprits who are then ritually killed in gruesome fashion.'

Brown was unsurprised at such barbarism but could not see what a little palace intrigue and ritual murder had to do with their expedition and said so.

'It's not just the palace that's involved, every bastard with a grudge uses the opportunity to murder their rivals often including whole families. I saw entire villages destroyed on my journey, livestock slaughtered along with men, women and kids. And don't think they wouldn't take a slap at white men if they thought they could get away with it. The whole country is either mad or drunk or both. I met one bloke who only just got away when he refused to surrender one of his workers to a bloodthirsty mob. I'm surprised nobody told you.'

Brown looked at Fitz questioningly, wondering if this was yet one more piece of information that Fitz

---

[11] King Bhunu of Swaziland had died in December at the age of 22. The probable cause was chronic alcoholism but it triggered waves of killing throughout the kingdom generated by witch doctors and local chieftains seeking supposed evil doers that had led to the King's demise.

had failed to mention but the latter addressed the Australian trooper directly:

'We had heard that the King had died and that there were some disturbances following the new Queen's accession but not much more.' If Fitz was concerned, it wasn't obvious. He smiled at the Australian and asked his name and his opinion as to whether the proposed journey remained viable.

The man looked at Fitz as if he had encountered an alien life form, which, in a way, he had, at least when Fitz was set alongside the people he was used to dealing with. His name was Dan Murray and his previous experience with British officers had been marked by their suspicion and condescension towards colonials in general and Australians in particular. Now, here was this Pom, as posh as a prince, asking his name and his opinion. He wondered if it was a joke or some sort of trap to have him make a fool of himself but something about the questioner's demeanour told him he was genuine. So he gave his name and his opinion, which was that it was unlikely that any insurgent natives would attack a well armed force of a dozen white men however drunk on booze or bloodlust they might be. He also explained that there was no rhyme or reason to the violence. It could erupt anywhere without warning and it was entirely possible that nothing untoward would happen near them and as time went on, it was quite possible that the killing would burn itself out.

If his words were intended to reassure, they were only partially successful, Fitz was in no doubt that the risk was manageable but then he wasn't going. Brown, on the other hand, was more doubtful but Wheatley and the others said nothing and were presumed content. After all, they were trained soldiers with modern rifles, more than enough for a few bloodthirsty blacks armed with assegais and ox hide shields. Just so long as there weren't too many of them at any one time as there had been at Isandlwana. [12]

All obstacles overcome, at least as far as planning was concerned. A day and a time were set for departure which would be on the next Sunday before dawn. Brown, Wheatley and two troopers would start from the consulate in the early hours, riding west with the horses and mule train. At that time, there would be few, if any others abroad, particularly on a Sunday and four armed men would deter all but the hardiest gang of villains. At intervals, the balance of the party would join them as they rode out onto the road west of the town and prior to making the turn south toward M'tini. Before the sun had properly risen they should be twelve strong and clear of LM. As Wheatley advised and Brown concurred: 'Riding with the attitude of men who have every right to be here.'

---

[12] The battle of Islandlwana fought on the 22nd of January 1879 was a stunning victory for King Cetshwayo's Zulu *Impis* against British troops. British forces under Lord Chelmsford invaded the Zulu Kingdom on the 11th of January 1879 as part of a British plan to absorb the Zulus into a federation of Southern African states under British rule. Chelmsford had little regard for the capabilities of the Zulus and split his force, leaving a mixed force of 1,800 including six companies of the 24th Foot in camp at Isandlwana. A Zulu force 20,000 strong attacked the camp on the morning of the 22nd. The Zulus were armed with spears and clubs, the British with modern breech loading rifles and artillery. The main Zulu force was discovered at about 11.00am, by early afternoon the British had been defeated with 1,300 killed by the Zulu forces.

It had all sounded good when discussed in the safety of the consulate, in practice it wasn't quite so simple to assemble a mule train and a dozen riders in the pitch black of a pre-dawn Lourenço Marques. There were a couple of wrong turns, and one missed rendezvous but eventually the whole troop and mules were together and on the right road in the right direction. The sun had risen just after they cleared the outskirts of the town and turned South. In the darkness, Brown had been nervous and had jumped every time that a mule had screeched, or any stranger had come into view, happily, in the darkness nobody noticed. Now that they were on their way and he could see their surroundings, he was more confident. He had ten tough looking troopers and the imperturbable Wheatley with him and one more inconspicuous associate, Crowe had sent his spy Patience with them to reconnoitre the land and warn them of any danger across their path. Crowe also wanted more information about the current conditions in Swaziland after the death of the King.

Patience moved on foot and mostly out of sight. He seemed perpetually cheerful and consequently the men treated him as they might an exotic pet although one or two regarded him with suspicion and kept their valuables close when he came near. He was relatively short and slight but moved with great speed and little noise. He wasn't certain of his own age but was probably not much more than twenty. He had little education but he spoke good English and Portuguese in addition to his own language. Skills that many of the white men in the party lacked but that people like Patience required for their very survival. White men had been in his part of Africa all of his life and that of his parents too. They were far more numerous now and much more mobile with the coming of the railway and to Patience, they were strange people that behaved in peculiar ways. The old people of his grandparents' generation muttered about a time before they had come but to Patience, they were a fact of life. He neither welcomed nor resented their presence, the casual brutality that some could display towards black people was another matter but in Captain Crowe he and his cousin had struck lucky. They were paid well, at least they thought they were, and fed and thus far nobody had raised a hand to them unlike other whites they had worked for. Uneducated he may have been but Patience understood that the British and the Boers were at war. The position of the Portuguese he was less sure of but he was not alone in that. His experience of the Boers had not been happy and the Portuguese had not been much better. Crowe and the other Britons that he had encountered had at least been fair although he had heard that even with Britons, this was not always the case. Yet here he was guiding these men and their horses and mules across his native land. Risking his life for scraps of food and a handful of coins. No one in Whitehall would have questioned Crowe's frugality here.

 Once clear of LM the road was mostly empty and such people as they did encounter were all natives. They all seemed friendly enough and Patience proved to be a skilled haggler where the purchase of food was concerned. The weather was hot but the cooler, drier days and nights were coming bringing a reduced risk of fever for both man and beast. While on Portuguese territory they could ride easy and the men bantered among each other and occasionally with Brown himself although not so much with Wheatley. He assumed correctly that they were trying him out, gauging his reaction to their familiarity, which was for the most part good natured but wouldn't have passed unnoticed in Aldershot. Brown took it in good part and remembering his past experiences, addressed each man by name and cracked the odd joke of his own without giving the impression of weakness. As they progressed South the confidence he felt in his command became mutual to the point where one of the Australians suggested to Wheatley that: 'the Major's not a bad bloke for a Pom.' Wheatley happily agreed but put it down to Brown's Irish roots. Overhearing the exchange, Brown couldn't help feeling amused. They were all part of the one empire but just like the blacks, they had their own tribes. The English, Scots Irish and Welsh and further abroad, the Australians and New Zealanders not to mention Britain's America, the Canadians. One great Imperial tribe all ranged against that other European tribe, the Boers. And within that great tribe, there were tribes within tribes.

It took five days to reach M'tini and the river Usutu, whose valley would be the entry point through the Lebombo Mountains that ran North to South along the border, protecting Swaziland from those to her East. On Portuguese territory they were able to ride easy and banter away but entering Swaziland, the joking stopped. Here the prized skill was listening rather than talking and keeping careful eyes open for hostiles, both human and animal.

Some of the latter came into view as they watered the horses and mules by the river. On a mid-river sandbank lay numerous crocodiles apparently sunning themselves peacefully. Quiet and somnolent as they appeared, everyone was aware that there might be others who were more awake. Brown watched them and wondered if their presence was some kind of omen, a warning perhaps not to push on into their country? Dismissing the notion, he found Wheatley and a couple of the older troopers and thrashed out a revised order of march and camp routine now that they had left Portuguese territory. The river valley they were to follow made him nervous, the hilly country and the vegetation still lush from the summer rains provided too many opportunities for ambush. They were only just inside Swazi territory and safe enough for the present but further on might be different. Resolving to be clear of the valley in daylight, Brown elected to halt there and push through the following day. Camp was made a safe distance from the river and its scaly residents and fires were lit to discourage any less aquatic predators from taking a close interest. Water was boiled for tea and for their canteens and guards were set. They were on a hard regime now, tomorrow would be stand to before the dawn and an early start that should see them through the valley to the plain beyond with daylight to spare.

There had been no marker to show where Portuguese territory ended and the Swazi kingdom began. In his mind's eye, Brown had half expected to cross into a world of burning villages and Boers lurking behind each bush. In reality, at first light, they found themselves riding through a pleasantly green valley, cool and quiet in the early morning and apparently deserted except for themselves and the abundant wildlife. The various antelope they saw they left unmolested. Until they had cleared the valley and were in open country, the risk of a shot drawing attention to them was too great. They rode alertly, and as quietly as was possible. Even the mules seemed to have caught the mood and walked on in a stoic silence. They had riders ahead and behind as well as a flank guard. When they had stood to arms before first light it was noticed that Patience was missing. There was some dark muttering among a few of the men that he had left them in the lurch, or worse, that he had run off to betray them. Brown quashed the complaints pointing out that Patience was often gone before dawn and always returned. Today would be no different and he would show up again as he always did, grinning happily and hopefully laden with fresh fruit. Brown believed in what he said about Patience's return but that would not stop him worrying about it until the little fellow showed up. He wasn't being emotional just practical. Patience was the best scout they had.

Happily, his faith was rewarded as the ever-smiling Patience made his reappearance just before they made a midday halt. He said he had seen no sign of any other white men and very few natives, all of which was welcome news. Brown was keen to be on their way before there were any changes to the scene but he knew that the horses had to be rested first. He fretted as the men smoked their pipes and chatted quietly while horses and mules enjoyed some rough grazing and water from the shallows of the river under the watchful eye of a trooper with rifle in case of crocodiles. As he waited impatiently it seemed that only he was conscious of the need to make progress out of the valley. Even Patience seemed relaxed as he chewed on a piece of biltong one of the troopers had given him. In truth, all were aware of the danger but losing a horse or mule to dehydration or exhaustion would be just as perilous. Eventually he ordered everyone up and mounted and the journey continued much as before. Patience went forward with their lead scout and soon vanished into the bush. As they rode, Brown alternately checked his pocket watch and the way ahead. Hoping that the land would begin to flatten out before the shadows grew longer. Sometimes he was convinced that they were almost there and on other occasions, he decided he would be trapped in the valley. He didn't relax at all until they rounded a bend in the river and there were hills alongside them but none to their front. Even then, he reminded himself that they had only reduced the odds of ambush and not eliminated them. Nevertheless, the tension that had accompanied their progress eased as the going became gentler. Soon the river turned away to the South and they left the river's course behind them with mixed emotions. It was a guaranteed source of water in what was a dry season, but their party were not the only thirsty creatures abroad. A variety of wildlife would make its way to the river some of which might be highly dangerous to man and beast. Murray noted that there were plenty of springs and when he had passed through previously, the dams used by the white farmers to hold water had all been nearly full. Looking around at the green vegetation, the signs were hopeful that water remained in abundant supply. Cheered by this and glancing once again at his watch Brown pushed the column on for the last few hours of daylight and a well-earned rest.

A suitable site for the night's camp was found and the evening routine commenced. For Brown, the relief of passing through the river valley and into the flatter bush beyond was now tempered by the deep darkness that descended. Away from the fire, the stars shone brilliantly but with no significant moonlight, movement needed to be cautious. Even the most experienced Africa man found guard stag a lonely and somewhat nerve-racking duty. To emphasise their remote location, every now and then a jackal would call or they would catch the roar of a distant lion but mostly, it was deathly still and silent and no less nerve wracking for that.

Everyone, Brown included, took their turn on guard duty and everyone was relieved when he finally gave the order to stand to. The sun was beginning to show red on the horizon, the fire was kicked into life for the morning brew of tea and each man began his own ritual of preparing for the day. There was no inspection, no parade or shouted orders. Each man took responsibility for himself, his horse and his equipment. Brown had observed them each morning and had no desire to interfere when no interference was required. They were competent men, proud in their own way and knew more about the bush than he did. He respected their skills and in turn they grew to like the Pommie Major, at least as much as they liked any officer. They hadn't seen him under real pressure yet but so far, he had not done anything obviously wrong and had done quite a lot that was right. Wheatley, due to his size, his Irishness and his experience had won almost instant acceptance which was only increased when it became clear that he was no parade ground sergeant.

Their departure was accomplished swiftly and quietly. Dawn came quickly but it was barely light when they set out. They didn't attempt to hide the campsite, there was little point. Twelve horsemen and accompanying mules would leave a trail that couldn't be hidden. The information they had was that Von Steinaecker and his group were operating to the North West of the kingdom, near to the Transvaal border. This would also be close to the LM to Pretoria railway and the bridge that they intended to destroy. This then also took them that much closer to enemy territory.

So they went on their way much as before, Patience had left before stand to although none of the pickets had noticed him. This was clearly an affront to the bush skills of the troops and soon wagers were being made as to who might first detect Patience coming or going out of camp. Wheatley grinned at Brown when he asked if he would be betting:

'Not a gambling man sir, so I'm not but if I was, it'd be the wee black feller I'd be betting on, not these people, however good they are.'

Brown smiled back and commended the Sergeant on his good judgment. He also didn't see any of the troopers catching Patience despite their obvious skills. They rode on in near silence for thirty minutes or so, until from ahead came the crack of a rifle which halted them in their tracks. It could have meant trouble but Brown had given the lead scout permission to shoot a buck if the opportunity arose. Fresh meat was hard to come by and where they were, the risk of a shot was worth it for the meat. It was almost certainly their scout but even so, Brown found himself praying that it was so and if it was not so that it had not been a terrible mistake to allow the shot. Certainly, they would not be moving before they knew the truth, one way or another. Happily after halting for some fifteen minutes or so, Trooper Harris came into view with an Impala slung across his saddle bow, neatly killed by a single shot.

The carcass of the Impala was transferred to a protesting mule after being swiftly field dressed and the column moved on, Harris trotting back to his position out in front of the main body. He had apparently seen a lot of game which suggested that there might be a spring or stream nearby but could also indicate the presence of predators. Once, Brown had been excited by Africa, the exotic plants and animals, the space and clean air of the veldt and the opportunities it presented. That was what seemed a lifetime ago. Now any piece of good fortune seemed balanced by an attendant peril. If it wasn't the Boers, it was bloodthirsty natives and if that wasn't enough there were dangerous animals and disease enough to send any sane man running for the first ship home. He wasn't insane, but he didn't have much time to dwell on the dangers, he had a job to do, responsibility for eleven other men and a valuable cargo so it was crack on and look to your front like a soldier.

They found a stream that was free of crocodiles and sunbathing lions and made a brief stop to refresh the horses and pack animals. According to Murray, who was the man with the most recent knowledge, there was little hostile activity this far South but further on as they neared the Northwest of the country, Boer patrols would be watching for any British activity near their border or the all-important railway line to the East. Their current situation was far from safe however and nobody was relaxing as they moved out once more. Several hours passed that might have been dull in other circumstances but in fact were tense and tiring as they scanned their surroundings for any signs of danger. For some minutes Brown had thought he had caught a suspicion of woodsmoke on the light air. He looked ahead and could see nothing but bush but sniffing again, he was certain he could smell smoke. He was about to call a halt when a small figure on foot appeared over the slight rise to their front. Patience had returned with news that explained the smell of smoke but that was unwelcome. Over the rise lay a shallow valley and a native village or rather what remained of it. Patience described a scene of savage desolation: burned huts, corpses lying where they had fallen and so recent that the vultures had yet to descend. That meant that whoever the perpetrators might be, they would be nearby. The random barbarism Patience described made it unlikely to have been Boers. They might treat the natives harshly but they didn't kill without cause and village massacres were certainly not their style. This left the likely culprits as being other natives 'killing off' to avenge a grudge or just for sheer devilry and likely, still in the area.

Brown considered his choices and quickly narrowed them down to three. They could halt for the rest of the day and night and hope that the killers had moved on before they continued, they could detour around the village hoping that they didn't encounter any hostiles or they could push on into the village trusting that their rifles would keep them safe from spear wielding warriors. None of the options were particularly appealing and Brown brought in Murray and Wheatley to seek their opinions. After a brief discussion all agreed that the safest course would be to seek out a suitable location for a defensible campsite and to hold fast there until the morning when they could push on with a good chance that the marauders had also moved on. They waited for the two men of the rearguard to catch up with them so that they could be briefed on developments and they could all then move together. The two arrived more quickly than anticipated and looking somewhat flushed. Dismounting in front of Brown, they brought him the disturbing news that despite being some distance from the Transvaal, there was a Boer patrol to their South East. They were unclear on numbers having sighted them at a distance but believed them to be at least a dozen strong. It was also not possible to know if they were following Brown's column or just happened to be in the area. What was not in doubt was that they would soon see the sign left behind as the column passed. What their reaction to the tracks of a dozen horses and some mules was uncertain.

Would they assume it was just a cargo of supplies for the mines to the North or would they suspect that it was a military column?

It was an unfortunate dilemma and had Brown's force trapped between the two elements they had feared most. The bloodthirsty native forces ahead and the enemy behind. Of the two, Brown worried about the enemy most. Even if they could fight them off, which was by no means certain, they would have been discovered, which would make their journey more dangerous and could have wider implications for operations with Von Steinaecker. If they encountered hostile natives, with luck, the natives would be unarmed other than for assegais. Deadly enough in sufficient numbers to be sure but they would have little enthusiasm or incentive for a scrap with well-armed professionals.

As Brown summed up to Wheatley and Murray: 'we have to avoid the Boers, even if it means taking our chances with the locals we'll have to detour round the village and keep moving.'

Murray nodded agreement but Wheatley's brow furrowed in thought.

Brown prompted him: 'Sergeant?'

'Well sir, if we have to take our chances with the blacks like you say, would we not be safer passing through the village rather than going around? Sure the Boers will smell the smoke same as us and might think twice about going that way for the same reasons we did.'

It was Brown's turn to think hard. Wheatley's words made sense and the chances were that the people that had torched the village and killed the inhabitants would have moved on anyway. If the Boer patrol was determined to investigate them, they would be no worse off and possibly, the ruined village might throw them off their track or at least slow them up. Deciding that Wheatley was right but also seeking affirmation, he turned to Murray and asked for his opinion. Murray had now become used to this new breed of Pommie officer and forgetting his original agreement with Brown, threw his weight behind Wheatley for the same sound reasons that the Sergeant had put forward but suggested they quiz Patience further on what exactly he had seen in the village.

Summoned to join them, Patience was very firm that the only humans he had seen had been corpses. The settlement was silent and he was quite certain that all of the murderers had moved on although, how far he couldn't say. Murray had listened to the diminutive black carefully, asking the occasional question but principally letting Patience talk. Once satisfied, he took off his bush hat and wiped the sweat from his eyes and forehead before speaking a few words in a native language which made Patience's smile even wider.

'You speak their language?' Asked Brown with some surprise.

'Not really sir, just a few phrases I picked up.'

'Well, what did you say, it seemed to make him happy?'

'I just thanked him and asked him to keep a sharp lookout. Not wishing to speak out of turn sir but I think he should scout ahead of us.'

Brown considered the proposal and saw it's wisdom but also the potential danger to Patience.

'If there's anyone there and they catch him they'll kill him.'

The Australian looked at Brown in wonder: 'Probably true sir and if they catch us the same might happen, which would you prefer?'

It was sound advice if badly presented. Wheatley had turned a shade of red but Brown seemed unperturbed by the seeming insolence. He was fairly certain it had not been intended to offend but was simply the way the trooper was used to expressing himself. It certainly wasn't the time or place to be having an argument over decorum. Brown contented himself with a nod to Murray and asked him to tell Patience what was needed from him. Turning to Wheatley, he issued orders for the troop to mount up and be ready to move. The two soldiers that had been rearguard estimated that they likely had a fair start on the Boers but they should not delay further in moving off, advice Brown was glad to take.

Patience had trotted off over the rise and had vanished among the thorn bushes and anthills. The column followed him slowly and cautiously with every man alert to odd sights or sounds that might mean danger. As they progressed, the smell of smoke grew stronger but there was no sound beyond their own movement. The going was now gently downhill and Brown guessed that any settlement was probably near water. Looking ahead, he noted a number of birds flying in a rough circle which indicated the location of the village and that it hadn't taken too long for the vultures to find their next meal. Shuddering slightly at the thought of the wicked beaks and claws ripping human flesh, he cast an eye backwards for any sign of pursuit but of course, saw nothing but the dusty troopers and mules following. Moving aside, he let the majority pass and then rode alongside the rear guard, now close in on the column, to satisfy himself that all was well.

Up ahead, things were not so good, as he discovered when he noticed a pause in the movement causing him to ride forward to find out the cause of the delay. He found out soon enough and wished he hadn't. Approaching a clutch of men apparently examining something they had found; he was about to rebuke them when he became aware of an appalling smell that worsened as he drew near and masked the scent of smoke. The source of the foul odour quickly became apparent once he had pushed his way through the dismounted troopers. On the ground was the body of a native man. His head had been shockingly battered probably by a knobkerrie and he had been disembowelled, his guts spilling out of his stomach and onto the ground. Brown winced involuntarily and swallowed hard. One of the other men turned away and vomited which did nothing to improve things.

Brown felt sick too, sick and angry but also fearful of the savagery that had passed this way and might yet be nearby. All of this he masked by yelling at the men to remount and get moving, which to his relief, they did. A little further and they came to the smouldering ruins of the village. The round, straw huts or rondavels as they were known were now just circular piles of still warm ash. The stockyard had been smashed and such livestock as had not been carried off appeared to have been wantonly slaughtered. The same treatment had been meted out to any villager that had been foolish enough to get in the way of the marauders. The corpses of men women and children lay where they had fallen, surrounded by black blood stains and buzzing swarms of flies. Even had they had the inclination, there was no question of burying them all, it would have taken days. At Brown's urging they moved on and through the village following a shallow stream for a short distance. Once satisfied that, at least for now, they were out of danger, they paused for water. As he looked around while the horses drank, Brown realised that much time had passed. Shadows had begun to lengthen and they would need to find a defensible camp site soon.

There was a slight rise in the ground to their North, the summit of which, such as it was, revealed a considerable plateau beyond. If the Boers were following them, there was nowhere much to hide. With the light failing and the necessity of fire to repel wild animals, they had to do the best they could and hope that there was no pursuit. In the end a stand of Marula trees was the best place that could be found. There was a reasonable amount of dry wood for a fire and even a little rough grazing for the animals. Each man knew his job and his place on the guard rota and before the very last of last light, animals had been secured, a fire lit and tea brewed and the first guards were on look out. While pieces of Harris's Impala were being cooked, those not on guard drank tea and talked quietly while cleaning weapons and checking harness. Brown was not the only one to have been shocked by the horrors of the village, even the hardest of the troop had been shaken by the sheer primitive bestiality of what had taken place. There seemed to be differing opinions on the event and its cause. Some said it was bad actors among the Swazis using the death of the King to settle old scores. Others maintained that all blacks were savages at heart and would murder anyone merely for amusement. Someone pointed out that Patience was not a bit like that and drew snorts of derision for his trouble.

'They're like wild animals' declared one of the Australians, 'you can hand rear 'em and they'll come to you for food and pretend to be your friend but show any weakness and they'll turn on you.'

Brown thought this a trifle hard considering the risks Patience had taken in warning them of the burned village and the fact that not long ago when these men had been brewing tea, Patience had been out scouting for any sign of Boer or Swazi pursuit. He was not about to enter a discussion of this nature with his soldiers but he was interested in how they saw the black people whose country they were crossing. For himself, he believed that if Patience was anyone to go by, with education, the natives' condition could be greatly improved. Currently, they were akin to grown children but with adult instincts and armed with spears and clubs. When unsupervised, inevitably horrors like today might occur. They could be taught better but only Great Britain seemed to have an interest in doing so. The victims of today and their murderers were under Boer protection which seemed of little value against either themselves or the Boers. The Boers were an inflexible people, particularly in matters of race and in Brown's view, their failure to adapt would finish them as it had so many other people who remained wedded to another time. It was unfortunate but they had no one to blame but themselves. With that thought, he rose to do his rounds of the guard posts preparatory to taking his turn on duty. Fascinating as the long-term solution to the native question might be, it was unlikely that anyone would seek his opinion on the subject and he had more important short term matters to attend to. Nevertheless, he would find himself wondering about the future for Patience and his brothers while keeping alert to the danger from the white men out there somewhere.

CHAPTER EIGHT

Brown's rendezvous with Steinaecker

While Brown was pondering the future for the native population and keeping his senses alert for non-native activity, in Lourenço Marques, Major Fitzherbert was dealing with a little local difficulty of his own. The man Forbes, who lived in Swaziland and had ridden with Boer Commandos against the Zulus was now interfering with the British war against those same Boers.

Despite the rebuff he had received at his attempts to raise the Forbes Lubombo Scouts, Forbes had persisted in his desire to lead an Imperial unit, preferably one bearing his name. To this end, he had somehow persuaded the army authorities in Cape Town to send a squadron of Canadian cavalry to Kosi Bay where they would land. Forbes would then lead them across Swaziland to Komatipoort to destroy the bridge that Brown and Von Steinaecker were intending to blow. In his role as intelligence liaison officer, Fitz had become aware of the plan and determined to stop it. He had not taken to Forbes and shared the view of General Buller that he was an amateur. More importantly, success by Forbes would take away any credit Fitz might have expected for his involvement. Fitz therefore sent word to the High

Command that the Boers were aware of the plan and had the bridge heavily guarded. As a result, the hapless Forbes waited on the Natal shore for his cavalry to disembark, only to receive a signal from the Royal Navy warship offshore that the operation had been cancelled. It was unfortunate thought Fitz but to have two British units roaming around Swaziland each unaware of the other could have had disastrous consequences. The fact that the bumptious Forbes had actually succeeded in having a force dispatched also underlined the need for an intelligence liaison such as himself to help the imperial forces work together rather than independently[13].

Fitz was quietly satisfied at his success in foiling the Forbes interference and demonstrating the necessity of a unified command structure. Whether his satisfaction was shared by Rear Admiral Harris, the Royal Navy Commander in the Cape and the sailors crewing the ships that had pointlessly sailed to Kosi Bay was more questionable. It crossed his mind that a man that knew the country, spoke the languages and had the necessary resource to divert a squadron of the Royal Navy might be a valuable asset. He swiftly dismissed the idea. The man's ego

---

[13] Somehow, Forbes had succeeded in persuading Rear Admiral Harris to sail with a number of ships and a squadron of Strathcona's Horse to Kosi Bay without General Buller or his staff becoming aware of the proposed operation. When Harris received a signal from LM advising that the plan was public knowledge and that the Boers had reinforced the bridge, he cancelled the operation. For whatever reason, the signal that Forbes received from HMS 'Widgeon' advised that the cancellation was due to weather too rough to allow a landing.

was out of control and he had the potential to be difficult. Fitz had his own man in place who would follow direction, he certainly didn't need loose cannons rolling around his deck. No, let him leave matters to Bill Brown and Von Steinaecker, under his guidance of course, and Forbes could be somebody else's problem. He had other pressing matters at hand, not least the location and interview of Johanna Reilly.

Waking in the pre-dawn out in the Swazi bush, Brown also had Johanna Reilly on his mind but for different reasons to Fitz. Brown was wondering what she was doing and wearing and whether she thought of him at all. He did suspect that she might not be quite who she claimed to be but he knew she could not be a Boer agent. Fitz, by contrast, was seeking to be certain that Johanna was no danger but if she was, to stop her in her tracks. Crowe's boys were on the lookout for her with instructions to rush news of any sightings to the consulate. So far they had drawn a blank. Crowe put the failure down to the absence of Patience but also conceded that she may have left town with Van Der Merwe, who was believed to have sailed out on a Dutch ship bound for Europe. Whatever the truth, if she was in LM, she would be found and if she had shipped out, like Forbes, she would become someone else's problem.

Shivering in the darkness Brown brought his mind to bear on more immediate concerns. The dry season was upon them and the nights were chilly. He had passed an uncomfortable night with limited sleep and a nerve straining guard stag. Yet nothing and nobody had come near them. The smoke of their own fires lingered and reminded him of the stomach-churning horrors of the previous day. He kicked the nearest fire back into some sort of life to take his mind off the images and smells in his memory and found some dry wood to impart life to the embers. Others followed his lead and with just a hint of purple in the sky, those who had been sleeping began to rouse themselves. The first issue that concerned him was the location of the Boer patrol, after that came any maddened natives and last of all the whereabouts of Von Steinaecker. With luck, they were only two day's ride away but that was if Von S was where he was expected to be and if they didn't have to deviate to avoid either of the first two. Worrying and wondering was not going to help so he cleared his mind of such things, found Wheatley and once more got his troop underway.

The land before them was empty except for the game they disturbed along the way, buck and zebra by the score and the occasional group of giraffes, trotting gracefully away when the column disturbed them at their breakfast. Nothing untoward was reported and they made fair progress across the plain. Once the sun was up properly and men could feel the warmth on their backs, their spirits rose too. Brown conferred with Wheatley and Murray as they rode and they agreed that the Boers had chosen to ignore them or had taken a different course. Now, all they had to do was locate Von Steinaecker and his few men in several hundred square miles of wild country. As one of the Scots fellows called Inkster pointed out, a sense of humour was an important military quality in such circumstances. With this in mind, Brown listened as the men around him cracked some very old jokes. However many times the stories had been told and retold, men still laughed. They were familiar and comfortable like a pair of favourite boots or gloves. They suited the mood and took men's minds away from the dangers of their job. These men did not, however lower their level of vigilance. They joked with their eyes open. After time though, the joking died away and they were left with only a hard and boring slog across rough plain to occupy their minds, that, and the element of danger that was never far away. The further they travelled, the more tired they became and as fatigue levels increased, so vigilance declined. As a result, the return of one of the scouts went unnoticed until he was almost upon them. If that didn't cause them to sharpen up, the report that he made to Brown certainly had them scanning the horizon. To their Southeast, was a party of horsemen. The trooper making the report stated that in his judgment they were on a parallel course rather than following directly behind. That could mean that they were just a party of civilians going about their business or more likely a Boer patrol, it was hard to tell from a distance when most people wore some variant of khaki and travelling any distance left you covered in dust. So, the question then was friend or foe and if foe what were their intentions? Brown called a halt and conferred with Wheatley, Murray and the scout.

The four of them considered the various possibilities and the conclusion that they reached was that barring miracles, whoever was out there was unlikely to be friendly. The best that they could hope for was indifferent but that seemed unlikely and carried with it the risk of whoever it might be talking about their presence to someone who was definitely unfriendly. So assuming that this was a hostile force, what was to be done? Laden as they were, they couldn't hope to distance them, stopping where they were to let them ride by might work if it was a routine patrol that was unaware of their presence. The only other possibility was to change direction away from the other group and hope that it shook them off. If they were being hunted, that seemed something of a long shot. In the end, they reached a form of compromise. The country to their left was more hilly than that which they were currently traversing and might provide better cover and safety for a group of their size. They would make for the higher ground and then halt for the night. Brown asked if anyone had seen Patience but he was nowhere to be found. Cursing the fellow for being absent when most needed Brown gave the order to change course and they began a slight left turn towards the hills to their West. It wouldn't take them too far out of their way and hopefully would shake off any pursuit. Unlikely thought Brown, nervously reassuring himself that his revolver was still strapped to his belt, but one lives in hope.

To Brown's surprise, the course alteration appeared to work, their rear scouts reported no sign of Boer activity behind them as they made their way further into the low hills and the shadows began to lengthen. Patience reappeared, seemingly out of nowhere and trotted along with them for a distance chatting with the friendly troopers and keeping clear of the ones that still harboured their suspicions. Brown sent him forward to find a suitable camp site, which he did with commendable alacrity. A broad, low hilltop near a small stream and enough vegetation to provide a source of wood and grazing. Although when they arrived the light was beginning to fail, it looked reasonably secure and seemed to command a view of at least some of the surrounding ground.

After a night spent cat napping between nerve jangling guard duties and the occasional disturbing animal noise Brown was tired but happy to see some colour in the sky. With luck and effort they should have a shot at finding Von Steinaecker today. Always assuming he was where he was supposed to be. Before leaving LM a rendezvous point had been agreed and Von S was to be there or nearby to await their arrival. That was assuming he had received the message and further assuming that they could find the correct location using the rudimentary maps and a measure of military skill. Crowe had assured him that the message to Von S had been coded and would be indecipherable in the event that the messenger was captured. Based on Brown's experience with Crowe's code in LM he expected it would take the average Boer about ten minutes to unscramble if he didn't just beat the information out of the messenger. If the messenger had been intercepted, he expected a welcoming committee of the Bremersdorp Commando. But they could worry about that once and if they got there. For now, they had to saddle up and ride out.

As the last tea was being drunk or poured onto fires, a black face appeared among them looking for Brown. It was Patience who had been following his usual practice of carrying out a pre-dawn reconnaissance but had unusually returned to camp before it was struck. That fact and the absence of the usual smile from his face had Brown convinced correctly that something was seriously amiss. In some agitation, the little fellow described spotting a Boer encampment across their line of march. Cleverly he had counted their horses which were illuminated by a watch fire. It was Patience's belief based on horse numbers that there were about twenty riders in the party, almost double the strength of Brown's troop and that much more mobile without their pack animals.

The news instigated a heated discussion that Wheatley had to silence. Everyone it seemed had an opinion including one man who suggested Patience was leading them into an ambush. Seeing that it was the Australian who had put forward the wild animal theory, Brown told him to stop being an idiot and to hold his tongue. Whatever thoughts of insubordination the man may have harboured were quelled by a look from Wheatley. Which was well and good but was not bringing his command any closer to the rendezvous. Looking around their location in better light, Brown could see that while the ground was not particularly high, it was high enough to provide some increased visibility and it wasn't overlooked by any other high ground, at least, not from anywhere close. Large enough to be defensible if they had to stand and fight but far from impregnable. However, he had no idea of what the Boers were about. Was their presence just bad luck or were they chasing the column? There was no point in standing mute and wondering so he called Murray over and asked if he would be prepared to scout the Boer positions and see if they had moved and if so in what direction. He wouldn't send Patience. Fleet of foot as he might be, he was no match for a mounted Boer and it would go hard with him if he was captured. Murray was well mounted and a good horseman, furthermore, he had proved himself a first-rate scout and probably the best man they had for this sort of work. He accepted the job without any obvious emotion and went off to consult with Patience for details of the exact place where he had seen the encampment.

Once Murray had departed, Brown and Wheatley set to putting their camp into some sort of defensive posture. If the Boers had gone it would be wasted effort but if they came looking for the troop, it might be invaluable. Shallow trenches were dug, bushes cut to provide some cover and all canteens were filled from a stream that would be outside the perimeter, such as it was, if they had to defend the hill. One man was issued with binoculars and told to keep his eyes peeled while everyone else made such preparations as they could. Then they waited, what else was there to do?

They didn't have to wait too long. A few tense moments followed the lookout's announcement that a single rider was approaching but to everyone's relief it turned out to be a dusty and sweat streaked Murray. He slipped from his horse and told Brown what he knew. He agreed with Patience's estimate of numbers but more importantly he had observed the Boers saddle up and ride East taking them away from Brown's planned line of march. Once he was certain they had departed he made a brief examination of the camp for anything that might give a clue to their orders or intentions but had found little of interest beyond an old English newspaper. This was a strange find but as Murray pointed out, they could have found it anywhere and kept it to alleviate the boredom of an uneventful journey or just for some news from the outside world. The significant fact was that they were out of the way and Brown could proceed more or less as planned. When he said as much to Murray, the latter struck a cautionary note. He was certain that the group he had observed were not the same as the one that had caused them to change course. Having crossed Swaziland on his way to LM not long before, Murray gave his opinion that the level of Boer activity was higher than he had noted previously. When Brown wondered aloud what they might be looking for, Murray grinned at him and said: 'people like us,' which was sufficiently blindingly obvious to cause Brown to flush with embarrassment and begin giving orders to prepare to move out.

Back in the LM consulate, Crowe's boys brought news of the increased Boer patrolling but, as yet no word on the whereabouts of Miss Reilly. Fitz was amused that his warning to the admiral appeared to be vindicated by events and doubly amused that blame for a supposed leak of information was being directed towards the consul. It was even said that a senior member of the government had commented that 'sailors can never hold their tongues[14].' Nobody, least of all Fitz, would repeat that to Crowe, although the sailor somehow became aware that the consulate was believed to have been indiscreet about a plan to destroy the Komatipoort bridge. He was furious at the suggestion but sensitive to the possibility that somehow something that had been said or done might have triggered the Boer reaction. Certainly it kept his spy networks busy to the point of overload as he dispatched them out to far flung points of Swazi territory and around the streets and taverns of LM.

The reports he received were not always reliable and were generally only considered so if two or three different sources reported the same or very similar things. Thus initially no significance was attached to an account of a high level of Boer activity in Northern Swaziland and along the railway line. Once the story had been repeated several times it was passed on to the High Command and if of particular importance, to the War Office in London. Fitz had anticipated events by making up his own account of a Boer presence on the railway without any shred of evidence but then he had a separate and distinct reason for the deception for which the Boers had

---

[14] Believed to have been Lord Salisbury

been kind enough to provide camouflage. One further happy if unexpected outcome of the Kosi Bay fiasco was that a number of reports indicated that the Boers believed there was a force of Imperial troops numbering several hundred operating in Swaziland rather than Brown's twelve and the six men with Von Steinaecker. Crowe worried about the possibility of either or both being killed or captured due to heightened Boer alerts and the mission to Komatipoort being exposed. But as Fitz said, even if that should happen, they would have tied down a lot of Boers that might otherwise be fighting Lord Roberts army which having recently captured Bloemfontein was now eyeing up a final advance on Pretoria to end the war.

Amused as he might have been by Crowe's discomfiture and his own cleverness, Fitz was also beginning to become bored with LM. Much of his work was routine and it certainly wouldn't win him any medals. He was keen to run down the Reilly woman and to see what she knew. He rather hoped she knew nothing and she could then provide some pleasant company to help him improve his knowledge of South Africa and alleviate the tedium of LM. Sadly, the failure to locate her suggested that she had indeed slipped out of town although a check of passenger lists failed to reveal her name. She had not been seen at the railway station either, where a close eye was kept on the West bound traffic heading towards the Boer capital. For the present then, Fitz was stuck with sorting and distributing the intelligence reports that came his way. He envied Bill Brown and Wheatley their freedom of movement and the chance to do some actual soldiering. His chance would come he thought, although the indications were that the Boers were crumbling. If true and

Roberts did take their capital, that would mean an end to the fighting and an end to any chance of Major Fitzherbert being able to distinguish himself. Nobody fought on after their capital fell, even the Zulus had understood that. Fitz could not shirk his responsibilities and wouldn't dream of doing so, he just considered how he could make those responsibilities get him closer to the actual fighting.

Whatever freedom of movement Fitz assumed Brown and Wheatley possessed had been curtailed severely by the need to keep clear of the Boer forces roaming Swaziland. The intelligence reports seen by Crowe and Fitz had been correct in stating that the Boers believed a force of 500 or so Imperial troops were in Swaziland. Brown, of course, was not aware of these developments and concluded that the Boers were simply on their guard because of the unsettled state of the country. Even had he known what Crowe and Fitz knew, it would have made little difference. He still had to find Von S and after that, there was the matter of the bridge. However well-guarded, a way had to be found to destroy it or at the least to disrupt the flow of materiel down the railway. Brown may have acquired some civilian instincts in his absence from military life but he retained a strong sense of duty. He had been given a job, it might even be said that he had volunteered for the job and now he had to see it through. With that in mind and the coast seemingly clear, he gave his orders and once more got his command underway. All of them now tense after two brushes with the enemy and the massacred village, the smell of which stayed with Brown even now. He watched his men, or at least the ones not acting as guards and scouts and while there was no obvious sign of nerves or fear, weapons were unholstered and eyes flickered. Even the impassive Wheatley had been licking his lips and swallowing as he rode, occasionally fingering his revolver or tapping the butt of his rifle, as if for reassurance that it was there. They were all good men but no one was immune to fear of being hit by a soft nosed bullet days from any medical facilities, not that they could have done much for you even had they been close by.

Brown had to balance the need to move with the need for caution, the effect was that they moved more slowly. The rolling terrain that they were passing through was no aid to progress and as no one knew what was on the other side of any hill, scouts or no scouts, progress was not only slower but more anxious. On they went however, cursing the odd braying of the mules and hoping that they would soon find Von S and a measure of security before anyone else found them. Brown was sceptical that they would be much safer as nineteen than as twelve but he kept that thought to himself. By nightfall, they were back on less challenging terrain but without any sign of the Von Steinaecker party. After they made camp, one of the troopers mentioned this. Brown pointed out that there was no sign of any Boers or man-eating lions either so he should be happy. It was weak stuff but it raised a laugh from the fellow's friends as they cleaned rifles for the umpteenth time and joshed him. Brown too carefully cleaned both his rifle and revolver before turning in. The constant repetition of the task without use made him feel a little like Lady Macbeth but rather that than having a dirty weapon misfire when you needed it most. Brown hoped fervently that he would not be required to take another's life but not as fervently as he hoped for his own preservation.

Fitz would have been only too willing to have an opportunity to use a weapon in anger but he could feel the likelihood slipping away like the Boer armies.

He clung to the slender hope that the Boer would prove as stubborn and tenacious as Bill Brown had said they would be. It was not a view shared by the majority of the army or the nation, particularly those who had not seen any fighting. Whatever the case, Fitz was stuck in LM for the present. His only consolation was that one of Crowe's boys believed he had seen Johanna Reilly go into the hotel where she had previously been staying. Walter, the hotel front of house man who was on Crowe's payroll, had confirmed that she was there but then he had also denied that she had ever left despite her not being seen for days. Fitz suspected Walter had more than one paymaster but that was unimportant now. His quarry had been sighted and he would do his best to run her down. maybe she was innocent of any involvement with the Boers, maybe not. he would do his best to find out. If nothing else, it would take his mind off his own situation.

Naturally Fitz would not approach the lady in an official capacity, he would just be a British businessman passing through the port looking for opportunities. Accordingly, Fitz donned civilian clothes and sauntered out in search of Johanna. In contrast to Brown's rumpled, linen, Fitz was in a well cut light tropical suit and gleaming shoes. Every inch the Briton abroad, he knew that he stood out but he couldn't have affected the look of a Bill Brown so he had to bluff his way as best he could. Taking a whisky and soda at the bar of the hotel, he kept an eye on the comings and goings in the lobby until he saw the lady he was looking for. He hadn't seen her previously, but Wheatley had and had given him a proper policeman's description before leaving. Putting down his drink Fitz walked casually into the lobby and in a strong Irish brogue that would have earned him a rebuke from his Mother, asked Walter the time. The

Portuguese simply pointed to the clock on the wall behind him but Johanna Reilly turned to look at him with a smile and asked if he was Irish. Replying with his most charming smile, Fitz began his own little campaign.

Brown was no longer rumpled, after days in the saddle and nights spent in the open, like all of his troop he was filthy. the red dust of the veldt got everywhere and the thorn bushes tore at the clothing of the unwary. Thus far, everyone had remained reasonably cheerful in shared hardship. Soldiers moan and there was plenty of moaning but no more than any commander might expect from tired men on a long journey with every prospect of encountering danger both animal and human. Given the circumstances, morale was good but Brown was concerned that it might not last if they did not achieve the first objective of finding Von Steinaecker soon. The trooper's comments of the previous evening had sharpened his anxiety. Wheatley was a godsend in these circumstances. The man was a well of useful advice and experience that he could call on and the men liked and respected him. In fact, the men liked and respected both of them but that wasn't obvious to Brown and he hadn't considered the matter. His concern was just getting them to where they should be without loss. He was sick of the veldt though, the landscape never seemed to change. There were ant hills and scrub as far as the eye could see and such changes in the contours that occurred were just significant enough to provide cover for a potential ambush without affording any sort of view over the countryside.

On their march they had passed through a couple of small native settlements whose inhabitants looked terrified by their presence. When quizzed by Murray, they denied seeing any other white men but the obvious fear they displayed made both Brown and Murray wonder if they were following instructions backed by threats of retribution. As Wheatley noted, the locals had plenty to be frightened of. Their own people on murderous rampages inspired by witch doctors, wild animals that stole their livestock or worse and now two warring tribes of white men tracking across their country. But then said Wheatley: 'On a positive note, you have to be alive to be frightened, so it's not all bad.' In which case, thought Brown silently: I am very much alive.

That thought came back to him when some distance further on, the sound of a single shot followed by two or three more had him spurring his horse forward towards the noise. He heard several voices shouting from both in front and behind. From behind, Wheatley was yelling at him to wait and dismounting from his horse from ahead, he heard an unfamiliar voice yell: *'wie is daar?'* And *'Wys jouself'*[15]

Staring at the dismounted Wheatley walking towards him with rifle in hand, he realised there was no sense in charging forward on his horse, it would just make him conspicuous. Dismounting, he unslung his rifle and worked the bolt to push a round into the chamber. He then went forward cautiously with Wheatley. He could have had Wheatley go alone or with one or more of the others, but this was his indaba[16] and he needed to see for himself what was going on ahead of them. They pushed through the dying autumn vegetation in a crouch towards the noise of further shouting and shooting and eventually found their lead scout, an Australian named Jennings

---

[15] Afrikaans 'Who's there, show yourself'
[16] Zulu 'affair'

taking shelter by a baobab tree. He gestured for them to keep down as a bullet passed overhead with a loud crack. Jennings grinned and gave them a very Australian situation report: 'Sorry sir, I think I just kicked over a bit of a hornet's nest. There's a load of the buggers down there and they ain't happy.'

Looking in the direction Jennings had indicated, Brown could see that there were indeed quite a few angry looking people pointing rifles in their approximate direction. They didn't expose themselves for long though. Each man would fire and then move to a different position generally out of sight. They seemed to know what they were doing and even though none of their shots took effect, they certainly discouraged movement. The ground fell away in front of their own position to what appeared to be a stream bed. Brown took his binoculars for a closer look at who and what they had stumbled upon. Wheatley took more practical action and loosed off a round at the opposition, causing Brown to curse with surprise.

It wasn't the first strong language Wheatley had heard not even the first strong language he had heard from Brown but he looked quite put out as he explained: 'Just keeping their heads down sir.' And then added in Jennings' direction: 'where did they spring from?'

A grinning Jennings responded drily: 'I don't know Sarge but I bet they're saying the same about us.'

Which was a good point. The trooper appeared to have had the misfortune to bump into a party of Boers watering their horses in a stream that the ground kept hidden until anyone passing was almost upon it. Neither Briton nor Boer knew of each other's presence until it was too late. Neither side knew how many or how few their opponents might be and Brown was as certain as he could be that the Boers had no idea of their cargo or purpose.

'Right Sergeant, we are going to bluff our way out of this with the aid of plenty of .303 rounds. go back to the others and tell them what's happening. Have them make some defensive preparations just in case we don't get away with this and send two of the best shots to Jennings here and myself and tell them to bring extra ammunition. If we can keep up a fierce enough fire on these fellows and make them believe we're stronger than we are, they may believe us and disperse.' He paused and looked at Wheatley seriously: 'of course, the opposite is also true. If we show signs of fear they will come at us, so we need to show plenty of aggression.'

'Very good sir' I'll be as quick as I can.' with that, Wheatley moved off with surprising speed and stealth.

Jennings fell to with a will, keeping up a steady fire from a convenient natural dip in the ground just ahead of Brown and to his left. Brown found his own position by a thorn bush that plucked at his coat when he crawled forward. They couldn't see much but shot at where they perceived their enemy to be. Modern smokeless powder made it hard to tell where the return fire was coming from and as far as they could tell, they didn't hit anyone but that wasn't necessarily the point. Soon they were joined by the two men sent forward by Wheatley, who deployed out on either side of Brown and Jennings and commenced firing. In theory they overlooked their enemy but the advantage was minimal. The Boer force took full advantage of whatever cover was available using the stream bed and associated rivulets to great effect and showing themselves fleetingly if at all. After some minutes of each side burning ammunition to no apparent effect, it seemed probable that the Boers would not attack. Brown began to wonder if perhaps he had been too timid and should summon some more men to perhaps work around the flank of the area from where most of the shots were coming but the mules and the need to protect the cargo they bore made that too risky.

Shortly thereafter, it seemed as if somebody had had similar thoughts. Off to their right came the sounds of heavy firing. Whether directed at their position or not Brown could not tell but he just hoped that Wheatley and the others had stayed put and not decided to mount a challenge of their own. After the initial outbreak, the shooting seemed to taper off and then resume again just as the fire they were receiving died away. There was some shouting and more shooting and then a distant beat of hooves suggested someone had decided to move and quickly. Brown and his half section ceased firing and waited. He gestured the men to silence but there was little to hear other than the noises of Africa reasserting themselves after the disturbance. He was loathe to move in case it was some ruse by the Boers to have them show themselves and congratulated himself on his caution when the noise of horses resumed and seemed to be heading in their direction.

Again, he signed to the men to keep down and raised himself slowly to look in the direction from where the sound came. There were a number of mounted troops that he could see advancing through the bushes, certainly enough to be a problem for his command and his spirits sank. All this bloody distance and now through sheer damn bad luck they run into a Boer force that will steal the very weapons that he had been ordered to keep from them. He wondered if perhaps they might pass by without contact but it was a vain hope, they were bearing down directly on his position perhaps three hundred yards away now, maybe a little more. A surge of anger arose in him and he checked his sights and determined to do some damage before the end came. He wasn't going to be humiliated by some blasted Dutchman and surrender but then he considered the men with him. They could decide their own fate he thought and stood up to take a sight on the lead rider.

Despite his desire to hit hard and fast something gave him pause. These men were in the usual khaki streaked with sweat and dust but there was something wrong. Hesitation he knew could get him killed but that looked a fair bet anyway. He let them come a little closer while attempting to remain concealed and then he realised what was wrong. There were only a half dozen or so and they weren't sporting the usual Boer bushy beards. In fact, the fellow he had decided to kill was the possessor of what might have been world's most ridiculous waxed moustache. If that wasn't enough to prove he was no Boer, he also seemed to be wearing a guardsman's cap and a sabre swung from his saddle. A preposterous sight he may have been but Brown swore with relief at the apparition and swore once more in thanks that he had let him live.

Brown was by no means a slow thinker but it took him a few moments to digest what had just occurred. The relief of surviving the combat combined with ears ringing from the effects of concentrated rifle fire were not conducive to a sharp analysis of rapidly changing events. Clarity began to dawn when he revealed himself to the approaching riders, waving his hat and keeping his rifle down. They came on at a trot and in any competition for scruffy looking soldiers, they might have edged Brown's own command but not by a lot. Their leader wore an outfit, it could hardly be called uniform, which had it been cleaner, might have suited a character in a comic opera. Aside from the guardsman's peaked cap, and waxed moustache he affected a long jacket and riding breeches. His men had their own idea of military attire too. They wore slouch hats like most colonial troops but with brims raised anyhow or not at all and some with tails from animals or bird feathers affixed to them. Had the Zulus ever lodged among the Apache, these men might have been a by-product.

The comic opera character reached Brown and reined in his horse. He didn't dismount but rather looked him up and down and then with elaborate courtesy addressed him in a heavy German accent:

'Do I hef the honour of addressing Major Brown?'

Laughing, even if from relief, was probably not the appropriate response but Brown couldn't help himself as he realised who he was looking at. He thought of Livingstone meeting Stanley but resisted the urge to say 'Baron Von Steinaecker I presume[17] ' for without doubt this bizarre figure could only be Baron Francis Christian Ludwig Von Steinaecker late of the Prussian Army and now the Lieutenant commanding the nascent Steinaecker's Horse.

---

[17] Dr David Livingstone was a 19th century British explorer who spent some years seeking the source of the River Nile. In the course of his exploration, he lost all contact with the outside world for a number of years. The New York Herald newspaper sent Henry Stanley to find him in 1869. Stanley was ultimately successful, running Livingstone to earth on the shore of Lake Tanganyika in late 1871, supposedly greeting him with the words: 'Dr Livingstone I presume.' A phrase that has now passed into popular usage.

Crowe had given Brown a very brief biography of Steinaecker before his departure from LM. He was a Prussian aristocrat who had served in that country's army in the 1870's. Following that, he had moved to South Africa and worked in a variety of unlikely jobs prior to the outbreak of the current war, becoming a naturalised British citizen in the process. When war came he had enlisted as a Private in the Colonial Scouts and rose swiftly to Quartermaster Sergeant. He then transferred to the Intelligence and was commissioned. General Buller had been impressed by him and had personally selected him for the mission against the railway bridge. Crowe had mentioned that the man was considered a little unorthodox, eccentric even but that hardly did justice to the figure that dismounted to introduce himself to Brown[18].

He was of medium height and slightly built, painfully thin and lacking most of his teeth. The moustache that had initially caught Brown's attention extended several inches either side of his face and seemed in no danger of losing rigidity despite their circumstances and the distance that Steinaecker had travelled. His chest was puffed out and he strutted rather than walked as he talked to Brown. The overall effect was of a rather under fed and over active pigeon. Despite his bizarre appearance and strange mannerisms, he exuded energy and confidence and the small group of desperados he had recruited were clearly devoted to him despite referring to him as 'Old Stinkey' both in and out of his hearing.

Introductions effected; a pair of Steinecker's men were dispatched to ensure that the Boers had gone. While they were away, Brown led the German and the

---

[18] In a war peopled by some extraordinary characters, Baron, and later Colonel Von Steinaecker DSO may not be the best known but should certainly be considered as one of the most colourful.

rest of his men plus his own three back to where Wheatley had established the bulk of the column. Steinaecker's roughnecks and Brown's had eyed each other up and decided that they would get along. The sight of any one of them would have given a British Sergeant Major an apoplexy but that was of no concern in the depths of the bush. A decision was taken to stay where they were for the night and all of them were soon building fires, brewing tea and bantering together as if they had been comrades for years.

One of Steinaecker's men was a Sergeant named Holgate who had grown up among the Boers in the Transvaal and had been obliged to make a swift exit when war broke out. He joined Wheatley and the two officers in an informal review of the action that had just taken place and each unit's most recent adventures. As Brown had surmised, Trooper Jennings had been unlucky enough to bump into a Boer patrol at rest by a stream. The fold in the ground concealing the water also concealed the Boers until it was almost too late. Fortunately for Jennings they had neglected to post guards and he just happened to come across one intent on answering a call of nature away from the main group. Each saw the other at the same moment but the Boer was the first to shoot, thus sounding the alarm. Not only did it alarm the Boers and Brown but it also caught the ear of Von Steinaecker who was in the vicinity casting about for the rendezvous. The sustained fire from Brown and then Von Steinaecker arriving on their flank, had been enough for the Boers who mounted and ran to the North toward the Transvaal border.

Holgate verbally sketched out the route that they had taken to find Brown after they had slipped across the Swazi border from Natal. Unlike him, they had seen plenty of evidence of Boer activity but had not had to take any evasive action. Brown noticed that while the review of each other's recent history was taking place, Von Steinaecker seemed distracted and was pacing the ground in an irritated manner. Eventually, he could contain himself no longer and said, 'enough of yesterday, let us plan for tomorrow.' Brown was about to remind him that he was not the senior officer but decided it would sound foolish, and anyway, he was right. Interesting as the stories of how they had arrived together might be, this was only the beginning. Now they had to plan for the next stage of the mission, the Komatipoort Railway Bridge.

CHAPTER NINE

Battle in the Botanical Gardens

While Brown and Von Steinaecker planned their next moves, in Lourenço Marques, Fitz was enjoying himself with Miss Johanna Reilly. Having introduced himself, he had little difficulty in initiating a conversation. Brown had told him of her Irish father and her apparent fascination with Ireland and its history. Accordingly, Fitz changed his persona to accommodate her interest. He was a little vague on some details but an eavesdropper to their extended conversation would have come away with the impression that Fitz was a prosperous Irish businessman, probably but not necessarily Protestant, who seemed sympathetic to thoughts of Irish Home Rule. His dress and mannerisms suggested time spent in England. No doubt he was a resourceful Irishman who had been able to do well in both countries.

Johanna Reilly was charmed as most people who encountered Fitz tended to be but in her case, he laid it on as thickly as he dared, ordering Champagne and joining her giggles as they watched the hapless barman send out for ice to chill the dusty bottle that he had unearthed. He told her of the Mourne Mountains and St Stephen's Green of the golden fields of barley and the fine seafood of Dublin Bay, which he compared favourably to the excellent shellfish to be had in LM. As they talked he was surprised that South Africa and the war that was raging there seemed to be of secondary interest to her. He pressed her on the subject a time or two and while she responded to his questions, she was soon back to talking of Ireland. Fitz was naturally a good listener so letting this charming lady talk was no difficulty. After all, he was there to hear her story, not to tell his own and among the family history and her thoughts on Ireland and the Irish, a couple of items caught his attention.

In discussing her background and history, she let slip that she had a number of acquaintances in the Transvaal government. Friends of her Father's to be sure but it seemed that she also had a surprising degree of familiarity with one or two important folk and had for a time worked as a secretary to Leydes, the attorney general. All this was of keen interest to Fitz and looking at the lady, he could well imagine that she would have little trouble gaining the confidence of even the sternest of the God-fearing Boers. His challenge was to conceal his interest but Fitz the master card player, had little difficulty with that. He feigned a simple interest in the lady and it wasn't entirely feigned. She was certainly interesting and had packed some interesting times into her twenty-five years. She may have been half Boer but her personality was all Irish. She joked and laughed and punished the Champagne in a way that would have raised eyebrows in the drawing rooms of Belgravia. Fitz hadn't met too many Boers but he doubted it would have been encouraged in Pretoria either. He wondered if he had gone too far when he attempted to press more Champagne on her and she politely declined and smiling made her excuses. He needn't have worried. In fact, all was well, Johanna had enjoyed herself hugely with this charming Irishman but had reached the limit of her tolerance for the Champagne, which was warm despite the barman's best efforts and was almost certainly the only bottle in the hotel, if not in all of LM. Before she left they made an arrangement to meet again for dinner the following night. As he settled the account with the barman, Fitz silently congratulated himself on a job well done and set off on a circuitous route back to the consulate thinking over what he had heard as he walked.

Arriving back content, Fitz planned his next move. Over a generous glass of the consulate's whisky he ruminated on the conversation that had just taken place. Thinking about what he had been told, again he was puzzled by Johanna's brushing aside her important and impressive familiarity with some of the decision makers in the Transvaal government in order to talk about Ireland. As a subject, it had been a useful introduction but whatever her Father's background, she had never even left Southern Africa, much less seen Ireland. Which reminded him that Wheatley had mentioned a Reilly in the Dublin Fusiliers that had been caught spreading false rumours. Highly unlikely to be any relation but perhaps worth an enquiry. He sipped his whisky and quickly scribbled a note for the telegraph office to send to London. The other question was what was she really doing in LM? He shared Brown's scepticism about her being sent away by her Father and also doubted the story of her secretarial and translation work in LM. Brown had said that she expressed some hostility towards Britain but she hadn't struck him as a fire breathing revolutionary, more of a wide eyed idealist. In the wrong hands mind you, even idealists could become dangerous. Ah well, he thought, the more they talked, the more he might find out and who knew where that might lead. Finishing his whisky he went down the hall to the telegraph to send his message.

The lady herself was having a quiet discussion at the hotel with a friend. After Pedro had been so horribly murdered, she had left the city for a few days riding up the coast for the air and to take her mind off the unpleasant events she had left behind her. She had kept the room on while she was away so Walter had not been completely dishonest with Fitz, she had the room so in the hotel's eyes, she hadn't left. As she described her recent encounters, the lady she was with listened and occasionally smiled at her descriptions of the men vying for her attention.

One she declared was not only charming and interesting but also fun. Unfortunately he was English even if his parents were Northern Irish Protestants. The other was Irish, so handsome and charming too in his own way. The first man she had not seen for some days while the second seemed to have just arrived in town. He had bought her Champagne and told her so many stories of Ireland. Her only complaint was that he seemed just a little too charming but where was the harm in that?

Her companion, an older Dutch lady cautioned her:

'Johanna, you must be careful, don't you think it odd that you encounter two British businessmen in your hotel in such a sort time? You know that they are busy trying to block supplies to the *volk*[19] and turning the Portuguese against us.'

Laughing, Johanna dismissed the older woman's fears:

---

[19] People- Afrikaans

'You see English agents behind every curtain Anna, I don't think either of them had politics on their minds. thinking about it though, the first fellow, the English one, was very concerned about the consequences of civil war in Ireland.'

Her companion started: 'You mean you discussed such a thing?'

'Not really' Johanna said thoughtfully, 'I think I said something of the expectations of the Irish people being that they would be free one day. He argued that if there was a rebellion the people that would suffer most would be the Irish because all of the fighting and destruction would be in Ireland and a rebellion would never be allowed to succeed.'

Anna looked at her wide eyed as if she had sworn in church: 'Why would you discuss such a thing with anyone here, much less an Englishman? Do you think he was looking for something?'

'Well if he was,' responded Johanna, 'he didn't find it. In any case, it was just a hypothetical conversation. It meant nothing.'

'Even so,' said Anna, 'even so, you must be wary of these people. You know what the English are like. They start charming and harmless and before you know it, they have a knife to your throat and your country in their pocket.'

Johanna laughed again: 'Not this one *Tannie*[20], he was as unlikely a danger as anyone you could hope to meet. He was so vague but funny too. No, far too amusing to be lethal and the other one far too charming and Irish. Don't worry, I'm careful with every man I meet just as Ma taught me.'

---

[20] Literally 'Auntie' but used of any older woman (Afrikaans)

Johanna laughed and Anna looked shocked. Really, she thought, these young girls from the city think they know everything and think of life as a laughing matter when it is so serious. A few years as a farmer's wife might teach this one in particular to be more respectful and more discreet. She said nothing, It would have been pointless. Johanna was very clever and had been of great assistance in LM. Her passion for all things Irish could be a distraction but despite that and her light-hearted attitude, she was certainly an asset.

Sighing quietly Anna gathered her things together and rose to bid Johanna farewell. The latter did not mention that she would be dining with the smooth Irishman that night and Anna had decided against asking if any further meetings were planned for fear of receiving an affirmative answer. She had delivered her warning and she knew that if Johanna was determined on something, she would do it irrespective of contrary advice. What Anna couldn't understand is why she would talk to an Englishman at all, even one claiming to be Irish. Anna loathed them all with a passion but then her husband had been killed at *Elandslaagte*[21], cut down by British cavalry from behind. If that were not sufficient fuel

---

[21] The Battle of Elandslaagte was one of the early (October 1899) engagements of the Boer War and an unusually decisive British victory. Fleeing Boers were cut down by a cavalry charge of the 5th Lancers and the 5th Dragoon Guards. A relatively small engagement, it was notable for one of the few successful cavalry charges made during the war and for the use of lances, which were soon to be exchanged for carbines. The Boer forces included a number of Dutch volunteers from Holland, including the brother of Vincent Van Gogh the painter, who was wounded and died soon afterwards.

for her hatred, not long after her husband's death, British troops had arrived at the family farm, looted it and burned it to the ground. Johanna had not yet suffered at their hands which would explain her laxity, yet even she had an Uncle kicking his heels in an English jail, the youngest of her Father's siblings, and for what? Just his politics. So much for the famous British notion of fair play.

Major Peter Fitzherbert, who was one of the two Irish Englishmen, being discussed was looking forward to his dinner with Johanna Reilly not just because the lady was extremely attractive and entertaining company but because the cable he had received from London suggested that there might be a lot more to her than met the eye. Anna had been correct that Johanna had an Uncle in a British prison but he was in Ireland not England. It was true that his politics had been influential in his imprisonment but what had really done for him was that he was a serving British soldier that had spread lies through the ranks of his regiment and attempted to induce men to desert. He was, in fact lucky to be in jail as the offences of which he was quite properly convicted could have brought him a death sentence. Major Fitzherbert, armed with this information viewed his dinner companion in a new light. Of course, being related to a guilty man was not evidence of complicity, particularly when you had never met him, as was Johanna's case but as Wheatley might have said, as a family they had 'form.'

There were a number of possibilities including that she was entirely innocent of any activity against British interests. Alternatively, she might be in LM to facilitate the passage of Irish recruits to the Boer forces. Dublin was awash with pro Boer sentiment and had been since long before the war had actually begun. An Irish Transvaal Committee had been formed and pro Boer demonstrations had attracted tens of thousands. There had been much talk of aid for the Boers but for the present, not much more than talk, at least in the eyes of British intelligence who were chasing every rumour from Cork to Belfast and beyond. They were kept very busy.

For himself, based upon what Brown had told him and the recent demise of Pedro Nunes, Fitz thought the most likely story was that Miss Reilly was indeed involved with a Boer enterprise involved in smuggling supplies through LM. He presumed her duties were purely secretarial or something similar but nevertheless, she might let slip all manner of seemingly insignificant details that taken together might lead to an intelligence coup for Britain and Major Fitzherbert. Walking out for his rendezvous with Johanna, in freshly pressed linen gleaming shoes and straw hat, Fitz mused upon the evening ahead. If war is hell, as the Yankee General Sherman had stated, he thought, then some parts were more diabolical than others.

It was unfortunate that he left the consulate before the second cable from London regarding Miss Reilly had arrived. Had he been able to read the contents, it might have made his conversation less difficult, not that Fitz had any difficulty conversing, he simply struggled to elicit anything worthwhile from Johanna in terms of intelligence. He quizzed her about her time with Leyds but she brushed it off as a mere secretarial role obtained for her by a friend of her Father. Fitz asked if it was boredom that had made her leave which caused her to laugh which in turn caused Fitz to be charmed by her looks and then irritated by her failure to say anything of substance. She went on to explain that the job with Leyds had ended when he was sent to Brussels as the representative of the two Boer Republics. For whatever reason Fitz thought this significant, he wasn't sure why that might be but made a mental note to discuss it with Crowe. Being a diplomat himself, he may have knowledge of Leyds and his mission in Europe that might establish a link to arms coming in to LM.

At the end of the evening, Fitz had charmed and joked, had poured much wine into both himself and his dinner guest but was largely returning to the consulate empty handed. His hand had been allowed to stray onto Miss Reilly's for a period it was true but she had not remarked on it and had withdrawn her own hand to consume a piece of fruit most charmingly. As the Major reflected, romance was not what he was there for. Even so, there was no question that she was dashed attractive. He hoped they were all wrong and she was innocent of any overt service to the Boer cause. It would be a shocking waste for her to be shut away in a prison, or worse when the war was over. He was shaking his head over that idea as he walked through the quiet streets back to the consulate, when he thought he had heard steps behind him that matched his pace. Rather than look, he turned at the next corner and found a convenient doorway to wait in while slipping the dagger from his boot and testing the point with his thumb. The steps went by innocently and he exhaled quietly and waited a minute before replacing his knife and resuming his journey. He chided himself for allowing thoughts of Johanna Reilly to lower his guard. Walking on, he wondered what might have come from a real challenge and almost regretted that there had been no danger. Forgetting Miss Reilly for the present, he mentally planned what he might do in the event of ambush. If it came, he would be ready.

The following day, Fitz was given the second cable from London regarding not only his dinner companion but also her former employer, Leyds. As Johanna had related, Leyds had relinquished the post of Attorney General of the Transvaal in favour of representing both Boer Republics in Europe. In this capacity, he did whatever he could to drum up support for the Boer cause among Britain's European rivals. He had many sympathetic ears but had achieved little more than sympathy. Britain was aware of all of this and was content to let diplomacy take its course. No European power was likely to threaten Britain at this time, however many penny novels were published about possible German or other invasions[22]. What had alarmed the intelligence people however, was the contact between Leyds and various factions of Irish nationalists. The Irish had nothing to lose by expressing open support for the Boer but had little practical to offer other than manpower. A particular firebrand of a lady called Maud Gonne[23] had been prominent in the Irish Transvaal Committee and had recently been with Leyds in Brussels. She was an unlikely recruiting Sergeant for the Boers but nonetheless, her meetings with Leyds had caused alarm in Whitehall and it had been made clear to Fitz that he was to extract any and

---

[22] For example 'The Battle of Dorking' by George Cheney (1871)

[23] Gonne was an Irish Republican and Suffragette who did indeed meet Leyds in Brussels to try and sell him on a plan to place bombs in the coal being used to fuel British ships. Leyds turned her down but did provide £2,000 for another Irish and pro Boer campaigner. Gonne married John MacBride, of the Irish Transvaal Brigade but subsequently divorced on the grounds of his drinking. She was also romantically linked with the poet Yeats.

all information that he could from Reilly about Leyds and any Irish connection he might have had.

Fitz smelled opportunity. He congratulated himself on establishing a direct link between a Boer agent and Irish rebels. Brown's part being conveniently forgotten. Here now was his chance to win distinction even if not on the battlefield. If he was successful here though, the High Command might allow him to choose his next posting. The question was, how best to go about the matter? His natural inclination was to carry on his subtle interrogation of Johanna over dinners and who knew what she might reveal? It was slow going though and Whitehall were clearly worried and expecting results. He considered an alternate plan of having her brought to the consulate and detained while he laid his cards upon the table and demanded answers to specific questions. if she refused to cooperate, he could threaten retribution against her captive Uncle. It wasn't really his style but London was impatient.

He chased these ideas around with Crowe, who as Consul, needed to know and also might have had thoughts of his own. He had not met Leyds however and knew no more of him than Fitz did. He did however see that London had a legitimate concern. Two enemies of the Crown meeting together rarely led to anything good. Crowe's view was that Fitz should pursue the subtle line of enquiry unless it was clearly not going to work and Fitz was certain that the woman was in possession of information that would be useful. Crowe wasn't enthusiastic about the possibility of the consulate being used as an illegal detention facility but was prepared to condone it if it seemed necessary. Should the Reilly woman decide to tell all in an attempt to cause embarrassment afterwards, he would simply deny everything. Any scandal would quickly blow over. The only harm that might come was to make life more difficult for his spy network but he could worry about that if and when the time came.

Deciding to follow Crowe's advice, Fitz left a note with Walter at Reilly's hotel, requesting the pleasure of her company at dinner. To his gratification but not his surprise, he received an affirmative answer some hours later and began to make mental preparations for the task. He could have used the time more productively. The attempted interrogation went nowhere. Fitz mentally compared it to bowling at a man who had no desire to make runs but refused to give up his wicket. The subtle questions were swept aside like a slow ball and quick ones aimed to take her off balance were left alone as the subject was changed. In the end, Fitz had expended a deal of time and the Consulate's money and received nothing in return. Out of sheer frustration, as they lingered over brandy and ices he decided on a little coercion.

He had been cautious about any discussion of Irish politics for fear of diverting their discussions from the war and any part she might be playing in it but now, armed with the knowledge of an Irish connection and with some background material provided by Crowe he dipped his toe into that murky water. He mentioned the Irish Transvaal Committee and that a prominent member was a woman. He wasn't certain but he thought he saw a flicker of recognition on Johanna's face. Proceeding with the theme he had chosen, he talked about the appalling conditions that Nationalist prisoners were held in and how much worse it was for the women. He didn't elaborate but he didn't need to, the pretty face was serious now but also attentive. He explained how he had friends within the prison service and thanks to that had been able to obtain an easier time for the son of a friend who had become mixed up with the Republican Brotherhood. He was now quite certain that he had her attention yet she gave nothing away other than that which he already knew which was that her sympathies lay with the Nationalists.

Fitz's demeanour as the debonair Irishman of means had been hard to sustain during the course of the dinner but he had managed tolerably well. It was in this way that he proposed a stroll in the botanic gardens the following day, explaining that he had a particular interest in tropical flora. He joked about the gardens being designed by an Englishman[24] but obtained her agreement to meet there in the afternoon. Fitz had little interest in horticulture but had strolled through the gardens and noted the number of shady corners to provide relief from the heat and cover for a kidnapping which was now what he had in mind. It was regrettable of course but she really hadn't left him much option. There was no doubt in his mind that Reilly was involved in something illicit. What was more, the way that she had deflected every question of any substance suggested that she either had received some training or was just naturally evasive. Had she not been a woman he might have suspected that she harboured political ambitions.

Returning to the consulate, he was irritated with himself for failing to extract anything substantive. Not so irritated that he failed to vary his route and to keep his ears alive to following footsteps. The experience of the previous night had not been lost on him and he determined to be more vigilant tonight. There was always a need for vigilance but tonight his walk home was undisturbed and he let himself into

---

[24] Thomas Honney

the consulate through the little wicket gate to the side to which he had a key. He took care to look around him as he did so but the darkened street was deserted and he saw nothing, particularly not the figure that moved out of the shadows after he had stepped inside.

The following day he explained his dilemma to Crowe and his plan to abduct Reilly from the botanical gardens. In essence, this involved Joseph being outside of one of the gates with the consulate buggy and two stout chaps lurking in the bushes for when Fitz gave the signal. They would grab Johanna and stifle any noises with a cloth bag over her head as they bundled her into the buggy. Joseph would then drive all of them back to the consulate. The bag would not only muffle any noise from the victim but would also serve to spare Crowe's diplomatic blushes as she would be unable to see where she had been taken. It wasn't ideal and it would mark Fitz down as a British officer but in his view, this might be his road out of LM to the battlefront. For Fitz, most clouds had a silver lining.

Fitz had given careful instructions to the two marines from the consular guard, he and Crowe had agreed that one couldn't have a white woman manhandled by blacks, and they should be in position now in the gardens. Joseph had been given precise directions as to where to station himself so all should be ready for Fitz's coup de main. He met Johanna at the hotel as arranged and he felt a pang of remorse as he saw her. She really was a delight but she would be less than happy to learn that her handsome Irish friend was in reality a British officer. 'A shame,' thought Fitz, 'I never really got to know her properly but then, if she is as deeply into Boer politics as we believe, I suppose I never would.'

They strolled happily towards the park and he chatted about the sorts of plants he expected to see, having quickly briefed himself on the topic from a volume in the consul's library. It wasn't a fascinating discourse but probably merited more attention than it received and Fitz sensed that he was boring the lady and her mind was elsewhere. He changed the topic to compliment her on her dress, which was indeed charming and that seemed to revive her attention at least a little.

The point that Fitz had selected for the abduction was a little in from the main gate but close by a smaller one leading onto a side street where Joseph and buggy should be waiting. They were close by in fact, almost at the designated point when the parasol Johanna had been swinging from her wrist slipped and fell to the ground. As he bent down to pick it up for her, Fitz was flattened by a powerful kick that caught him in his ribs and sent him sprawling and gasping for breath. He knew he had to regain his feet and rolled with the blow reaching for his dagger as he did so. He had the blade in hand as he bounced up looking for his assailant and found that the world around him had exploded into burly struggling men.

The two Marines having seen their officer attacked had leapt from their concealment and set about the two men responsible in fine style. One was streaming blood from a blow to the nose and reeling away from his cursing adversary while the other was trading blows with the second Marine until he saw Fitz coming at him with dagger in hand. Screaming something indecipherable he made to flee and Fitz was about to give chase until he spotted Johanna attempting to slip away.

Fitz was after her in an instant yelling: 'Jones with me' as he went. It was no contest. Fitz was on her in three paces with a restraining hand on her shoulder and Marine Jones catching her arm and holding her in place. Of the two who had attacked Fitz, one had gone after a glimpse of his dagger and the other, bloodstained but still looking troublesome suddenly decided that discretion was indeed the better part of valour and quit the field at speed. Marine Wilson made to give chase but Fitz had him stand fast.

'Let him go Wilson, we've got more important things to attend to.'

'Very good sir. Orders?'

Nodding towards Johanna whose open mouth was covered by a hand Fitz gave instructions to get her out of the park and onto the buggy. It was a short but cramped ride with three men and Johanna on board and was conducted in silence. Johanna wasn't entirely certain what had just happened. She had not expected the bodyguards assembled by her to attack Fitz quite so savagely and the sudden appearance of his two rescuers had just added to the shock. The truth was that each side had a nose for a good place for treachery and as a result had picked the same spot. How the four men had not bumped into one another would be explained by Marine Wilson. He and Jones had carried out a walk-through reconnaissance of the park early and picked their moment to take cover in the vegetation. Not long before Fitz and Johanna had appeared, the others arrived and made their own arrangements. The Marines watched them hide and were well prepared for what came next. In Wilson's own words to Fitz: 'We knew they was up to no good even if we weren't too sure what but when they went after you sir we was ready' and he grinned as he proudly displayed a brass knuckle duster.

Johanna had only once attempted to quiz Fitz as they rode to the consulate but he had waved her to silence with the assurance that she was in no danger and all would become clear shortly. The lady was no hot house flower who would have a fit of the vapours in such a situation but the speed and the violence had been shocking. She had recovered her calm immediately after the brawl in the gardens and was busy taking note of her surroundings and also her travelling companions. Fitz had changed from the charming man about town to someone far more blunt and to see him wield a dagger was certainly nothing she had anticipated. Aside from that, his voice was different, much more upper class Englishman than educated Dublin and the two men with him looked and sounded like soldiers and obeyed his instructions without question. Johanna wished she had paid more heed to Anna's warnings but Fitz had learned nothing from her and could not possibly have any inkling of her real purpose in LM. In fact, now that she gave the matter some calm consideration, and with a flash of anger at his duplicity, she wondered if she might in fact learn more from Peter Fitzherbert than he would from her. His questions would inevitably indicate what the British were worried about and he couldn't detain her for long or hurt her. Despite her detestation of the British, she had no fear of harm in their hands. So, she relaxed as best she could and pondered the best facade to display, outrage, distressed female or puzzled and sarcastic. She settled on the last as being easier to sustain and awaited developments.

Fitz was feeling very chipper, he had been on the edge of a scrap, had successfully lifted a Boer agent and would hopefully soon find himself back in uniform again when LM became to hot for him. He had abandoned any attempt at concealing their destination as pointless and when the buggy drew up in the consulate grounds, he directed the two Marines to guide Johanna to one of the interior rooms he had picked out and to see that she had such refreshment as she wished. They could toss a coin for first guard stag and either stay in civilian clothes or revert to uniform as they or their Sergeant saw fit, just so long as there was always one of them outside the room containing Johanna. Leaving Johanna in their capable hands, Fitz went to see Crowe to keep him updated and to regale him with his tale of the battle of the Botanical Gardens. Fitz's fun with whoever was protecting Miss Reilly was not as important to Crowe as preserving the diplomatic status of the consulate from any embarrassment and protecting his spy network. He asked Fitz what he intended to do with her and was greatly relieved to be told that she would simply be questioned and released then returned to her hotel courtesy of the British Consul. Before Fitz took his leave of the Consul, Crowe observed thoughtfully:

'You know, we have all been concentrating on the Irish supplying manpower to the Boers, supposedly, the Gonne woman even had a plan to smuggle dynamite into the coal bunkers of British ships but Reilly is here in LM where goods are not only imported but exported overseas too. What if the Boers were working to supply the Nationalist Irish with the means to start trouble in our own backyard? After all, the Boers have plenty of money in their treasury. Leyds might be meeting with Gonne and others in order to start another uprising while our backs are turned.'

Fitz heard him but took little notice, he had his strategy for questioning Johanna and he did not want to be diverted from that. Hours later as he found himself getting nowhere with Miss Reilly regarding the import of contraband to aid the Boer cause, he wondered about a more Irish connection and with a certain trepidation, played his trump card, Johanna's Uncle and his prison status. He reminded her that her Uncle's situation was already uncomfortable and suggested that it could be made more so and even that the charges against him could be revived as inciting a mutiny which would carry a death sentence. Fitz was reasonably certain that the law would not tolerate such a thing but his voice carried conviction and he could see that he was getting her attention. This was the stick he had with which to beat her. That and a degree of fatigue. Later would come the carrot encased in Fitzherbert charm and juxtaposed against the threat to her Uncle. For after all, if a prisoner's condition could be made worse and new charges could be made against him then the opposite must also be true, that the same forces might be used to make him more comfortable or even to secure an early release. Fitz being Fitz, he neither threatened nor promised directly but his meaning was entirely clear.

It took some time including breaks for refreshment for both parties, taken separately and without alcohol, but eventually Fitz's persistence began to show results. Slowly the spectre of the Uncle that she had never met but who was always in her Father's thoughts began to change her attitude. When the realisation that she was in a position to save or end his life dawned, she began to talk candidly to Fitz. As she told him what she knew, he not only listened carefully but began to formulate a plan that if successful would win him great plaudits.

Fitz was only briefly put out to discover that Crowe had been on the right track. Johanna had nothing to do with the import of supplies or fighters for the Boer cause from Ireland or anywhere else. She supported the Republics in their fight against the British but all of her energy while working with Leyds and subsequently had been directed towards inciting and financing a rebellion in Ireland that would benefit the Boers by distracting Britain and would hopefully lead to freedom for the Irish. She was in regular communication with both Leyds and the Transvaal government and had based herself in LM for easy access to the mail ships and a cable service that Britain could not cut. She would slip back into the Transvaal from time to time for conversations with the government and it was where she had been after Nunes was killed. All of which was most interesting but what fascinated Fitz particularly was that Johanna had been asked to work for the government as secretary and translator. She had been in two minds, about the prospect, as she enjoyed unusual freedom of movement in LM and was less enthusiastic about the prospect of an office existence. However, it gave her great access to the members of a government friendly to Ireland and made pleading Ireland's case that much easier.

Fitz's saw his opportunity to have an informer at the heart of the enemy's government. It would be a tremendous coup and might just hasten the end of the war in Britain's favour. Of course, a certain amount of trust would be required but Fitz was reasonably certain that with her Uncle in their hands, Miss Reilly would fall into line and cooperate. He could also issue assurances that her parents would be safe when Pretoria fell, the converse of which might also be true if she did not cooperate. Overall Fitz wanted her as a willing player, not one that had to be threatened and coerced, so he began to outline the good things that would result from her cooperation, not just to Johanna and her family but to South Africa and Ireland too. An end to the fighting would benefit the Boer people. It would stop the destruction of property and loss of life in what had always been a hopeless cause. The Cape was essentially self-governing, a post war federation of South Africa would maintain Boer independence even if notionally under the Union flag. If she would work with Britain to end the conflict in South Africa, she would save many Boer lives and help in the creation of a new nation run by Boer and Britain for their mutual benefit. Fitz made no mention of the natives and Johanna didn't ask.

He applied the same argument to Ireland. That Home Rule had almost succeeded under Gladstone and would inevitably come sooner or later. Surely better that than more bloodshed that might actually slow the process of Irishmen running their own affairs? In the process, a grateful government in London would surely be able to turn a blind eye to the indiscretion of a young Private Reilly. Had he had deeper thoughts than just the job in hand, Fitz might have considered that what he was suggesting might be planting the seeds for the destruction of the empire as he knew it. If subject people were to be allowed to run their own affairs, how long before the teeming millions of India might expect the same dispensation? For that matter what about the other nations now under British rule? Had that thought been raised, doubtless, Fitz would have pointed out that self rule would only work where the population was up to the job and Britain would be the arbiter of that.

He was most persuasive and he held all the cards. Popular heroines of the penny novels that abounded in railway waiting rooms would have clutched their pearls and bade Fitz do his worst and let their Uncle go hang, possibly literally. Johanna was an intelligent and thoughtful woman who had been raised by her Father on tales of British iniquity in Ireland. Tales of burned farms and starved tenants and terrible retribution meted out to those who had dared to resist. She had visions of her Uncle chained in a British dungeon and threatened with unspeakable violence if she did not play her part. In fact, her Uncle, while not exactly comfortable in Kilmainham Jail could have been a lot worse off. Her Father, by his stories played a significant part in her conversion from would be Irish rebel to British agent. It was hard and it took all of Fitz's persuasive talents but eventually she asked what might be expected of her if she agreed.

Fitz felt his spirits soar with this indication of triumph but maintained his usual air of calm joviality as he explained that all she had to do was take the proffered position within the Transvaal administration and send Fitz fortnightly reports of war planning and anything else that might seem important. She would be instructed on where to deposit these so that they might be retrieved and forwarded by one of the lower level informers the British had working in the enemy capital. She would be handsomely paid for her work but what was more important was that she was doing the right thing and helping her family at the same time. Tell someone the same thing over and over and often they will believe it. Johanna wanted to believe Fitz, in the end, she had to believe him, otherwise how could she square what she was going to do with all that she had held dear? She told herself that she was saving lives and the battle would be won by other means.

The timing of Fitz's coup was inspired. By the time Johanna was to take up her post, the Transvaal government had abandoned Pretoria in the face of the British advance from the Orange Free State.

Kruger and his ministers had run East down the railway line to Machadodorp from where they would continue to direct the war. This put them much closer to the Portuguese border and made Johanna's move that much easier. It also meant the reports she sent would be read by Crowe and Fitz much sooner than had they had to come from Pretoria. To ease Johanna's conscience, Fitz arranged for a cable to be sent concerning the prisoner Reilly and stating that he would not be required to perform hard labour. He had never been so burdened but it pleased his niece when she read it. The extensive network of British informers and sympathisers within the Transvaal was trawled for a reliable courier in the Machadodorp region and a local wheelwright was found whom the Boers tolerated for his skills which were much in demand. He would retrieve Johanna's notes from a loose brick in a garden wall and see that they were passed on to Crowe in LM. A system of signals was arranged to indicate when a report was ready or alternately if there was a message for Johanna. Typically a small scrap of cloth would be left on a specific thorn bush near the station, green for outgoing, khaki for inwards messages for Johanna. If anything very urgent was in the wind or Johanna felt in danger, the colour would be red. In a place like Machadodorp, which was a small settlement, it was risky but it was also the best idea available.

Johanna was able to pass off her decision to join the government in Machadodorp to Anna and the small LM Boer contingent as a reaction to her abduction by the British agent Fitzherbert. The story tripped from her easily, how terrified as she was, she had told him nothing about the financing of an Irish rebellion but had stuck to her cover of being just a secretary and translator at a small import agency allied to the Transvaal government. In reality, she hadn't been terrified but Anna, knowing the wicked British believed her. And she agreed with Johanna when she said that she was probably being watched so assisting the cause in another way far from prying British eyes seemed best. Resisting the temptation to scold her for ignoring advice, Anna agreed that what she had planned was probably for the best and helped her prepare for the journey.

So, on a bright day, Johanna boarded the train from LM to Pretoria that would rumble across the Komatipoort and Malelane bridges before ascending the steeper parts of the track that would lead to Machadodorp. The passenger coaches were full of people from many different places speaking English, Portuguese and Afrikaans. Johanna did her best to avoid conversation with anyone lest she give anything away and because she was nervous of what was to come and what she was doing. She still believed it was for the best but without Fitzherbert's cheerful encouragement her resolve was tested. For now she wanted to be alone with her thoughts and to ward off would-be conversationalists, she took out a book and pretended to be absorbed in its contents. Rarely had she ever engaged in so many falsehoods and deceptions and she was concerned that they were becoming second nature. 'The war will soon be over,' she thought, 'and then so will this strange business. It was just a question of patience.'

Her thoughts of patience would have resonated with Bill Brown and Sergeant Wheatley who had spent days observing the railway line and associated bridges and who unknowingly watched Johanna Reilly pass over the Komatipoort bridge en route to her new position as secretary to the Transvaal government and British spy. In the event, she was very fortunate in her timing.

CHAPTER TEN

Malelane Bridge

After their successful rendezvous Brown and Von Steinaecker planned their next move with an eye to the destruction of the Komatipoort Bridge. Steinaecker had decided on making an operational base at Nomahasha to the East of their current location. The local tribe was ruled by a chief sympathetic to the English and the area was not too far from the railway but remote enough to be largely safe from Boer patrols. The joint command of Brown's and Von Steinaecker's men duly set off in that direction and on the way, Brown had the opportunity to consider his fellow officer in more depth.

His heavy accent and Germanic mannerisms made him difficult to understand at times and he lacked any sense of humour, particularly if he thought he might be the target of a joke or remark. This absence was counterbalanced by an overwhelming sense of ego and self confidence. He never doubted himself but in military matters, the confidence was more than justified. Brown wondered how he had fared in civilian life and would not have been at all surprised to learn that the answer was disastrous. He had tried farming without success and the failure of a subsequent business had seen him declared bankrupt. the outbreak of war shortly thereafter gave him the opportunity to show off his real talent for soldiering.[25] Brown as senior officer was in overall command but as Von Steinaecker was going to be commanding these men in this territory after Brown had completed the destruction of the bridge, he largely deferred to the German on most day to day matters. If occasionally he had to be restrained for some of his outbursts about discipline. In Brown's area of expertise, the relationship was akin to that of the Chairman of a company and his Managing Director, the former was the titular head but the latter gave most of the orders. It worked well enough, the men seemed content and from Brown's perspective he wasn't called upon to soldier too hard.

Nomahasha, the location Von Steinaecker had chosen for his base, was on the Swazi Portuguese border and just South of the Transvaal. The land was rough and contained many steep escarpments which would assist in spotting any unwelcome visitors. The native Chief Mahlalela was also happy to provide information about any strangers that his people might encounter. All things considered it was as safe a refuge from Boers and even wild animals as could be found and the men set to making it as comfortable as the circumstances and available materials would allow. Von Steinaecker exuded energy and drove the men hard but they could see the sense of it, the benefits to themselves and there were few complaints. The presence of natives provided not only an additional labour source but also a welcome improvement in available food.

As the camp took shape, under Von Steinaecker's direction, Brown's thoughts were on the bridge. He decided that he and Wheatley accompanied by

---

[25] After the war, Von Steinaecker again failed to adapt to civilian life ending his life as a handyman for one of his former troopers. On the outbreak of the First World War he took poison and died before he could be interned.

Patience, who Von Steinaecker described as 'a good little fellow' would go and see for themselves the state of the bridge and the guards and what might be required to drop it into the river. Von S suggested additional men but they declined. This was strictly a reconnaissance to be executed swiftly and stealthily. Two and a native scout were more discreet and could do the job just as well as a larger force. The three of them left Nomahasha in the pre-dawn some days later, heading North to the Transvaal border keeping the mountains to their West and Portuguese territory to their East. They slipped into enemy territory and rode briskly through the mountain passes to the plain beyond. There were few people moving about outside of the native settlements in their path and Brown began to hope that they might find the bridge unguarded.

Hope may spring eternal but in this case it was misplaced. They were still some twenty miles from the bridge itself when they were forced to lie up to avoid a patrol of a dozen or more Boers. Brown had spotted them with his binoculars from a reasonably safe distance making it easy to avoid them but it didn't bode well for their reconnaissance. Slowed and slightly apprehensive from eluding the patrol they arrived at a point conveniently overlooking the bridge just before nightfall and settled in to rest themselves and their horses for the night. No fires, so no hot food and worst of all no tea. Just a little biltong and fruit for sustenance and rock hard ground for a bed. They took turns to watch and listen and when they slept it was briefly and intermittently.

When the sun rose, they were able to view the bridge and the river that it spanned and using the binoculars they could pick out detail quite clearly. It wasn't a comforting sight. It seemed that the British had not been alone in recognising the strategic importance of the bridge. There were sentries at either end and more walking on each edge of the bridge between the ends. Smoke curled up from cooking fires and put a sharper edge on their hunger. As Wheatley said, the smoke suggested that however many guards they could actually see, there were plenty of other personnel in the vicinity. It looked hopeless at first glance but they were there to gather information so they watched the bridge and its guards, taking note of when the guards were relieved and the numbers at each end. They watched and noted any patrols riding out and the condition of the men and horses. The more detail that they could accumulate increased their chances of finding some chink in the defences that might afford a chance for a determined party to sneak in and plant some charges. After two days of continuous vigilance, Brown decided they had seen enough and what they had seen was far from encouraging. The Boers were alert and patrolled not only the bridge itself but the surrounding area too. They had plenty of men and they even performed checks on trains coming in from the coast. Perhaps anticipating a sneak attack by rail as Brown joked to Wheatley.

Patience had been performing some long-range reconnaissance of his own by approaching the Boer camp and asking for work. He had been lucky enough to be engaged to clean cooking pots and thus was able to get a sense of the number of Boers in the area which he put at about fifty. He stayed just long enough to steal some food and then scampered away into the bush and back across the river to where Brown and Wheatley were encamped, dodging the crocodiles as he went. Native labour came and went all the time so he would not have aroused any suspicions but his estimate of numbers was far from encouraging. Unless something changed dramatically, there was no chance of being able to successfully bring the bridge down. The Boers were far too strong for any force Von S could field. Brown was irritated, he had no desire to report failure. Desperately, he racked his brains to find some point of weakness that might afford an opportunity but could think of nothing. Disheartened, he was ready to order an ignominious return to Nomahasha when he had what might be termed a eureka moment. Komatipoort was just one bridge on the line and the last within the Transvaal before the territory began to flatten towards the coast. Deeper into the Boer Republic the land contained greater elevations which would necessitate further bridges. Further into their own land, the Boers would feel safer and may not guard the bridges. Kicking himself for not thinking of this fairly obvious point, he explained to Wheatley that he wanted to follow the line Westwards and try to find an alternative place to cut the railway. Wheatley agreed with alacrity and pointed out that even if unsuccessful, they would surely pick up useful information along the way.

Whether the Boers felt safe or not, when they moved out, the three moved cautiously. Patience scouting ahead, they followed the railway into the Transvaal, keeping a careful eye out for hostiles of any description. Fortunately, they encountered no trouble from either man or beast and after some hours they found just what they were seeking. Near the settlement of Malelane, the railway crossed the river by means of a single span eighty feet high bridge. Patience reported that the bridge was unguarded other than for a native watchman who looked after the adjacent pump house. Despite this, Brown elected to repeat what they had done at Komatipoort, watching the bridge and surroundings for enemy movement and making notes of everything that they saw. In the two days they were there they saw but one small party of Boers who passed over the bridge Westwards without halting. When he was satisfied that the Boers had no regular presence in the vicinity, Brown called a halt to the surveillance and on Patience's return, confirming all clear, they set out on the long ride back to Nomahasha to advise Von S and to plot the destruction of this second bridge.

On arrival in Nomahasha, after seeing the horses looked after, Brown sought out Von Steinaecker to explain the situation and resultant plan for Malelane. The German listened carefully, cocking his head to one side occasionally as might a bird, waxed moustache gleaming in the sunlight. He waited until Brown had finished and stared hard at the sketch Wheatley had made of the bridge, sucking air in over his brown and broken teeth as he did so. Then he sprang to his feet and paced about, presumably deep in thought and ignoring the red dust all over his boots. When he spoke at last it was with great excitement and approval for the plan. His energy and enthusiasm were boundless and as Brown told Wheatley later, it was almost as if he wanted to set out straight away. Enthusiastic as he was, Steinaecker also knew that there had to be a plan, how many men and which ones? How many horses, how much explosive would be needed and what would be the safest as opposed to the quickest route to the bridge and return?

Between them he and Brown decided on the number of men and which ones would be used. Brown and Wheatley of course as the explosives experts, Holgate for his scouting and linguistic talents and troopers Duncan and Inkster as escorts. They had sufficient fresh horses for the journey so long as they took care of them. Africa was very hard on horses as the army was discovering on its journey to Pretoria, losing over 300 a day on average. Without horses, operations against targets like the Malelane Bridge would be impossible, so great efforts were made to nurture and protect them from the various perils that they shared with the men who rode them[26]. The horses they would take were the fittest that they possessed, the intent being to reach the target, do the job and then get back to Nomahasha at speed to evade any pursuit. Von Steinaecker was insistent on being a member of the party and Brown saw no reason to dissuade him. Despite his obvious eccentricities, he was a skilled and experienced officer who understood the country.

The planning took a day and included all those to be a part of the mission. When all the details of route, means and method were settled and understood by each man involved they turned their attention to the equipment to be carried with them. All of the command assisted in checking and loading explosives, fuses and detonators. Weapons were stripped and cleaned, ammunition distributed and saddlebags loaded with necessary supplies. Three days after Brown and Wheatley's return they found themselves once more riding into enemy country, this time with a specific task and the means to carry it out. Patience was despatched in another direction

---

[26] Horses succumbed to enemy action, disease and overuse. Over the course of the war, the remount department would furnish the army with over 500,000 horses from all over the world.

with a message for Crowe explaining what they were about and another native was brought along for scouting and camp duties. Whatever his real name was Duncan and Inkster being Scots nicknamed him 'Jock' and it stuck. Von Steinaecker appeared in full comic opera garb including the massive sword that swung in a scabbard from the saddle of his horse. Brown looked at him in disbelief as they prepared to set out, opened his mouth to speak but thought better of it. Inkster and Duncan saw the look on Brown's face and grinning nudged each other. Like the excellent NCO's they were, Holgate and Wheatley said nothing and kept their faces expressionless.

The men left behind turned out to see them ride out and gave them a thin cheer as they did so. It was well meant and lifted Brown's spirits which were already excited at the thought of finally doing something tangible and something he could share a little credit for. The party intended to take a slightly indirect route, heading West initially through thick bush, then crossing the Krokodil River to the West of the settlement at Kaapmuiden and being most careful to avoid the amphibians the river was named for. They moved at a steady pace mindful of the welfare of the horses and were careful to ensure that the animals were well fed and watered when they halted. It was on one such halt by a secluded stream South of the Krokodil and miles from any human habitation that the operation was almost derailed. The horses were quietly grazing or drinking from the stream and Brown had taken out pipe and tobacco. He was in the act of lighting the tobacco when his hand was grabbed by Wheatley who held a finger to his lips to stifle any protest. Far from protesting, Brown was momentarily frozen, only his eyes moved, following Wheatley's arm pointing towards an agitated Inkster who was waving distractedly towards them from the lip of the ground above the stream bed. Grabbing his rifle, Brown crawled forward to the Trooper's position and lifted his head just enough to look in the direction Inkster was indicating.

There was a group of mounted Boers perhaps a hundred yards distant who were moving at a forty-five-degree angle to the direction that the British party would be taking once the horses were ready. The Boers looked relaxed and were chatting among themselves clearly believing that they were alone and secure behind their borders. From the look of them they were at the end of their patrol, caked in dust and moving slowly. If it came to a fight, they were too few to take on Brown's group with any prospect of success but simply the discovery would have been a Boer success in itself and probably the end of the mission. If all of Brown's party stayed quiet until the Boers were well clear then all would be well but the Boers were in no hurry and even a loud snort or whinny from one of the grazing horses could alert them to the British presence.

Brown silently cursed the Boers for their idleness and then started at the click of some fool's rifle bolt. To Brown's ears it was as loud as a shot but the Boers failed to react and carried on their agonisingly slow progress to the North West. For what seemed like hours but was in reality a few minutes Brown watched until the patrol was out of sight. He waited a couple of minutes more to be safe before giving a silent all clear. He gave thanks that they had kept the party down to a small number, any more of them in that situation would have increased their chances of discovery with more men and horses to silence. He also gave thanks for the discipline of all involved who, even after the danger was past, did their best to keep noise to a minimum while they prepared to resume their own journey.

When they did set out once more, it was a quiet and anxious band of men. Duncan and Inkster on their usual form could have joked their way across the Sahara but now all was deadly serious and the closer they came to Kaapmuiden, the more each man looked about him and rode closer to his fellows. They forded the river as planned and without incident to the West and then swung East riding as long as they dared between breaks for the horses. The light went and they rode on cautiously finally arriving in the vicinity of the bridge well after dark. A careful reconnaissance confirmed that the structure was unguarded and the work of preparing the explosive charges began. Brown and Von Steinaecker took the bridge itself, while Wheatley and Duncan set out for the pumping house nearby, the rest doing their best to keep a watch for Boers or trains that might interrupt.

Cutting fuses and connecting detonators in the dark was difficult and it took an hour or more before Brown and Von S had placed the charges to their satisfaction and connected the fuses. Wheatley and Duncan confirmed that they too were ready to go and the demolition parties warned the guard party of what was to come then lit their fuses.

First to go was the boiler house. A mighty explosion sent debris flying everywhere and had everyone lying flat on the ground. The only actual casualty was the native attendant who Brown had assumed to be absent but was in fact sleeping in the bush nearby. He awoke with a piercing shriek and ran off clutching an arm damaged by flying brickwork. Before anyone could react to that, the bridge charges went off and in what moonlight there was, it was apparent that they had done their work well. A large part of the embankment had been destroyed and the bridge span lay one end in the river, the other flat against the wall of the bridge like an enormous drawbridge that had collapsed. The rails themselves were bent and twisted upright from the force of the blast and for some seconds afterwards there was the sound of debris returning to earth. Each of the men gaped at what they had done, almost in the manner of naughty children who had broken one of their Father's windows and were fearful of parental retribution. Von Steinaecker came to his senses first clapping Brown on the shoulder and proclaiming in his fractured English 'vot a triumph' the whole thing was. Everyone breathed and began to laugh and point at the destruction until Holgate pointed out that it was quite possible that the sound of the twin explosions would have alerted every Boer for miles around and they would probably be coming their way. That settled them all down to picking up any spare fuses, detonators and explosives, packing them away and then saddling up for a rapid departure. Before they left they cut the telegraph wires to slow up any pursuit and made off South for Nomahasha leaving Jock behind to see what the Boer reaction would be and if any trains would be destroyed crossing a bridge that no longer existed

They rode most of the night cutting any other telegraph lines they happened upon, only halting in the early dawn to save the exhausted horses. The sense of elation returned despite their exhaustion and Brown was no exception to the triumphant mood. He found himself grinning to himself as he recalled the night's events. While it wasn't the bridge they had set out to blow, its destruction would halt rail traffic for a time and deny the Boers their most important link with the outside world. He had selected the target and made it happen with the help of Von Steinaecker and the others while Fitz had been kicking his well shod heels in LM. Surely, now he could make a case to Fitz for his release from the army and a return to civilisation and Elizabeth. Thoughts of Elizabeth, to his shame, led to thoughts of Johanna and he wondered what had become of her. Had he known that she had crossed the bridge he had destroyed just days before he would have been horrified. Fitz might too have been concerned but for very different reasons. However, Johnna was safe but there would be consequences of their night's work as they would discover when Jock reported back to Nomahasha.

The main group's return to base camp was uneventful bar another close encounter with a Boer patrol just North of the Transvaal border. Some friendly natives had tipped them off that there was a party of mounted white men in the vicinity who had stolen some of the natives' livestock at gunpoint. Armed with this knowledge, gained at considerable risk to the natives concerned, they were on the lookout for the Boers and Holgate's scouting ahead enabled them to lay up and let the patrol pass by. It was a good reminder that one blown bridge would not end the war and they were still traversing country with an active enemy presence. Chastened by another close call, they pushed on South in silence and found their way back into the Lebombo country in the early evening.

There was much story telling by those that were there to their fellows who weren't but attempts to stretch events and a player's part in them met with good natured derision from all sides. Beer and rum were issued and enjoyed and Brown and Von Steinaecker sipped their ale quietly and let the men enjoy themselves. As Brown said, they had earned it and things had gone better than he could have expected, now they waited for Jock to report on developments and perhaps to consider another look at Komatipoort. The Boers had seen that the British could and would strike far into their own territory, it was possible that they would stretch themselves too thin in an attempt to guard everywhere at once, if that happened there might be an opportunity to seize the greater prize.

Brown and Steinaecker had a long conversation into the night about their backgrounds and hopes for the future but also regarding more immediate concerns such as Komatipoort. Brown wondered about the possibility of recruiting natives, not merely to perform menial camp tasks but to act as guards freeing more of the white troops for other tasks. He pointed out the success of Patience and Jock as scouts and the courage of the natives who had warned them of the Boer presence. Von Steinaecker agreed that in theory there was some merit in the suggestion but cautioned that in his view, blacks like Patience and Jock were the exception rather than the rule. As evidence, he cited the example of the fellow that had been supposed to be minding the pump house at Malelane but who actually slept through the whole business until he was wounded. Trooper Inkster overheard Brown making sympathetic noises and suggested that it was the man's own fault for sleeping on the job. He and his fellows raised a great laugh at that. Although Brown shook his head he caught himself smiling at the jibe despite himself. Holgate had joined the conversation and gave his view that the natives could be used more but if they were captured, the consequences for them would be dire.[27] Having lived among the Boers, he could testify

---

[27] Despite the fact that the war was fought over what could

to the casual brutality with which they treated natives. Holgate's words only served to increase Brown's regard for natives such as Patience and Jock who were risking everything for people they barely knew and for little reward. The matter was left there, largely unresolved. Thinking about it and considering some of the native behaviour he had seen, he could see why many whites on both sides of the present conflict considered the natives as good for very little other than unskilled labour, he just wondered how much anyone had tried to change that by way of education. It was not his problem; he had come to destroy a bridge not change the world and on that thought he retired for a well-earned rest.

A day or so later Jock returned with news of Malelane. Apparently only an hour or so after they had made good their escape South, an Eastbound train pulling five trucks had plunged into the gap killing the driver and stoker. Unsurprisingly, the

---

be argued to have been their land, neither Boers nor British wanted to involve the native population and certainly not to arm them. Necessity quickly changed attitudes. At the siege of Mafeking, Colonel Baden-Powell armed three hundred blacks to man gaps in the defensive perimeter. This prompted a furious response from the Boer General Cronje who described it as 'an enormous act of wickedness.' Blacks that worked for Britain in any capacity could expect little mercy from the Boers and Lord Kitchener stated that: 'Cold blooded murder of natives by Boers is frequent.' By the end of the war both sides had not only employed blacks but also armed them when they felt it necessary. General De Wet wrote of 'the ungovernable barbarity of the natives' was the reason that they received no quarter from the Boers. Whether he saw any irony in employing barbarity like shooting unarmed prisoners is not recorded but seems unlikely.

destruction of a train as well as the bridge had put the Boers into uproar and patrols were now up and down the line between Komatipoort, Malelane and beyond. There were also feverish attempts being made to repair the wrecked bridge using timber from the Selati branch line which was brought by train from Komatipoort. It was inevitable that the Boers would attempt repairs and the zeal with which they went at it showed the value of the line to their fight. The Malelane bridge was single span and would be relatively easy to put back into operation given sufficient men and materials. Komatipoort was a much longer, multi span bridge that would be more difficult to repair. That thought and their first success brought some changes for Brown and Von Steinaecker. Firstly, a congratulatory note from Crowe and the promise of reinforcements for Von S. Second, the promise of additional man power and the lure of the Komatipoort bridge caused a gruelling routine of reconnaissance patrols to be instituted, looking for any chance to drop the bridge or some part of it into the river beneath. Lastly, they learned the news that was already known to Crowe and Fitz, that the Boers believed their force to be several hundred strong. Whether the Boers really thought that or they did not wish to admit that a small unit was causing them so much trouble didn't matter much, they were aware of trouble in their backyard and were doing their best to prevent any repetition. Von Steinaecker's men thought it most amusing and gave a great cheer when he told them.

Even with more men, the patrolling was tiring and with the Boers up in arms, was also potentially dangerous especially in the vicinity of the railway. The reports were all depressingly familiar: Boers all over the Komatipoort bridge and little or no chance of making a successful raid. Had Von Steinaecker the numbers of men the Boers imagined, he might have been able to seize the bridge and surrounding facilities long enough to plant and detonate the charges but with the men he actually had available this was impossible. The focus on the railway meant Brown had had little news of the greater war. They learned of the fall of Johannesburg and the Kruger government's flight to Machadodorp through a message sent by Crowe. Next they learned that Pretoria had fallen and surely that suggested that the war would soon be over. Yet the fighting continued. Brown pondered the futility of the Boers continuing the struggle and then considered what he might do in their situation and decided that they might be right.

If Roberts was advancing down the railway he wouldn't stop at Pretoria, he would want the whole line to the Portuguese border to be in British hands. Perhaps the diminutive Field Marshal and the main force of the army would be the ones to take Komatipoort after all. Maybe that would be for the best. Brown wanted to go home but would have preferred to do so off the back of a larger success than Malelane. It didn't matter what he thought though, it was out of his hands. So he buckled down to leading the odd patrol, writing reports for Crowe and Fitz and reading the incoming messages. The paperwork was fairly dull enlivened only by patrol duty but even that was becoming monotonous. Then one day a patrol came back in the usual condition: filthy, hungry and tired but unusually merry too as they were accompanied by two prisoners. One was a stalwart fellow named Commandant Van Dam who took his capture stoically, his companion was a dour and angry Sergeant named Shribley who cursed in Afrikaans and occasionally spat on the ground to emphasise his displeasure.

There were two reasons that Van Dam's demeanour was more amenable than his Sergeant. Firstly, he was a European Hollander not a Boer born in Africa and perhaps more importantly had been saved by one of Steinaecker's men from an angry Swazi warrior intent on severing his head from his body. Apparently, these two and a companion had strayed away from the main body of their commando and into the vicinity of Chief Mahlalela's *kraal*[28] where they were confronted by a group of Steinaecker's men and some Swazis. Their companion had foolishly attempted to draw his gun and was shot dead. Van Dam, recognising a lost cause, had surrendered but the Swazis' blood was up and an axe wielding warrior came at him. He was only saved by the bravery of Corporal Gray who with great presence of mind and personal courage, leapt between the two with rifle levelled at the Swazi.

Van Dam as an officer was naturally of interest and when he let slip that he had been sent from Johannesburg to patrol the railway line that interest increased dramatically. Unfortunately for Brown and Von Steinaecker, who attempted a little gentle questioning over dinner and despite Brown's liberal application of rum, he would not divulge any more information of use. The pair were held at Nomahasha in a fairly relaxed captivity. One thing Van Dam had agreed to over dinner was to give his parole not to escape. He cautioned that Shribley would give no such word and could not be trusted. While that may have been true, unless he could steal a horse he had no chance of getting away anyway and even with a horse he would have had to evade not only Von

---

[28] Village or enclosure

Steinaeker's men but also the local tribesmen. After Van Dam's experience Shribley thought better of it.

A message had been sent to LM about their guests and a response requested that they be brought across the Portuguese border to a general store on the road leading to LM on a certain date when Crowe, Fitz and an escort would meet them. The message also required Von S and Brown to be there to receive instructions. There was no hint as to what the instructions concerned but with the evolving military situation in the West, there were all manner of possibilities, including perhaps Brown's recall to civilian life. Comforting a thought as that might be, Brown did not allow his hopes to rise too high. He couldn't see Crowe coming all this way to give him a thank you and a one way ticket to Southampton, particularly after his insinuations about Johanna.

On the appointed day, a party of eight men set out from Nomahasha. Brown, Von Steinaecker and Wheatley, the two prisoners and an escort of three troopers. Holgate was left in charge at Nomahasha. The two prisoners were unbound but Shribley was told with great firmness by Von Steinaecker that any attempt at escape or even anything that might be seen as such an attempt would result in his death. He didn't seem much put out by the threat but neither did he attempt to escape.

The Nomahasha party reached the rendezvous first. A ramshackle store with the usual corrugated metal roof, it was run by a friendly Swiss who chatted happily to Von Steinaecker in German while having water boiled for tea. He took in the different characters in the party and while he said nothing, it was clear that he had Shribley figured as a bad egg from the beginning. Not that it was hard, the man looked like a difficult fellow, if he spoke it sounded like a snarl but mostly he sat in truculent silence.

Another indicator for the storekeeper might have been the way that at least one of the troopers always had a rifle trained on him. They had taken Von Steinaecker's threats to heart and having also taken an immense dislike to Shribley were rather hoping he might bolt but Shribley knew better than to try.

After an hour or two spent in the shade of the gum trees that provided a little shade, a small group of mounted figures appeared from the East who proved to be Crowe and Fitz and an armed escort from the Marine guards. To preserve the diplomatic niceties, Fitz and the Marines were in an approximation of civilian dress in the sense that they wore khaki without unit or rank badges. All of them were well armed however, and even Crowe carried a revolver. Sergeant Shribley's reputation had preceded him and nobody was taking any chances. Crowe was curt but polite and while Fitz's eyes widened slightly at his first sight of Von Steinaecker, he was all affability, pumping Brown's hand and offering congratulations to all on the success of the Malelane operation. The two Marines were taken off by Wheatley to meet their prisoners and the troopers guarding them with whom they soon had an easy rapport.

Crowe, Fitz, Von Steinaecker and Brown commandeered a rickety table to the side of the store and over tin mugs of tea Fitz laid out what was on his mind and the mind of the High Command. They all listened in silence as Fitz gave a succinct summary of the current military situation, the taking of Pretoria and Kruger's flight to Machadodorp together with his government and all the money and bullion from the Transvaal treasury. Yet despite this abandonment of the seat of government the Boers for the most part were still fighting. Several thousand had surrendered in the Brandwater Basin but they had been excoriated by many of their fellows who sneeringly referred to 'hansoppers.'[29]. The assessment of the High Command was that the Boer armies in the field would fight on until they were overwhelmed by the British or they ran out of food and ammunition. It would take time and many casualties on both sides but there was a chance that the collapse might be accelerated.

Brown and Von Steinaecker listened attentively, delighted to be brought up to date but wondering why they were being given this high-level intelligence briefing and now intrigued as to the nature of the catalyst that would hasten the end of the war. Fitz had paused in his delivery to be sure that he had their full attention. He cautioned them that what he was about to reveal was of the utmost secrecy and must not be spoken of to anyone. It had to be said even if the opportunities for indiscretion were limited in Nomahasha. Warning delivered; Fitz resumed his briefing.

The High Command had good reason to believe that President Paul Kruger was preparing to flee the country. Fitz paused again for effect. Their information was that he would board a train at Machadodorp which would take him to LM from whence he would take ship for Holland. Brown and Von S looked at each other as they considered the possibilities. Brown spoke first and asked if the intention was to kill Kruger or capture him. Until now Fitz had worn the serious face of the officer delivering his briefing, Brown's intervention brought back the easy smile as he responded.

'Don't be so bloodthirsty Billy. Kill an old man and his civilian companions? Whatever would they say about that in the papers?'

---

[29] Literally people with hands up i.e. Surrendering

'Possibly that he was our enemy and had instigated a war against Britain and her people that caused thousands of deaths?' Suggested Brown drily.

'That might be true of the Daily Mail' said Fitz 'but it won't wash in New York or Paris or Berlin. We would be painted as the bully that picks on the old and defenceless and there would be questions asked and protests lodged. No that would never do.'

'So capture then?' Persisted Brown.

'Jaysus no' laughed Fitz 'that would be worse. What would we do with him? Put him on trial? Lock him up? Look, either of those courses of action makes Kruger a martyr and would probably prolong the war. If he leaves the country and goes into exile of his own volition, he can be portrayed as having run out on his people and left them to their fate while he enjoys a comfortable life courtesy of the Transvaal in Europe.'

'So we just let him go? In which case why are you telling us all this?'

'I'm just coming to that Billy and like so many aspects of this war it's a little complicated so bear with me.'

Both Brown and Von S looked attentive as Fitz launched into the meat of the business.

'Firstly, don't blow up any more bridges. We don't want any accidents. The bridge that you did blow is back in action on a limited basis, well done again there. The repairs were effected with timbers that were cut for the Selati line which runs North from Komatipoort to the gold fields and farms up towards Rhodesia, or at least it would had it been finished. The line is a hundred odd miles of track that ends near the Sabie River. The Transvaalers were taken advantage of by some sharps from Europe and work stopped when the money ran out.[30]'

Warming to his story, Fitz continued: 'You may recall that I mentioned that when Kruger left Pretoria, he took the contents of the treasury with him. We believe that when he sails for Europe, the money will sail with him. This provides a handy opportunity to portray Kruger as stealing from his people to fund his retirement. In reality, the Boers are just trying to keep it out of our hands.'

'Our information is that a substantial sum of the Transvaal's money will not go with the old man but will, in fact be diverted to fund a rebellion in Ireland.' Fitz allowed himself a grin at the surprised look on the faces of his listeners.

'When the train carrying Kruger reaches Komatipoort, a coach will be detached and will then be coupled to another engine which will take the coach and the individuals inside North up the Selati line. Your job will be to ambush the Selati train and to capture the occupants and the money.'

Von Steinaecker looked up and asked why the Boers would send the money up a line that went nowhere. Fitz explained that the train would be met by a party of horsemen at the Sabie River. Following that rendezvous, both cash and people would transfer to horse and would then ride to Chiveve in Portuguese territory to take ship for Ireland. That

---

[30] The contract to build the Selati line became a byword for corruption and financial mismanagement. A Frenchman named Oppenheim bought the support of corrupt Transvaal politicians to obtain the contract. Work began in 1892 but by 1895 the spiraling costs and whispers of false accounting led to an inquiry. The project collapsed in a storm of lawsuits leaving the Transvaal with a line going nowhere at a million pounds cost. Oppenheim was sentenced to three years prison, but no politician was charged.

way, they would escape any scrutiny from the British consulate in LM and there could be no embarrassment caused to any European host nation who might be accused by Britain of helping foment rebellion.

Brown had stayed silent and was looking at Fitz while scratching his head in a distracted manner. It was a lot of information to absorb and of a most dramatic nature but he wondered how Fitz could know all this with any degree of certainty so he asked the question. Fitz's reaction was odd, almost a look of triumph. It would have been strange on anyone but so unusual of Fitz to reveal anything that he was thinking. It could have been bravado but when he filled in this piece of the jigsaw, it was plain that he was pleased with himself. He explained that the Intelligence Department had recruited an agent that they had succeeded in placing inside the highest reaches of the Transvaal government in Machadodorp. This agent had provided regular reports regarding the thinking of the administration including Kruger and their plans for the conduct of the war. Close to despair at the evacuation of Pretoria there had been some talk of making terms with the British but the Transvaal had been rallied by President Steyn of the Free State who bluntly accused his allies as proposing a 'selfish and disgraceful peace.' Transvaal sinews suitably stiffened, it was expected that the Boer armies would fight on by living off the land and conducting small scale operations against British forces when they saw the opportunity. To prevent his capture and to raise support for the Boer cause in Europe, Kruger would leave the country travelling by rail to LM and then taking ship for Europe with some of his staff.

'What about the money for the Irish?' Asked Brown, 'who will be arranging for that to travel North?'

'Our agent in the government will see to that and will be on the train carrying it. She will provide us with details of timing and the number of guards travelling with her, which will make your part in all of this that much simpler.'

Brown looked quizzical: 'Did you say 'she?' The agent you have in place is a woman?'

Fitz smiled his amused and ever so slightly superior smile: 'Ah yes, I didn't mention that before but then there was no need. Our agent is indeed a lady and a very resourceful one too. She hasn't been working with us long but her reports have been immensely helpful. But you know her Billy, it's Johanna Reilly.'

Brown suddenly became aware of the heat, the cracks in the table and a fly buzzing around his tea mug. There were too many questions, none of which he wanted answered by Fitz and some of which he probably didn't want answered at all. Conscious that Von Steinaecker and Fitz were both looking at him curiously, he flushed and tried to pretend it wasn't happening, then composed himself. Crowe had said nothing during Fitz's narration but now broke the silence.

'I think we misjudged Miss Reilly before' he said to no one in particular. An observation made as if to himself. For a moment Brown thought it might almost be an apology but then decided it was Crowe justifying himself. The first thought he had was: 'Yes you bloody well did' but that was cut off by another more urgent thought that overcame even his desire to be rude to Crowe.

'Johanna Reilly had no love for the British, you didn't misjudge that. I don't believe she was a Boer agent but there is no way in hell she would work for us and certainly not to interfere with the prospect of a rebellion in Ireland. I cannot believe that she is spying for us in any way.'

Fitz nodded and spoke softly, even sympathetically: 'Now Billy, I can see why you might think that, I really do and certainly the lady had to be persuaded but there's no question in my mind that she is conscientiously working for the Queen in the heart of the Transvaal government.'

'But why and when you say persuaded, what do you mean?'

So Fitz filled him in on the rest of the story, how they had established the link between Johanna and Leyds and found that she was working to persuade the Boers to finance rebellion in Ireland to divert troops from South Africa. That they had found out about the uncle Johanna had in Kilmainham jail and how Fitz had persuaded her that her uncle's life could be improved or possibly even saved by her cooperation. He didn't mention Johanna's kidnapping or the brawl in the botanic garden but gave Brown just enough to have him convinced of the truth of the matter.

'So there it is Billy' Fitz stated firmly 'Johanna is working for us to shorten the war and save lives on both sides and to stop a pointless and bloody insurrection in Ireland where all of the blood that would be spilt would be Irish.'

'Are you certain that the lady can be trusted?' Von Steinaecker asked 'If I understand you correctly Herr Major, she has achieved her goal of finding Boer cash for an Irish revolt. Vy shouldn't she just take the money and go to Ireland as planned?'

Fitz's eyebrow raised as he gazed at Von S, who was looking at him intently.

'A very reasonable question Baron' he replied, all affability 'but you will be there to make sure that whatever temptation she may feel, she will not act upon. Remember also that her uncle, her Father's youngest brother, is in jail having been convicted of a very serious crime. If new evidence were to be discovered linking him with yet more serious acts, it could go very hard for him. I have confidence in the lady.' He paused as if in thought, then added: 'But it does require a deal of trust, I do agree with you there and as the responsibility rests on my shoulders, I shall be coming with you.'

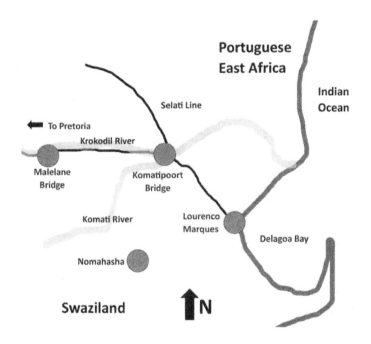

CHAPTER ELEVEN

Holding up the train

The party that rode West into the lowering sun had shed two prisoners and gained another officer. The other party riding East was led by her Majesty's Consul General in Lourenço Marques, who was chatting casually to Commandant Van Dam of the South African Police or *Zarps*[31] as they were known colloquially who was accompanied by the more taciturn Sergeant Shribley. Shribley wasn't talking, which was probably just as well given what he was thinking and that his escort of two Marines were just longing to fire their weapons in anger. With the exception of the Sergeant, the Eastbound group were probably more relaxed than their Westbound fellows. Brown was worrying about Johanna and what Fitz might have done to bring her into British service. Knowing her as he did, he was even more concerned at the consequences if she decided to change her mind and somehow confound Fitz's grand scheme. The British Empire was hard on people that let it down and Fitz would not take kindly to having his plans upset. Brown had seen the steel

---

[31] The *Zarps* or properly the *Zuid Afrikaasche Politie* were a paramilitary force rather than a traditional police force and started life as part of the artillery. During the second Boer War they fought with great distinction earning the acclaim of friend and foe alike.

and it worried him. For the rest of the party, Von Steinaecker was incapable of relaxation, Wheatley was concerned about Brown whom he could tell was shaken by Fitz's tale. As for troopers Duncan and Inkster, they wondered about the new Major and whether he would prove as easy to deal with as he appeared. Only Fitz rode serene and content, his opportunity for great deeds unfolding so neatly before him.

Further West yet in Waterval Onder where the Transvaal government had moved from Machadodorp, preparations were being made for the final departure of Kruger and select aides and separately, Miss Johanna Reilly and three members of the Transvaal Irish Brigade who would be escorting the lady and a significant sum of money to a rendezvous near the Sabie River. Fitz was a clever man but his self-confidence had marred his judgment in the case of Johanna Reilly. The time and distance between them and the way events had begun to unfold made Brown's concerns absolutely justified. She was even now thinking of ways to abscond to Ireland with the Transvaal's money that would not get her Uncle hanged or her parents imprisoned but the fear that Fitz had instilled into her on both those counts was a steep mountain to be climbed. So far she was stumped but she was a clever and resourceful woman and as the great political events unfolded around her, she clung to the hope that an opportunity would emerge from the earthquake that was about to shake Southern Africa.

The following day in Nomahasha, plans were being laid to execute Fitz's scheme. maps were consulted and consideration was given as to the ideal spot at which to ambush the train that would be on the Selati line. Unfortunately, the map did not how the course of the line in any detail but those making the plans knew that it began at Komatipoort and ended at the Sabie River so somewhere between those two points lay the ideal spot. It would be best to do the job nearer to the Komatipoort end as that would mean less distance to travel both out and back and less chance of interference from any Boer patrols in the area. This sounded good in theory but had a number of practical difficulties. Firstly, there was no time to ride to the area and pick a likely spot. The reports from Waterval Onder suggested that departure could come within ten days or a week which made sense based upon Roberts' rapid advance eastwards. The second issue was how to stop the train? If you had enough time, you could block the track or even cut it but there was no certainty that they would have the luxury of time to prepare anything so elaborate. On the more positive side, Holgate commented that as the line had not been used much other than by the Boers hiding rolling stock, it may well have been neglected and any train would have to travel cautiously to avoid derailment. It satisfied Fitz who had seen Buffalo Bill's Wild West Show and could see himself riding alongside a train of fugitives, revolver in hand in the manner of an American train robber. Brown was more concerned about the safety of Johanna Reilly and was disturbed at Fitz's indifference to her fate.

'She knew the risks when she agreed to do this' was his answer when Brown asked how she would fare in a train crash.

'But she couldn't have known about this' persisted Brown.

'Billy, it doesn't matter, she doesn't matter. Keep your mind on stopping the train and keeping the cash from getting away. Johanna more than likely will be fine. We don't know that the train will derail and even if it does, she won't necessarily be hurt.'

There were many things that Brown could have said in response, but Fitz was in charge and he was right. Getting the job done was the priority but Bill Brown was determined to do everything he could to ensure Johanna's safety in the process. He didn't know how but he was resolved that she should not become an unwitting casualty of war or Peter Fitzherbert's ambitions.

Whatever encouragement the Transvaal Boers may have received to keep fighting, the British kept landing blows. The town of Belfast some one hundred and twenty miles East of Pretoria fell and when General Botha attempted to hold a defensive line further East, at Bergendal Farm, his troops were swept away by artillery and the bayonets of the Rifle Brigade and Inniskilling Fusiliers. This put the British within twenty-five miles of President Paul Kruger and his government.

Isolated as they were in Nomahasha, the details of the Boer defeats didn't reach Brown and Fitz. It wasn't important because the pattern had been established and the only question about the complete collapse of the Boers was when it would happen. The same applied to the flight of Kruger and what Fitz insisted on referring to as the 'Great Train Hold Up.' A title he found highly amusing but which irritated Brown and confused Von Steinaecker and the men, most of whom had a rather literal view of the world.

Irritating or not, Fitz was thorough, he went over various different scenarios over and over again until everyone concerned knew what they had to do in each situation. They rehearsed stopping a train with an obstruction and how to board it from ahead and behind. They considered what they might do to stop a train if they had nothing suitable to bar the line and various other permutations of the challenges they might face. Time was likely to be against them so Fitz ensured that they prepared as well as they might for whatever may lie ahead. The men that had not encountered Fitz previously were wary at first but like their companions who had met him and partly because of them they soon came to like him. His willingness to work hard alongside them was one thing and his good sense in commanding with a light touch was another. Whatever thoughts they may have had about Brown's position, nobody was in any doubt that Major Fitzherbert was running things from now on. Von Steinaecker although perhaps disappointed at no longer being in command, recognised a fellow professional and followed his directions happily, occasionally offering thoughts and suggestions of his own but content to acknowledge Fitz as senior officer. This frenzy of activity had everyone tired but confident however, had it been much longer in preparation would have dulled the edge of the dagger. As it was, the word came at the right moment and they were ready and sharp.

The note that arrived from Crowe indicated that they would need to be in position in two to three days. Fitz cursed the vagueness of the timing but made plans for an immediate departure. Hard riding could put them North of Komatipoort in a day and a half but they would have to nurse the horses as best they could. Now though, they were able to enjoy the fruits of all the aggressive patrolling that had been carried out previously. The route was familiar and the location of streams and water holes was known and mapped. In addition, after so many close encounters, they knew the most likely Boer patrol areas and to either stay clear or stay extra alert.

Preparations for departure were completed quickly but not hurried, there was too much at stake to rush things. For Fitz and Von Steinaecker there were medals to be won, for Brown there was the hope that the war would soon end and for all of them, there was a keen desire just to survive the next few days and come back intact. All of the men were keen to be part of the operation. Fitz and Von Steinaecker agreed that they should ride out in force and so few were disappointed. Only three were left behind to maintain the camp and all of them were ill or injured in some fashion.

Once the force left, they rode swiftly through the day and the following night. They encountered no Boers and the natives they met along the way confirmed that they had seen none in the last few days. They were a little way off from Komatipoort when the sun rose and it was broad daylight by the time they were close enough to see the bridge. Fitz and Von Steinaecker studied the structure at length through binoculars and pronounced it free of enemy troops.

'It's odd' observed Fitz, 'with all those guards they had in the area, you'd think they would give the old fellow a send off.'

'Maybe they believe your stories' said Brown, 'you know, that he left them all in the lurch and made off with their money.'

Fitz laughed and agreed that it was entirely possible but not until the Presidential train had left the country.

After a brief reconnaissance to ensure the area was free of Boers, they rode across the bridge into the station area which too was deserted. While they poked around looking for signs of life and anything worth stealing, Brown walked down the track a little way looking for the Selati branch line, which he found after a few hundred yards. There was an odd tang in the air which he recognised as the sulphurous smell of coal smoke. From passing trains he thought or maybe just in my imagination, whichever it was it contrasted unpleasantly with the clean air of the bush to which he had become accustomed. He turned to walk back to the others thinking that they should probably get on their way down the Selati line and establish their ambush when he heard raised voices. There was a small group of troopers and Von Steinaecker surrounding a terrified looking old native who was bobbing his head and gesturing in the direction from where Brown had just arrived.

Fitz strolled over to join the group listening to the old fellow's wide-eyed answers to the German's questioning. His story was that he was a labourer on the railway. He had been snatching an illicit rest in a paint store and had awoken to find all of his companions gone and a small force of Boers in the vicinity. Fearful of retribution if discovered, he stayed still and silent only occasionally daring to look out of the soot grimed window. A train had arrived and halted and there seemed to be a great fuss around both of its carriages. A second engine that he had not seen used before was brought from a siding and the one of the carriages from the original train was coupled to it. He had seen both of the trains depart one after the other. He waited until he was sure he was alone and then emerged from his refuge only to walk smack into Von S. Further questioning established that the fork in the line leading North to Sabie would not have been visible to him so he could offer no assistance on where each train was going only that one train arrived and two had left.

It seemed certain that this was the train they were looking for but a day early. Had Johanna played Fitz false? It didn't really matter much if Johanna had not long departed. They would follow the line to its ending at or just beyond the Sabie River, moving as rapidly as they could. According to the rudimentary map they had, the line at one point curved West to avoid some low hills and then resumed a Northward path. If there had been no trace of the train at that point, they could split their force and send a party over the hills to try and get ahead of their quarry while the remainder could continue to follow the track. Time was no longer on their side; they needed to meet and stop that train before it could be met by the Boers who were to escort Johanna and the cash to the coast. So Northwards along the track they rode, looking for the tell-tale plume of smoke that would show the train. For miles, nothing disturbed the blue of the late winter sky. They passed great piles of abandoned building material discarded by the engineers when the Selati project was cancelled, stark against the empty bush and like the rails themselves, showing the signs of neglect.

The ground undulated and mounting a slight rise, Holgate's scout's eye spotted smoke in the distance. Just a smudge on the horizon but there could be only one source. Fitz urged them on and they pushed the horses as hard as they dared alongside the track towards the smoke. Their current position was well South of the Sabie which was the meeting point for the Boer escort to the coast but the train was a long way off and continued to roll. The iron horse ridden by the Boers had the advantage of unlimited stamina unlike the horses of the British and carried its own fuel and water. To Brown's eye, it seemed that the distance between them and the smoke was too immense for them to catch up but they had no choice but to try. Fitz must have felt the same thing as he urged everyone forward again. Looking back briefly,

Brown saw that they were kicking up an enormous cloud of dust and wondered if the party on the train realised they were being followed. Even if they didn't, they must be alive to the possibility, but it wasn't incumbent on them to be alert, they were on a fixed line and could only hope that they could make the rendezvous without interference. Fitz and his party had to not only catch up with the rolling train but find a way of halting it too. Short of driving a herd of elephants onto the track, Brown was beginning to wonder if it would be possible.

They pressed on towards the train and like Brown, Fitz was trying to decide what exactly they would do once they had caught up to it. If they were decreasing the gap now, it meant that they could get ahead of it and perhaps block the line forcing a halt but how would they block it? Men and horses would be swept aside and it seemed unlikely that they would have time to place anything substantial across the track, even if there was anything suitable to hand. It didn't matter though, unless they got ahead the whole question was moot. So they rode on watching the blob of grey against the blue grow slowly begin to grow larger with each passing mile. When the track began a Westward curve around the low hills on the Eastern side. Fitz gestured to Brown to ride up alongside him.

'I'm going to take five men, Holgate, Steinaecker, Duncan, Gray and Foster and ride over those hills to try to cut them off.' Fitz was shouting above the noise of the horses, like everyone else, filthy with dust from the ride. His uniform breeches were ripped from contact with thorns and his hat was jammed down hard upon his head but there was no doubting the excitement on his face.

'I want you to press on with the rest of the men. There's no reason we can't stop them but if anything should go wrong you must carry on and stop them yourself, either along the line or at Sabie. Don't deviate and don't concern yourself with anything except that bloody train. Is that all clear?'

The words and the instruction was perfectly clear and if Brown's doubts showed, Fitz ignored them. Brown gave him an 'Understood' followed by a 'good luck' because what else could he say? Then he watched as Fitz gathered his little subgroup and veered slightly right and up and over the hilly ground, vanishing into the scrub.

Taking command of the remainder and bulk of the force, Brown led them along either side of the railway. It wasn't too long before they were rewarded with a glimpse of the train itself down a straight section of track before the line curved away again. The sight encouraged them all and the pace of the pursuit accelerated accordingly. The horses seemed to have caught the mood too and while no one was about to shout charge, the pace quickened perceptibly. Brown was looking at the horses and praying none went down injured or lame. It was going to be a long walk home for anyone without a horse but that was only going to be a worry for the living.

Two minutes later they could see the train again and much more clearly, the change of pace had made a great difference, and they would soon be caught up and then what thought Brown? A shout of 'halt in the name of the Queen?' Maybe 'stand and deliver' would be more appropriate in the light of their ultimate intention. The train stayed in sight and as they closed the gap, Brown noticed something odd. The angle between engine and coach looked wrong, too sharp, as if attempting a right angle turn and then he realised that while smoke and steam continued to billow from the engine it was diminishing. There was no movement, the engine had derailed. It wasn't surprising, the further they had come down the line, the more the fruits of shoddy workmanship and exposure to the elements had become apparent. It was a desperate plan of the Boers that had gone desperately wrong. Or was it? What if it was something more sinister like the bait in a trap? Taken by that thought Brown slowed his troops down and bade them spread out more to present a harder target. Why should anyone go to such elaborate lengths to ambush a command they believed to be several hundred strong? He couldn't imagine but he didn't want anyone to die through carelessness. They moved wide and they moved cautiously. As they drew closer, there was a shot and a scream from ahead. Brown ordered a halt and a dismount. They would move on foot from here on, Boer style, leapfrogging from bush to bush and rock to rock. Three would move and three would cover them on either wing with Brown in the centre of the track, rifle ready.

There was more firing and rounds could be heard striking the engine and fizzing away again. Fitz and his men had achieved their objective of getting ahead of the train and now were announcing their presence to the train crew and passengers, who they expected to include Johanna Reilly. The firing was between Fitz's group and the train. The train's riflemen didn't seem to be aware of Brown's presence in their rear area. That might have changed when a man jumped from the engine and was promptly shot by Trooper Inkster. It wasn't a fatal wound and the man lay alternately screaming and moaning. Nobody else emerged and the screams and cries of the wounded soon subsided. Brown paused his men and waited but receiving no return fire they continued their steady advance towards the carriage in silence allowing Fitz to make the running with the defenders.

It wasn't an even contest and it couldn't last long. There were unlikely to be more than a half dozen aboard the stranded train one at least badly wounded and maybe another too. There were nineteen armed troops approaching from two different directions and those inside had nowhere to run to. They also had a limited ability to fire on Brown's group without disembarking due to the angle of the coach to the track which was shallower than that of the engine. When they were a good hundred yards off Brown halted his men and had them take cover as he considered next steps. Looking at the carriage, it was upright but off the rails at the end nearest the engine, the rear wheels being half on half off the track. It was an old civilian design, possibly used to transport railway or mine workers short distances. No armour plate and mainly wooden construction. A .303 round might or might not penetrate the wood but the noise any round would make on striking the exterior would be horrific for those inside. Working on the theory that his opponents would quickly recognise the hopelessness of their situation; Brown ordered his men to give the carriage five rounds apiece to provoke a surrender. He prayed that Johanna had the sense to take to the floor and stay there.

Splinters of wood flew as the rifles did their work and there was some shouting from within the carriage but nothing intelligible above the shooting. The firing ceased and Brown's men reloaded. In the silence that followed he shouted a call for those inside to surrender. The only response was a wildly inaccurate shot. Brown heard a Scottish voice from behind him say: 'I think that means 'no'.' Instantly hushed by Wheatley. Insubordinate or not, it was a reasonable assumption thought Brown but what did the bloody idiots think they were going to do against these numbers? More importantly perhaps, if they insisted on carrying on this pointless fight, what were he and Fitz going to do to compel a surrender?

Up ahead, Fitz and his group were conferring as to their own next steps. They had taken some fire from both engine and carriage, happily without any lethal effect but as Von Steinaecker and Fitz agreed, they would have to act reasonably quickly or risk the arrival of Boer reinforcements. Kruger may have left the country but the war was still being fought and they were well inside enemy territory. However unlikely a Boer rescue might be, Fitz wanted no upsets. Hearing the sharp volume of fire from Brown, Fitz took a swift decision. Concluding that the best course of action would be for his group to draw the fire of the Boers while Brown charged the train from behind. He decided to send Trooper Foster to Brown to tell him what was required. Foster mounted and elected to swing around to the Western flank of the train in order to avoid riding back over the hill to the East which looked more exposed to enemy fire. He may have been correct but he wasn't lucky, a shot from the carriage knocked him out of the saddle into a clump of bushes where he lay cursing. His horse, seemingly oblivious to his fate or any immediate danger cantered on a few more yards and then stopped to graze.

Fitz saw Foster fall and cursed the man for an idiot. It was an unfair slur and Fitz was at least partially at fault for putting the man in harm's way without more thorough planning but he was in a hurry to win this fight, retrieve the money from the train and get back to LM to tell the story. Noting that Brown's men had resumed shooting and gathering his small group together, he told them to ride West but ahead of the train then dismount and fire to attract the attention of the enemy and draw fire away from Brown. He was gambling that Brown was sufficiently competent an officer to see what was happening and would order his men forward as the enemy fire turned on his own position.

Had Fitz been able to see the interior of the carriage, he might have been more patient. The members of the Transvaal Irish Brigade sent to escort Johanna and the Transvaal's cash were shaken enough by the derailment. The effect of Brown's concentrated fire had been to set them railing at one another. The calmest person aboard was Johanna, although she wasn't feeling it but busied herself binding up the wound of one man who had taken a bullet to the shoulder. The other two thus far unscathed were loosing-off wild shots in between cursing each other, the people responsible for them being there and the engine driver for derailing the train. Foster had been particularly unlucky to fall victim to one of their better shots but at least he lived. The train driver was not at fault for the derailment, but was in no position to respond to criticism, having been killed by a round from Fitz when he first opened fire. His stoker had succumbed after Trooper Inkster had shot him as he panicked and tried to run from the engine.

Inside the carriage the noise was close to unbearable, both of the impact of incoming rounds that smashed into the exterior and from the return fire. The stink of cordite made eyes water and hung in the air, made worse by every shot fired. Johanna could see that the fight was a hopeless one and wondered how best to convince her defenders to throw in the towel. They were Irishmen that had been convinced to travel to South Africa to fight for the

Boers. As Irishmen, they were also British subjects and liable to a charge of treason for taking up arms against the Crown. The fact that they were also in charge of a sizeable sum of money destined to fund rebellion in Ireland was not going to make them any more popular with the British authorities. Johanna tried to reason with them, pointing out that continued resistance meant certain death but surrender at least gave them a chance. The men had heard the stories about British justice to rebels, the same tales that Johanna had been fed by her Father and that Fitz had played on. Surrender they declared was not an option.

The rounds kept coming causing splinters of wood and glass to fly around the interior of the carriage. Johanna's attempts to make her companions see sense were having little effect. Of the three men, Donaghue, lay nursing his wound, babbling prayers among the chaos, the other two, Finnegan and Burke were of a more secular bent and cursed as they fired, sending shot after shot in the general direction of their tormentors and substituting volume of fire for accuracy. This had the effect of keeping the heads of their opponents down but this could not be sustained for long. Something Burke realised when he reached into his ammunition pouch and found that it was almost empty. He grabbed at Donaghue's bandolier bumping him in the process and causing him to scream in pain. He cursed the man to silence and cursed him again as he recovered only a handful of rounds. Finnegan raised his head briefly to look forward and then checked his own ammunition to find he too was down to a very few bullets.

As Burke reloaded his rifle, Johanna noted Finnegan's gaze travel to the leather bag containing the gold coin destined for Ireland. As he looked,

Johanna began to wonder what he might be thinking. An incoming shot interrupted, sending a chunk of timber into Burke's head, which put him on the floor and caused a prodigious flow of blood but little serious damage. Johanna cleaned up Burke as best she could and as she did so, Finnegan risked a further glance outside but kept his weapon down. He then turned his attention back to the inside. As two more shots landed in quick succession, he pushed Johanna out of the way and grabbed the bag. He strained to move it and instead effected an entry with a clasp knife and proceeded to fill his pockets and empty pouches with gold coin bearing the portrait of Paul Kruger.

'Don't you think the British are going to search you when we surrender?' Asked Johanna.

'No Miss Reilly because I'm not going to be here. There's a loose horse among those bushes not twenty yards away and he's my way out of here.' As he said it Burke looked up and called him a thief.

'Well, maybe I am and what of it? And thinking about it, I'll take that too' and he grabbed Burke's ammunition pouch from him before vaulting out of a broken window.

Finnegan was a lucky man. His sudden and unexpected appearance caught Fitz and his men off balance and he was almost in the saddle of Foster's horse before anyone could react. When the reaction came shots flew past him but none found their mark and he was urging his newly acquired mount into a sharp gallop West away from the fight.

Brown and his men were unsighted and largely unaware of these developments. They heard the scatter of shots and noted the absence of any return from the train. Brown only paused for a moment before ordering his men forward. He halted them once more twenty odd yards from the carriage and was preparing to order a volley followed by a charge onto the coach when a white cloth appeared through a broken window attached to a rifle barrel. Ordering a cease fire, Brown made to move forward to accept the Boer surrender when he felt a restraining hand on his shoulder. The hand belonged to Wheatley who cautioned him from entering alone.

'Let me come with you sir. There have been stories about the Boers abusing white flags before, it might be a ruse. I can cover you going in, just in case.'

Brown nodded and the two went forward together. Reaching the rear door of the carriage, Brown announced their presence and their intention to enter. For good measure, he praised their good sense in giving up in the face of the overwhelming odds that had them surrounded just in case anyone inside was feeling heroic.

He needn't have worried, battered by noise and choking on cordite, the two remaining men were wounded and almost out of ammunition. Any desire to carry on the struggle had fled with Finnegan. Even Johanna was dishevelled and bleeding from some minor injuries she hadn't noticed until now. She had been responsible for the white flag, which she now relinquished under Wheatley's stern gaze.

Brown looked at her partly with relief and partly regret. He was relieved that she had escaped relatively unharmed but concerned at what part she might have played in the rescheduling of the train or any of the other events leading up to the little skirmish that had left two men dead. There was a moment of silence broken by Wheatley asking: 'are you alright Miss?'

Johanna managed a weak smile and a nod and Wheatley begged her pardon as he relieved her of the rifle bearing the white cloth. He then turned his attention to the two wounded men and disarmed them too. Donaghue was in no case to offer any trouble and the bloodied Burke knew that the game was up. Wheatley ushered them outside to be watched over and given water while Brown renewed his acquaintance with Johanna.

When Johanna had been recruited by Fitz, he had not mentioned Brown or his part in matters to her. She had always thought Fitz too smooth to be totally honest but had never suspected Brown of anything untoward. Here he was though in uniform and clearly a British officer just as Anna had suspected. So much had happened since their last meeting in LM: Pedro had been murdered, she had left and returned encountering Peter Fitzherbert who had charmed her, abducted her, and finally convinced her to act as a British spy against all the instincts of her upbringing. After all of that, a train wreck and a gunfight, meeting Billy Brown in the midst of all this horror was surprising but hardly inconceivable.

'Billy is that really you?'

'It is Johanna but how are you? You're hurt.'

'Not really, just a few cuts and bruises.' She sighed and looked up at her rescuer or possibly captor, she couldn't be sure.

'So you have been a part of this all along?'

'Possibly, it depends on what you believe 'this' to be.'

'Don't play games with me Billy, I'm too tired for more games. It is just what it looks like, another bloody British plot.'

Brown raised an eyebrow: 'one in which you played an active and important role.'

Looking momentarily angry, Johanna shook her head 'it's not that simple but I expect you know that. I suppose you know Peter Fitzherbert?'

He nodded but he had no need to answer, she knew that it must be so. Gently, Brown asked if she could stand. She responded by doing so and smoothing her dress. Her hair was tousled and contained splinters of wood and glass. Her clothing bore the marks of the journey and its ending and Brown suspected that it had supplied the makeshift bandages for her wounded companions and the flag of surrender. He wondered at the strength of the woman. She left the carriage ahead of him, stepping out into the sunlight and the appreciative gaze of the soldiery who paused in their work of weapon cleaning and fire building to look at her, most of them with open admiration. Wheatley approached her to offer assistance and she asked what would happen to the two prisoners.

Wheatley explained that they had been given water and had their wounds looked at. They would be offered tea and some food once the fire was ready and would she like some too?

A thin smile returned to Johanna's face: 'I was thinking more of the long term.'

The big man looked grave and said that was not for him to say but he imagined thy would be put in a prisoner of war camp until the end of the war.

'Shouldn't be for long now Miss.'

Further conversation was interrupted by the noise of Peter Fitzherbert riding up in a spray of dust, rifle in hand. He slid out of the saddle gracefully and slapped at the dirt crusting his breeches with his hat.

'Johanna, Billy, I apologise for my late arrival. I was trying to get our runaway but I couldn't catch him.' He added thoughtfully even wistfully: 'and try as I might, I failed to kill him.' Recovering himself he looked around at the derailed coach and engine bearing the scars of battle and the men preparing to light a fire.

'Don't light that yet' he ordered, 'we're further along the line than I realised, not too far from the river in fact where the rendezvous was planned.' He looked around at the closest men and the rising ground behind them his gaze lighting on Wheatley.

'Sergeant Wheatley, could you post a couple of chaps on the higher level to maintain a lookout?'

'Already done sir' answered Wheatley 'Duncan and Inkster.'

'Excellent Sergeant' grinned Fitz 'keep the Caledonians together. Don't let 'em go haggis hunting though.'

Wheatley smiled at the old joke. 'Indeed no, sir.'

Fitz was laughing at his own witticism and seemed to be enjoying himself, then he looked at Johanna and the smile changed, it didn't vanish but what was left failed to convey any hint of amusement, much less pleasure.

'Johanna my dear, I think we have some matters to discuss. Come with me a little way where we can talk in private' and he indicated a small grove of trees a little way off with his rifle. Johanna said nothing but looked apprehensive and her eyes looked around as if seeking some rescue or support from someone, her gaze coming to rest finally on Brown. Fitz noticed and replacing his hat, said: 'You had better come too Billy, I'm sure you have some questions of your own.'

The three of them walked to the indicated trees, Johanna noticeably pale but looking less concerned now that Brown was with them and then Fitz pounced:

'No doubt there's a perfectly reasonable explanation but why did your message indicate that the train would move tomorrow and not today?' The tone was superficially light but no one who knew the questioner or the circumstances would miss the overlay of menace. It certainly wasn't lost on Johanna who shook her head at the question and replied in a shaky but forceful voice, the vehemence intended to hide the tremor, not entirely successfully.

'I didn't know it would happen like this, the date was set then changed at the last moment. There was barely time to pack a bag, much less send a note to you, which wouldn't have reached you in time anyway.'

Fitz held her gaze and he tried without success to decide if she was telling the truth or attempting to mislead him. Then he continued:

'So what were you going to do? Take the slow boat to the Emerald Isle and join the rebellion as you had planned?'

Johanna's eyes darted to Brown hoping for relief but found little comfort there, it wasn't only Fitz that had been shot at today and Brown was just as keen to learn the truth as was Fitz. So alone as she was, she told the truth: 'I didn't know what to do. I couldn't tell you; I couldn't stay behind either, I just had to join the train and hope something would happen that would give me a chance to escape.'

'Escape eh?' Fitz sounded far from convinced 'escape to where? Well, for now, let's leave that on one side. We will return to it though but there are more urgent questions for you to answer. Firstly, other than the two we have here and that vulture that bolted from me were there any others on the train?'

'The two crew'.

'No need to worry about them, they're both dead.' It was said in a matter-of-fact voice and sounded the more brutal as a result.

Johanna recoiled at the words and shaking her head again said: 'both civilians.'

Fitz grinned at that: 'hard to tell from a distance amid all that gun play but their own fault for getting involved. The fellow that stole Foster's horse and got away, did he steal any of the money?'

'A little, yes but he just filled his pockets and ran when he could. I doubt he got more than a few hundred.'

Fitz considered then asked the obvious question: 'where's the rest of the cash?'

'In a leather bag in the train carriage.'

'Is it now? Well we'd best make it safe' and calling Wheatley once more, he bade him guard the now open bag of gold coin and was gratified to learn that once again the Sergeant had anticipated his orders and had the matter in hand.

'So much for the past and present' said Fitz with apparent good humour, 'now, let's look to the future. How many men were to meet you and take you to the coast and what was the exact, and I do mean exact, rendezvous point?'

'We were to meet a mile South of the river and go on horseback from there. Apparently the track was unsafe beyond that point. As for the escort, I don't know how many, I wasn't told.'

'You weren't told? Well let's ask that fellow, maybe he has more information' and he pointed at the injured Donaghue and shouted for him to be brought over. One of the men helped Donaghue to his feet and escorted him to Fitz. He looked pale and in pain from his wound and walked slowly and with difficulty. When Fitz tapped his injured shoulder lightly with the barrel of his rifle he recoiled in fear. It was warm in the sun but not hot, yet the man was perspiring heavily.

'Don't be nervous old chap, what's your name?' Enquired Fitz in a friendly tone.

'Donaghue.'

'Well, Mr. Donaghue, Miss Reilly here says she is ignorant of the number of men who were to meet you and escort you to the coast. Do you share her ignorance or were you told some details? It would be so helpful if you could give us a little more information' On the surface Fitz might have been making a polite enquiry from his scared prisoner for directions but as Johanna and Brown looked on, he shifted the grip he had on his rifle. With no warning he then used the butt to deal Donaghue a savage blow to his wounded shoulder. The wounded man screamed in agony as the blow felled him and caused a ripple of turned heads from the soldiers nearby.

Johanna gasped at the unexpected brutality and Brown cursed: 'Jesus Fitz, he's a prisoner and wounded. You can't treat a man like that.'

'I am fully aware of his status and his unfortunate injury. What I don't know is how many of his friends we might expect to encounter if we're unlucky enough to meet them. That's quite important to the success of this operation and the safety of my men, including you. Johanna professes ignorance so I turn to someone who might know. Unless Johanna you have remembered something?' He looked away from the prostrate and groaning Donaghue and back to Johanna who was staring open mouthed at the man on the ground.

Getting no change from Johanna, Fitz spoke to all three: 'If this fine fellow would tell us what he knows, he will be perfectly safe from further injury. So Mr. Donaghue, what can you tell me?'

Donaghue was struggling to speak and with difficulty repeated that he knew nothing about the escort. Fitz paused thoughtfully then asked the man if he was certain. Receiving a yelped response that Donaghue was indeed sure, he responded with a kick at the man's ribs. Once the screams had subsided into sobbing pleas that Donaghue had nothing to tell. Smoothing his hair and replacing his hat, Fitz smiled his charming smile and addressed Johanna: 'I suspect Mr Donaghue's telling us the truth about the escort and naturally my dear I accept your story too. One thing we do know thanks to you is the location of the meeting point. While it's hard to be sure from our rather elementary maps, I suspect it is too close to our position to be comfortable. The trouble is, we have acquired three extra people not to mention some valuable cargo but we have also lost a horse. What would Mr. Micawber say I wonder?' And the smile widened slightly at the joke.

Johanna stood glaring at him with her fists clenched in fear and anger but could find no words. To see genial, charming Peter Fitzherbert treat a helpless man with such brutality had stunned Johanna. She had considered in LM that there was something not quite right about him and had called him too smooth but then she had been concerned about his motives. Even after he had abducted her and talked her into what felt like a betrayal of both her countries, she had seen no sign of the cold ruthlessness on display now. Having looked a little into his soul she felt a brief chill pass through her despite the bright sun.

Fitz's expression by contrast remained one of amusement: 'Not keen on Dickens? You really should give him a try sometime. He was a great storyteller.' poking away, he turned his face to the sky and then to Brown. 'It will be dark soon Billy, the horses and the men are tired and we have some transportation problems to solve. We'll camp on the high ground here tonight and then move out at dawn. Let's go and find Von Steinaecker and get the men organised.' He tipped his hat to Johanna and turned then looked back at Donaghue and as an afterthought added: 'I'll send someone to help you with him, a cup of tea and he'll be right as rain.' He might have been offering a lift to someone in Piccadilly it was said so easily, even jauntily.

Brown looked at Johanna and was about to speak when Fitz cut him off: 'Come on Billy, we've work to do.' It was said in an even tone and Fitz's demeanour suggested nothing untoward had just happened. There was no hint of regret or remorse nor even any suggestion of sadistic pleasure. Fitz just walked back among the men engaged in various tasks and gave a cheerful word here and a joke there and while most laughed or grinned as he passed, Brown noticed there were some odd looks too and the prisoner Burke shrank from his presence as he passed. For Fitz however, it was over. He had done what he felt was necessary and that was all.

Walking up the gentle gradient to the top of the small hill where Duncan and Inkster were keeping watch they encountered Von Steinaecker. If he was concerned at Donaghue's treatment he didn't remark on it. While Fitz had been conducting his interrogation, he had come to the same conclusion that they had to rest where they were for the night and had begun considering the best layout for the camp. Having been joined by Fitz, together, they outlined a perimeter and locations for sentries, where the horses should be held and other essentials. Holgate had discovered a small watercourse a little way off that would enable replenishment for the night but was sufficiently distant to present no problem from wildlife. Brown took little part in the discussion but let Fitz and Von Steinaecker get on with it. His mind was distracted by the events and violence of the day and like everyone else he was exhausted. When the evening meal came, he ate with little appetite but forced himself, knowing that he would require the energy the following day. Despite his tiredness, sleep came with difficulty too but eventually he slept, adding his light breathing merging with the other sounds of the camp including the groans of pain from Donaghue.

CHAPTER TWELVE

Battle at Krokodil River

It was still dark when Brown was roused from what seemed like a few minutes' sleep by the toe of Fitz's boot nudging him. Fitzherbert had rifle in hand and quietly but firmly told Brown to join him and Von Steinaecker for a council of war, the first time Brown had heard those words used seriously and in the appropriate setting. Rubbing his eyes and scratching he followed Fitz's shadow to where Von S, Holgate and Wheatley were standing. The air was still and chill and he couldn't help wondering how Johanna and Donaghue had fared during the night. Fitz, however, had other things on his mind, principally getting his command and its valuable cargo away from any Boer forces that might be looking for them.

If the Boers were looking for them, they wouldn't be hard to find, follow the railway line and turn right at the wrecked train. You really wouldn't need to be a skilled scout to do that. Rolling these thoughts around his still fuddled head, Brown could see why Fitz was so keen to establish the numbers of the escort that were waiting for Johanna. Just a half dozen could be fought off with ease, more might be problematic. Added to that, they would be slowed by insufficient horses and the burden of the bullion. Fitz was speaking and Brown realised he was canvassing the group's opinion for the next move. It seemed pretty clear to Brown that they couldn't stay where they were for long even if it was a defensible position and that was by no means certain. On the other hand, they were much more vulnerable against a mobile force if they were on the move. it wasn't military genius, merely common sense but one way or the other, a decision had to be taken. He offered the suggestion that as the Boers knew Kruger had fled they might not be too keen to risk their lives in a lost cause. The silence following his suggestion was ended by Wheatley's gravelly tones observing that might depend on how much they wanted the bullion. Von Steinaecker nodded his head and added that merely because 've belief zeir cause is lost, does not guarantee zeir agreement.'

All good points as Fitz acknowledged but interesting as the speculation might be, they had to get themselves and their cargo from where they were to Nomahasha and at the same time, they had to plan for some form of Boer intervention to stop them. The horses were reasonably rested but they now had four more people than horses and about ninety pounds extra weight of coin to carry. To add to their troubles, three of their number could not be expected to walk any distance: Foster and Donaghue were wounded and then there was Johanna. Fitz wondered aloud if the prisoners could be left behind.

Holgate looked appalled: 'may as well shoot them sir as do that, it would be quicker.'

Another officer might have reacted angrily to an NCO criticising his orders but Fitz merely looked quizzical: 'Shoot them Sergeant, whatever can you mean? We'll leave them some food and there's water available, their own people will find them soon enough and they can take care of them. If they're after us, that will slow them down rather than us.'

'If they come sir and if the lions or the jackals don't find them first.' Holgate was distinctly uncomfortable. He was a good soldier and a hard man but he knew the bush and the danger that lurked there for the unwary. He also had a firm view of right and wrong and in his mind, he knew what Fitz was suggesting was wrong. Before Holgate could commit a disciplinary breach, Brown interjected his own concern.

'And Johanna Fitz? Is she to be abandoned too?'

Fitz stroked his moustache and arched an eyebrow: 'Johanna is not a prisoner Billy, why ever would you think that?'

It was a question that might once have embarrassed Brown but in the chill pre-dawn, tired and a little disturbed at the turn of events he was angry and didn't care to hide it, not that he had much talent for concealing emotion.

'Just wanted to be sure we understand what you're proposing, sir.' The last word was intended to offend and everybody knew it. It just triggered the natural defences of its target who nodded serenely and agreed that orders should be both clear and clearly understood. Both of them were dissembling beneath a cloak of military discipline and it wasn't healthy. Fitz sensed a rising dissent and moved swiftly to crush it.

He turned to Wheatley: 'right Sergeant Wheatley, let's prepare to move. We need to spread the bullion around. Preferably over a relatively small number of saddlebags and ideally those of the most honest and authority respecting soldiers. There's not much incentive for thievery out here but let us not lead anyone into temptation. We will have to travel at walking pace with two walking at any one time excluding Foster and Miss Reilly.'

'Very good sir' answered Wheatley 'and the two prisoners?'

'Show them where they can find water and provide them with enough food for two days, we can't afford much more.'

Wheatley's face was impassive: 'what about a rifle sir? In case of wild animals.' Considering the previous exchange with Holgate, Wheatley knew what the response would be.

'Certainly not Sergeant, if anyone has a spare knife they can have that but I'm not giving away a rifle to two bloody traitors.' He couldn't afford to stretch loyalty and discipline too far and so he softened his tone and pointed out that the two Irishmen would be for the gallows if they were taken and in the event of a fight with the Boers, they could cause mischief. He couldn't tell whether or not Wheatley was convinced but he agreed and with that, Fitz knew he would have no problem from the men. While Burke and Donaghue's fate was being discussed, Von Steinaecker had remained silent. he paced a little impatiently but said nothing. Now he spoke for the first time and urged a swift departure. When the others looked around, sure enough, there was a hint of light and the occasional animal noise could be heard. Nature works to her own immutable timetable and soon it would be light and they would be exposed.

Fitz began to issue orders via Holgate and Wheatley, the time for consultation had come and gone and he was going to get his charges home, come what may. Two riders scouting in front, Holgate and one other some distance behind. Bullion with those riders in the middle which would include Johanna. It was brisk and efficient but to Brown left a couple of things in doubt, in particular, his place in the column.

'Billy, you're a fine horseman, I'd like you to be a free agent on either flank as you feel appropriate.'

'Very well Fitz and where will you be?'

'I'll be in the centre with the main body.' Which was entirely sensible. Have the command by the core of what you're trying to protect provides for a quick reaction to danger. It also meant close proximity to Johanna which illogically caused Brown concern. Orders, however are orders and when danger may be near, everybody has to play their part according to the agreed plan, not their own theories. Accordingly, he put his worries aside, which were undefinable anyway and went to see to his gear and his horse.

The camp was alive now and the smell of woodsmoke carried on the air as tea was hastily brewed prior to abandoning the site. Wheatley was standing over Donaghue and Burke and telling them in a surprisingly gentle manner what was intended for them. Donaghue was still in some pain and said nothing while Burke just looked hard at Wheatley before saying:

'British mercy, God love us all. You're going to abandon us in the middle of nowhere, surrounded by wild animals and with no way to defend ourselves. Have you no soul man?'

Wheatley responded in the only way possible, he simply stated: 'those are the orders I have, your friends will find you and you'll be safe then, so you will.' Burke could see argument was pointless but he cursed Wheatley and he cursed Fitz and he was on the brink of cursing all things British from the Queen Empress down when he looked at Wheatley's imposing bulk and shut up. There was some dark muttering from some who had learned of the prisoners' fate but others were all for it. It didn't matter anyway; they were too busy preparing to get on the march to have time to worry about two Irishmen who only yesterday had been shooting at them.

Brown wondered what Johanna's reaction would be, he couldn't imagine she would be happy. Damn it, he wasn't happy but Fitz had spoken and Fitz would take any consequences, although not the same consequence that the two captives might face. Whatever she thought or said, she said it quietly and when the column finally got under way she gave him a brave smile as she rode past just behind Fitz. Brown had elected to hang back with Holgate and Trooper McKay at the rear and the three of them stood by their horses, scanning the ground North towards the Sabie for signs of hostile movement and seeing nothing. The horses tails flicked at insects as the sun rose properly and the silence was only broken by the occasional curse flung in their direction by Burke. After forty minutes or so they mounted and moved off. It was a relief to be moving. The two men most sympathetic to the prisoners had been forced to oversee their abandonment. It had been a most uncomfortable and unpalatable task but now it was done and all that was left was to hope. They rode in silence McKay off to the left, Brown to the right and Holgate centre. Every thirty minutes or so, they would stop and look to their rear but all that moved was the occasional herd of zebra or Impala that would move off at their approach.

It was a slow tedious journey and Brown was grateful to Fitz for his roving commission between rearguard, flanks and the advance party. When he rode to the front, he found Von Steinaecker had also joined the advance guard and they rode together for a period.

'You know, zat vos hard thing the Major did zere mit der prisoners.' Von Steinaecker observed a propos of nothing. Brown said nothing and the German continued: 'But you know, I zink it vos right. Ve had few horses und zey could hef caused trouble.'

It was hard to tell if he was justifying it to himself or trying to convince Brown. If it was the latter, he had no doubt of the practicality but to him this failed to trump the wickedness of abandoning two men to the wilderness, one of whom was wounded. They rode on with Brown deep in thought about the matter. He didn't wish to speak but he did not want the Baron to be insulted so finally he said: 'You're quite correct but forgive me if I maintain that it was wrong. Those men were our prisoners, they were in our care and we abandoned them unarmed in the middle of the wilderness. There may be no formal rules to war but this is not conduct that is a credit to our country.'

Von S watched him carefully then asked: 'und if one of zem had taken a gun and killed one of our men? Or given avay our position to the Boers? Vot zen?'

'Then he could have been dealt with appropriately at the time. It doesn't matter now it's all one but I still think it was a damn shabby piece of work. I'm not in command however and neither are you, so our views don't count for much.' They continued on their way for a time without further conversation. Their eyes on the ground ahead for any sign of danger but all was quiet other than for the wildlife that either ran or eyed them with curiosity as they passed.

Progress was slow due to the walkers, which included Fitz taking his turn as did Brown and Von Steinaecker. Holgate had volunteered but had been told to remain where he was being more valuable there. As the day passed with no sign of pursuit spirits rose, although it reminded Brown that if the prisoners were not rescued, they would surely die. He hoped they had been found but their rescuing party were too few to hope to take on the British column. Winter was over now and the sun was hot by midday.

Shoots of green vegetation were beginning to appear and soon the rains would come. They wanted to be over the Krokodil before any serious precipitation in case the bridge was unusable. It was an odd time in the war, Kruger had fled and Pretoria had fallen, but not all the combatants would know and even if they did, it was no guarantee that the Boers would go gently into the negotiating chamber. Certainly the mixed bag of Scots, Irish, Australian and English escorting a goodly chunk of gold South were taking no chances.

On the third day, there was still no sign of pursuit and Komatipoort was only a few blistering miles to the South. People were too tired to be cheerful but the prospect of getting out of the Transvaal at least gave some hope to the weary troops. But, as Brown, Fitz and Von Steinaecker discussed, there was the question of getting the bullion to Pretoria and relative safety. It would be secure in Nomahasha, but what then? Mule train to LM and steamer to Durban or would Britain have seized all of the railway line by then and the gold could thus be loaded on a train at Komatipoort for delivery to Pretoria. The only answer was to get to Nomahasha and see how the land lay but first, they had to get across the river.

Sweating and brushing the dust from their faces, the column pushed on. Von Steinaecker, keen to be the first to find the crossing, rode ahead with the forward scouts and when the river was finally in sight came back to the column in great excitement which communicated itself to all. Smiles of weary relief appeared on grimy faces and Fitz called a halt to allow the rearguard to catch up which they did with some bad news. Holgate and McKay rode in with the news that there was what looked like a body of thirty or more riders following their path along the railway. Smiles quickly evaporated as the news sank in. Fitz pressed for more details and then asked: 'Where's Major Brown?'

'He stayed back sir to get a better picture but he wanted you to be aware and to know that it's a strong party that's coming. He's found a *kopjie*[32] to watch from, says he'll catch up as soon as he's got more definite information but I don't think they're friendly sir.' Fitz knew Holgate was right. Any group of riders coming down the railway line would be hostile and suddenly he was exhilarated. This was what he had been waiting for, his chance to take his place in the annals of Fitzherbert history.

'Well now, at least your friends will be safe from the vultures' said Fitz with a grin. 'Captain Von Steinaecker, how far to the river do you think?'

'Vun mile, maybe a little more. But you know, ve are still some distance from ze bridge.' Von S was excited too, his cap was pulled down tight, moustache at attention and vibrating like an expectant Labrador. He continued to describe a bend in the river that formed an inverted 'u' shape that could create a defensive position with each flank anchored by the river. Fitz nodded thoughtfully then traced an appropriate shape in the dirt with a piece of wood and asked if he had the dimensions right. Von S made some minor adjustments and the two set to roughing out a plan of defence while Holgate and Wheatley looked on. Satisfied that they had the basis of a plan if it came to a fight, there was then the question of getting the column there with two men walking. Being well aware of the military axiom about not splitting his force, Fitz initially struggled with doing just that but in spite of the perceived wisdom, decided that the solution was that Von S should take

---
[32] Afrikaans - small hill

the mounted element to the bow of the river and organise the defence while he would stay behind with one other to await Brown. They would then fall back to join the others, if necessary making a fighting withdrawal. Wheatley politely but firmly told Fitz that what he was suggesting was a non-starter.

'You're the commander sir, you shouldn't be risking yourself out here when you should be in charge of the main body with the Captain.' Fitz's face betrayed his surprise at Wheatley's admonition and the Sergeant quickly added an embarrassed: 'if you don't mind me saying so sir.'

Fitz was conflicted, he knew Wheatley was right but he had seen a chance for distinction and was loathe to let it go. Wheatley clinched the argument by volunteering to give up his own mount.

'Inkster and I will wait a little to see if the Major returns and will walk back either with him or without him. If we have to, we can hold any hostile force up a little and give some extra time for you to prepare a position.' As ever, he spoke matter-of-factly and logically and Fitz was forced to agree. The Scot Inkster, a short, hard type who combined an ability to laugh at anything with an extraordinary resilience let out an oath at hearing his name. It was perhaps louder than he had intended as Fitz and Wheatley both turned to stare.

'Aye, yon's a grand plan Sergeant. Never fear, if ye get hurt I'll carry ye.' It got a laugh from his comrades. He might as well have offered to carry a horse, the disparity in size was so great but his joke broke the rising tension and Wheatley's growl was lost in a flurry of orders dispatching the column in the direction of the river and eventually leaving the bulk of Wheatley and the diminutive Scot Inkster looking North for signs of Brown or possibly his captors or worse. Both men had checked their pouches and rifles for full magazines as well as a chambered round apiece. The ground to their front was fairly flat and dotted with scrub beginning to bud. To their rear, it was much the same until it fell away very gently to the river.

Fitz and Von Steinaecker led the balance of the force away to their rear and enjoined the Sergeant to exercise caution and to avoid being caught in the open if possible. If the Boers came, they were unlikely to dash in any old how. They were a wily people that were cautious with their lives and played to their strengths using bushcraft and marksmanship to their best advantages. If Wheatley and Inkster could get off a few rounds at their approach, the chances were good that they would pause and advance on foot, giving the pair a chance to effect a fighting withdrawal while buying their comrades time to consolidate some elements of a defensive position.

Wheatley wasn't the ideal build for a light infantryman, but he was a good shot and within his limitations surprisingly nimble. Inkster was ideal for the role, short and fast and a more than competent rifleman. It was a tactic that in the British Army dated back to the Seven Years War. A screen of marksmen holding ground in front of a prepared position to delay or break up an enemy advance, if two men could be designated a screen. The worst aspect of their position was the unknown. They had no idea if the enemy would come at all, or if he did, from precisely which direction. They separated and put about seventy five yards between their individual positions and waited. The sun grew hotter and insects circled signalling the oncoming fever season and causing each man to slap at them in irritation. With the departure of their comrades, there was no sound but the odd bird cry and nothing much to be seen, even for Wheatley who had the advantage of field glasses loaned by Von Steinaecker and so they waited.

After thirty minutes had passed with no sounds or signs of anything or anyone, Wheatley began to fear the worst. He glanced at Inkster who was off to his right and saw all was well there. he checked the shortness of the shadows from the bushes which confirmed what he already knew that the sun was at its zenith and now was the time to begin retiring to the river. The Major's absence confirmed the presence of a hostile force but little more and he turned back towards Inkster, to signal him to move. Before he could do so, there came the distant sound of rifle fire. A single shot then several more suggesting that his fears for the Major were premature. He could see Inkster react and the pair held their ground and awaited developments.

After the initial smattering of shots came silence. No other sounds came from any direction and Wheatley slapped at a distracting bug and tried to decide the best thing to do. He hated to think of Brown dead or captured but if the first shots indicated his being alive and well, the lack of any further fire suggested the opposite. Staying in their present, exposed position wasn't going to help him one way or another and he waved to Inkster to begin walking down towards the river.

The two men were experienced soldiers and moved one at a time cautiously from bush to bush whilst the other watched the rear making the best of whatever cover might be gleaned from the mostly bare branches. They kept a watch in all directions as they walked, occasionally even turning and taking a few steps backwards to look for any sign of pursuit. Approximately half way to rejoining their fellows, Wheatley sensed movement off to his flank and halted to make use of the field glasses. At first, all he could see was dust and scrub but then he saw a single rider coming on at a canter, rifle in hand. Letting go the glasses, he slipped the safety catch off his own rifle and waited to make a positive identification. As the distance narrowed, he realised it was Brown but he kept his rifle ready in case the Major had unwelcome company.

Brown spotted Wheatley and waved his rifle, slowing his horse as he did so then sliding out of the saddle when he reached him. His eyes looked around and back to the impassive Sergeant.

'Where's Major Fitzherbert and the rest of them? And what are you doing here on your own.'

'Inkster and I have been waiting for you sir in case you needed any help. The Major has taken everyone down to the river and is holding there in case of trouble. We heard the shots and then nothing and decided it would be best for us to rejoin the others.' The implication that they had given up on him was obvious but Brown knew they had done the right thing and said so.

'Right Sergeant let's join the Major and the rest as fast as we can. I counted thirty five mounted Boers. I let them come close to make sure of the numbers but misjudged it and had to shoot. Didn't hit anyone but caused just enough confusion to allow me to get away. I tried to lead them in the direction of the bridge but whether they bought that or not I don't know. If they didn't, they could be on us quite quickly.'

'Very good sir, well, the river's that way, you ride down there and Inkster and I can follow on foot.' It was the right thing to do but Brown wasn't about to ride in alone leaving two men behind possibly facing a hostile force.

'No Sergeant, three rifles are better than two. I'll walk in between you two. Now let's get moving while it's quiet.'

Not long after, the white of the sandbars in the low waters of the river became visible and then they were gesturing to the outlying posts not to shoot as they approached. Once safely among friends, Brown told his story to Fitz and Von Steinaecker. They listened attentively and when was finished, the German congratulated him on his escape. Fitz's eyes were fixed in the general direction of the bridge, too far away to be visible but not that far if the Boers had gone in that direction and finding nothing decided to scout the river bank. The troopers had taken up positions across the top of the 'u' shape in the river and had scraped out a number of shallow scrapes from which to fight with the river at their back and sides. The water was shallow and muddy and not much of a physical obstacle to an attack from the rear but it was better than nothing.

Looking around, Brown could see that if a stand had to be made, here was as good a place as any. They couldn't have reached the bridge and even if that had been possible it might have been guarded which would have had them potentially sandwiched between two enemy forces. Here, they had water, they had some cover and they had one advantage, they knew more about their enemy than their enemy knew about them. That was about to change however.

Holgate saw them first, a group of three riders coming from the East, some way distant from the river's winding course. They were spread out and looking for sign of the British force. Fitz enjoined everyone to silence. If they stayed still and quiet, it was just possible the Boers might pass by without being aware of their presence, unlikely but possible. They might have got away with it had not one of the

Boers turned in their direction just at the moment one of their horses whinnied in alarm at some imagined danger. The Boer yelled to his chums and pointed in the direction of the encampment. Had the man had more discretion, he might have survived. As it was, the need for silence having passed, he fell to Holgate's first shot, fired without orders but timely and effective. Fitz raised no objection but congratulated the Sergeant on his marksmanship.

The other two Boers barely spared their fallen friend a glance as they hauled their ponies around and ran. There was no cause for any general celebration among the British troopers, now that the Boers had found them, it was only a matter of time until they returned in force. Fitz moved from man to man having a quiet word with each and even making the odd joke. There was no other sound except for the occasional click of a rifle being checked or the gentle noise of the horses moving on their hobbles. Brown had adjusted the sights on his rifle a dozen times and then noticed Von Steinaecker checking the loads for his revolver so he did the same for his own sidearm. On inspection he found that the weapon was fully loaded as he knew it would be but he couldn't help but make certain. All any of them could do now was wait, no doubt those of a strong faith prayed too. Hands wiped away sweat from eyes and faces and the same eyes scanned the land for signs of the enemy.

They heard the drumming of hooves before they saw anything, then, out of the Northeast came a swarm of Boers mounted on the tough little ponies they favoured and pouring a wild but heavy fire towards the British positions. Whatever their reputation for skilled shooting, firing accurately from the back of a moving horse is impossible and they hit nothing except for the one lucky round that found

Major Peter Fitzherbert just as he decided to stand up. Brown saw him fall and ran to where he was lying, a spreading bloodstain on the upper left side of his chest. Fitzherbert was silent and for a moment Brown thought he was dead. The obscenity that escaped Fitz as Brown bent over him reassured him on that score. Telling Fitz that he would be fine Brown looked up for inspiration. He had no idea of how to treat a wound and didn't want to make anything worse. Fortunately, he was not alone, Johanna had also seen Fitz go down and rushed over to help, pushing Brown out of the way and ripping open Fitz's shirt in order to staunch the bleeding wound.

Relieved of that responsibility, Brown swiftly moved to the bush where Wheatley was lying, expertly aiming and firing as an opportunity presented itself. The Boers having looked as if they were about to launch a full-scale charge had sheered off left and right and were now engaged at sniping the British position. So far, Fitz was the only casualty, but the Boers kept up a hot fire and they didn't miss by much as the dirt kicked up and their rounds showed. It was only a matter of time before the shots began to take a toll. The British were already well outgunned, and each casualty would only make matters worse. Wheatley enquired after Fitz and then asked Brown what his intentions might be, a question that brought him up sharp with the realisation that he was now the senior officer and was in command of what was shaping up to be a very nasty situation.

Looking around him as the shots cracked and flew, Brown saw that his options were limited. The bow of the river was a natural defence that enveloped them behind and on both flanks but it also made movement very difficult. The Boers were able to see their forward positions but there was enough depth to allow some movement at the rear that would not be targeted by the Boer snipers and in fact Johanna and a couple of troopers had already proved this by moving Fitz away from his exposed position. That was all to the good but they were still outnumbered by two to one and their mobility was severely constrained by lack of horses and the need to transport the bullion. The Boers only needed to keep them bottled up in their current position and wear them down slowly. There were about four hours of light left, four hours for the Boers to chip away at them before night came to give them some protection.

Rolling away from Wheatley, Brown sought out Von Steinaecker and the pair found a fold in the ground screened by some bushes in which to talk. Brown laid out the situation as he saw it and put forward a plan that he thought might get most of them and the bullion away. The river was shallow and after dark, a party holding the bullion could slip across the river while their fellows stayed behind as if nothing had happened. With luck, they could effect a crossing the following night. It sounded good as he laid it out until Von Steinaecker pointed out that the river was called 'Crocodile' for a reason, any crossing attempted would fall foul of the reptiles lying in wait for their next meal. Shuddering at the thought, Brown agreed that a river crossing was probably out of the question. This left him bereft of any plan other than standing and fighting where they were and hoping to outlast their enemies. It wasn't much of a plan and there had to be an alternative. Leaving Von S with an admonition to be careful, Brown made a crouching run towards the river to see conditions for himself.

It was a broad bed with channels of water flowing slowly between sandbanks. He could see at least two dark streaks on one of the banks of white sand which were crocodiles basking in the afternoon sun. He could see no others but that didn't mean they weren't present. Estimating the distance between the riverbanks at about one hundred yards, he looked up and down the river for inspiration and found none. There had to be better options available than a last stand at the Crocodile River. As he looked, he noted that the vegetation was thicker near the river affording more cover although, due to the season, it was far from thick but it was something. In addition, the ground dropped away quite quickly even at the edge of the river, carved out by the flows in the rainy season. He followed the course West a little way and then retraced his steps and went to look for Von Steinaecker.

Whether Von S was exceptionally lucky or the Boers didn't shoot at him because they couldn't believe he was real was hard to tell. While he was only of middle height the ridiculous cap should have marked him out and he was exposing himself quite recklessly, having moved forward from where Brown had left him. Now he was moving from position to position giving encouragement to each man he spoke with and occasionally pausing to peer through his field glasses at the Boer positions. Brown quickly yelled at him to get down and then waved him back to an area of comparative safety. Having got him where they could talk Brown asked for his assessment of their situation. He ran through the basics, so far, they had been lucky, other than Fitz only McKay had been slightly wounded but that was unlikely to be the case for much longer. They had good supplies of ammunition, each man having eighty rounds and some reserves in saddlebags. In short supply, food was available so not a critical consideration but the water supply was at the whim of the crocodiles, which in the heat might present a bigger problem. When Von S finished, Brown reflected on their situation. It wasn't ideal but it could have been much worse had not Von S spotted the tactical advantage of their current location. If the Boer force had caught them in the open they would have been done for but they were still in peril. The river that cradled their position also held them firm. If they couldn't get away across the river, they would have to think of an alternate plan. They could hold the Boers off for a time but numbers would tell eventually and then the whole enterprise would collapse. Meanwhile, shots continued to be exchanged, reminding Brown that time was far from an infinite commodity. Sooner or later men would be hit and the balance would swing further towards the Boer force.

He felt Von Steinaecker looking at him expectantly and he called out to the nearest trooper to find Sergeants Holgate and Wheatley. Desperate times call for desperate measures. He had one idea that might extract them from their current impasse, but it needed some discipline and coordination. The two Sergeants were sensible, experienced men who would approach the matter with open minds but wouldn't hesitate to expose obvious flaws or to offer advice.

The Sergeants brought in; Brown reprised Von Steinaecker's situation report. He then looked at ways out noting that the river acted in the office of both moat and prison wall and moved on to what he considered to be the only viable way out. He and Holgate would take a party of five men on foot along the edge of the river on the Western side, using the dip in the ground and the vegetation as a screen until they were close to or at the Western edge of the Boer positions. The main force would hold their positions and when the flanking force let fly from the West, the others would join in firing as fast as they could in the hope that the Boers would think a new force had arrived and that they were in danger of being surrounded.

When he had concluded explaining his plan there was silence. Wheatley and Holgate exchanged glances and Von S waited, head cocked on one side like an expectant bird listening for a mate's song. Wheatley spoke first, commenting that the plan relied on the Boers believing that the British had been reinforced and thus causing them to panic. Brown agreed but pointed out the limited range of options available to them:

'We can stay here, hold on and hope but we risk dying by inches from a superior force. We cannot cross the river in the dark. Even if the horses would make the crossing we would be bound to lose a couple to the crocodiles and the Boers could pursue us at their leisure. This way, if we can pour fire into them from two different angles at great intensity, they may just believe that we are much stronger than they had realised. They are used to single shot, aimed fire, we will just pour in rounds as quickly as we can load and fire making it appear that it is a troop firing controlled volleys into their position. Even if they don't run, we should take a few down and we'll just have to press home an attack as best we can.'

Brown had read of the forlorn hopes of the Napoleonic era, how sheer ferocity had served to sweep away superior forces in prepared defences. This was not quite the same and was certainly on a lot smaller scale, nevertheless, he felt confident that a minute or so of intense rifle fire using modern weaponry to its full capacity could swing the struggle in their favour particularly if the attempt at enfilade was successful. He could see that Wheatley and Holgate had their doubts but the decision, in the absence of Fitz who was in great pain from his wound and would be taking no further part in proceedings, was his to make. Not only the decision but also the consequences and on that thought, he began to issue orders.

He left it to Holgate to select the right men to accompany them. Von S was to command the rest of the force, holding them in place and ensuring they responded appropriately when the time came. The operation was set for first light the next day and those selected by Holgate given the details of what was expected of them. Brown emphasised over and over the importance of the rapidity of fire even at the expense of accuracy. Heads nodded and nobody raised any question, although the laconic Inkster muttered something about 'wasting ma time on the range when any fool could just shoot.' Holgate shushed him and Brown laughed and promised him extra rum for each target he hit. But for all his brave face, Brown knew this was a desperate gamble and people would die. Hopefully other people, not his men but he was putting them in harm's way, which was an officer's burden. It was no time for doubt but rather for preparation and planning which would prevent the doubt from creeping in.

As the sun vanished and the air cooled, fires were lit which would provide welcome tea and hot food from their dwindling supplies. More fires than were needed were lit serving to suggest to any watching Boer that they were facing a larger, confident enemy. Sentry posts had been dug-in in an effort to prevent infiltration by the Boers.

It was another cloudless night, chill yet beautiful and still as a counterpoint to the noise of the afternoon's shooting. Guard duty was a strain on everyone, with Boers to one side and reptilian horrors in the river behind them. Despite what was coming, Brown was pleased and relieved when the sky began to turn pink once more. Overnight, some cloud had formed obscuring the stars and giving an indication that summer with downpours, steamy heat and deadly fever was just around the corner. Encouragement enough to see Brown finding his men and readying them for what lay ahead with Von S doing the same for his own section.

It was not properly light when they set out along the edge of the riverbank. Holgate was in the lead watching for wildlife, moving slowly but doggedly his head constantly turning to spot any danger before it came close. Brown was relieved to have him scouting ahead but it didn't do much to relax him or any of the others as they crept along alternately peering through the vegetation for any sign of the Boer positions or looking to their left for any danger from the river. They were well spaced out and mostly silent until Brown tripped on a tree root and cursed. It wasn't much noise but they all froze in place until Holgate gestured for them to continue. Brown flushed with embarrassment and felt the sweat on his forehead. Dabbing it away with a sleeve he carried on but to his irritation he continued to sweat. It had been cold not long ago, but now it felt warm and humid. He put it down to nerves and tried his best to ignore it, wiping his eyes and forehead as needed.

It took some time but eventually Holgate halted and waved to Brown to come forward. The Sergeant was peering through a gap in a bush and gestured to Brown to look. Sure enough, there was a small group of Boer commandos kicking a fire back to life and lighting pipes. They were bearded and unkempt after days in the saddle, not unlike their British opponents. They also looked in dire need of a meal and Brown noted more than one pair of trousers secured by string around a waist. Whatever sympathy he might otherwise have had for fellow humans suffering hunger and discomfort, he quickly put aside as he and Holgate brought their riflemen into firing positions. The light was still bad and the shadows long but there wouldn't be a better chance of springing a shocking surprise. Von S and his men should by now have crept forward to where they could make good use of their rifles and should be waiting for the first shot from Brown's men which would be the signal for general rapid fire. Standing by Inkster, Brown told him that if he could drop the tallest of the visible Boers first shot there would be a double rum ration. The Scotsman grinned and asked Brown to be careful because 'if you're kilt sir who will gie me ma drink?'

The seven men quietly slid their rifle bolts back and then forward, pushing the first round into the breech. On a whispered command, all raised their pieces to cover the targets they could see and any that might appear. Brown waited and then calmly but clearly gave the order: 'fire, fire at will.' Seven rifles discharged as one and all of the visible Boers were hit and down, some still but at least one screaming. Without hesitation, the seven continued shooting and Von S and his men joined in on cue. A maelstrom of fire was now sweeping the site of the Boer encampment from two directions. The noise was extraordinary but beyond the Boers he had seen fall, Brown could see no other movement. He was suddenly grabbed with doubt. The Boers hadn't fallen for his ruse and his troops were just burning ammunition for no reason. This would be the end, they would be killed or captured and the bullion would be lost and as he saw the end of everything, he suddenly remembered Johanna - God what if they knew she was a spy? What would happen to her? The thought only served to deepen his despair and the cacophony of rifle fire sharpened thoughts of the disaster that he had set in motion. Angry and desperate he carried on, firing rounds as fast as he could to where he hoped the enemy might be. It was useless, he realised, a foolish gamble that had been doomed from the beginning. He was about to order his men to fall back when he heard screams and yells and then spotted at least one bearded figure fleeing to the rear. He took a bead, fired and missed and then there were more some armed, some but not all running for their lives. The sight of the enemy intensified the shooting and suddenly blood was pounding in his head. Wiping sweat away, he reached into his bandolier for more ammunition and heard himself yelling rubbish and cursing as another figure ran off in the distance out of his sight. For whatever reason, this angered him and he was about to give chase after the retreating foe when he felt Holgate grab him.

'Not that way sir, you'll be shot by our own chaps, let's just move further up the tree line and see what else breaks cover.'

It was sound advice and they were able to spot a number of Boers mount and ride off at speed encouraged by further shots. As the firing slackened, they looked around and emerged from the bushes cautiously. The Boers had gone, the live ones that is. There were a half dozen corpses scattered around including Inkster's first victim and Brown felt sickened by the casual way he had made a bet over a man's life. Moving on in the direction that the Boers had gone, they came across some abandoned weapons and other pieces of kit which they examined for anything useful, taking what they wanted and discarding the rest. One saddlebag abandoned in a hurry, had a heavy family bible with various inscriptions in Dutch. Brown leafed through it and wondered about the man who had brought his family bible into battle. With some regret he discarded it and hoped that it might be retrieved and returned by some kind person. It was unlikely but stranger things had happened. Of more practical use were the two ponies that they found. They would supplement the horses that the column had and make their escape that much easier.

While they were searching the bodies and equipment, they heard a thin cheer from the direction of the river which turned out to be Von S leading an advance towards them sword and pistol in hand and cap neatly in place albeit stained rusty red with dust and mud. The German was grinning his broken toothed grin and wiping his blade with a coloured handkerchief he put sword back in scabbard and proffered his right hand.

'You did it!' He exclaimed shaking his head and laughing. 'By Jove, you did it. I thought you ver mad but zen I thought ze Major is a thinker and he must hef thought long and hard about zis und I vos right! You hed thought hard and your plan vorked. How many did ve kill?'

It was kindly meant but just reminded Brown of his responsibility for the day's deaths. He just waved towards the nearest corpses then went into the bushes to be sick.

CHAPTER THIRTEEN

Komatipoort revisited

Whatever Brown's nausea and disgust at the events of the morning, they had to be put aside as he turned his mind to the practicalities of getting his force and its cargo away and over the river into Swaziland. First, there were the dead Boers to be buried, so he put Wheatley in charge of overseeing that unpleasant job. It would be an exaggeration to say that the Sergeant stifled all grumbling but he kept it to a minimum. Brown watched them begin then left them to it and went to check on Fitz's condition. He found him semi-conscious with a concerned Johanna standing over him still bearing the signs of the journey. To Brown's eye she was still lovely despite the grime but there was a look of fear on her face.

'He's lost a lot of blood' she said looking at the pale face on the ground. 'He needs proper medical attention or he could die. I'm sure there are things we could do but I have no idea what they might be.' Brown regarded her with concern. She was tired and worried and his heart went out to her. Looking at Fitz, although he was no medic, he guessed she was probably right. Where a doctor was to be found close enough to save Fitz was difficult to say. The nearest settlement was Komatipoort but it was still a mile or two off and what if the Boers had occupied it? Scratching his head in thought, he decided to defer the question for the present, simply asking Johanna if she had eaten and promising to have some food sent to her. Having beaten off the immediate threat, he now found himself with a set of new difficulties to overcome. It was hot and somewhat humid and looking skyward, he saw that the clouds he had noted before had multiplied and were growing into great towering shapes in the sky. It would be rainy season soon but surely not yet? He put the thought away and went to find some food for Johanna and Fitz if he could manage it.

On his way, he considered the overall predicament and wondered if a river crossing might be attempted now that it was light. If it could be achieved safely it would enable them to take a shorter route to Nomahasha. He put the matter to Holgate who was dubious.

'We've got wounded sir, if the horses get spooked or are attacked by crocs, anyone going in that river will be as good as dead. Best to try the bridge at Komatipoort, no reason for the Boers to guard it now.'

'Not unless they're looking for us' countered Brown but he knew the Sergeant was right. It was not that much further than chancing the river and assuming they could get Fitz there without killing him they might be able to find a doctor to look at him. So once again, he took charge, ably assisted by Von S and the two Sergeants. By taking charge and keeping busy with the orders for the journey he avoided worrying about the responsibility he had been obliged to assume. Neither did he have time to dwell on the events of earlier but threw himself into logistical matters, looking at the welfare of the horses, redistributing ammunition and generally making sure everyone was ready and reasonably equipped for the journey. By the time they were ready, the weather had become hot and sticky and the clouds were darkening ominously. At his word, the column got underway, riding East towards Komatipoort and keeping eyes and ears tuned for any sign of a Boer return. They made a slow progress slapping at insects and wiping away sweat as the humidity closed in on them. They followed the great bow of the river until they found themselves looking at the few metal roofs of Komatipoort in the distance. Brown halted them and consulted with Holgate. All was quiet in the little settlement, no trains, no signs of movement, not even any smoke from cooking fires. The heat was oppressive and the air still, men and horses twitched and the men cursed at the swarms of insects that were attacking them, the only creatures to be thriving in the heat.

Brown turned to Holgate: 'What do you think Sergeant? Is it clear or not?'

'Impossible to say sir. It certainly looks clear but if the Boers are waiting for us they wouldn't show themselves. I think I should take a closer look if you don't mind.'

'I don't mind you looking Sergeant, but I do object to you getting shot.' It was the sort of flip comment that Fitz might have made and he was surprised at himself. Holgate was grinning at him but before Brown heard his response, there was a yell from behind them and they both turned to see a native being hauled along none too gently by Trooper Duncan.

Duncan was another short, wiry Scot but from the slums and grinding poverty of the Clyde. He had made a new life and probably a much longer one for himself by enlisting and getting away from the filth and disease that curtailed so many lives in industrial

Glasgow[33]. He had the black man with him, who was somewhat taller than him in a firm grip by his right arm and was propelling him forward to where Brown and Holgate sat their horses. Neither the native, nor his captor spoke easily intelligible English. Brown could just about understand that Duncan had found the man when he emerged from some bushes nearby but couldn't understand a word the black was saying. Holgate addressed the man in his own language and a brief conversation ensued, at the end of which Holgate ordered the native released. Duncan released his hold reluctantly, muttered something and spat while the native grinned happily and said something further to Holgate.

Turning back to Brown, Holgate gave a summary of their conversation: 'he says that there are white men on the bridge and in the village' Holgate explained. 'He watched them from a distance and doesn't think that they're Boers.'

'What's he doing out here?' Asked Brown, 'you don't think he's a spy do you?'

'Most unlikely sir. He says that he heard there had been a fight between two groups of white men and that the Boer party had run away. He wanted to find us and warn us that someone was on the bridge ahead of us.'

'But how would he know we would come this way and warn us of what exactly?'

Holgate gestured towards the sky and the darkening clouds. 'When the rain comes, the river will quickly become impassable even on horseback. He's a local man and says he likes the British he thought we would have to come looking for the bridge

---

[33] Life expectancy in Glasgow at the time was only 42 and considerably less in the poorer parts of the city.

and he wanted to tell us of the presence of other men around it.'

Brown thought for a moment before responding. 'Do you think he's genuine?'

Holgate tipped back his hat and wiped away perspiration. 'I'm sure he is sir. Why bother coming to find us and warn us of men in the town? If he was a spy he wouldn't have revealed himself to Duncan, he would just have watched us and told his masters what we were doing.'

It was a reasonable point, and now that they were aware of a mysterious group of whites on the bridge, what were they to do? Whoever these people were, they were curiously inactive. Or were hiding themselves. Out here at the Southeastern edge of the Transvaal, it was unlikely if not impossible that they were friendly or even a neutral party of hunters or prospectors. The black might not think they were Boers but who else could they be? Brown shared these thoughts with Holgate as Von S rode up and asked what the plans for entering Komatipoort might be. Brown brought him up to speed on the native's message and before they could weigh up the options before them, they felt the first raindrops fall. It was a gentle rain, not significantly hard but the sky had darkened and there was going to be a lot more quite soon. The only road to Nomahasha and comparative safety lay across the Komatipoort Bridge, the bridge they had invested so much time trying to destroy and currently held by a group of mysterious white men.

The rain drops began to grow in size and ferocity blown by a wind that had suddenly sprung up. The weather brought a sense of urgency to Brown's decision making. Staying put or going back were neither of them reasonable options, the only way was forward but how to do so safely? Holgate suggested that he ride in as close as he dared accompanied by the black and then send the black in to see the lie of the land.

'While the rest of us sit here exposed to the elements and any Boers that might be riding by?' Brown knew Holgate's plan was well intentioned but if the rain kept up it would not be good for Fitz or any of them for that matter. There seemed only one thing to do and that was to walk toward the bridge, spread out for safety and hope that whoever was in front of them would be friendly. The odds were long but with the rain running off his slouch cap and down the back of his neck, Brown thought them better than their chances if they stayed where they were. A distant flash of lightning followed seconds later by a rumble of thunder would have made up his mind, had not some even more pressing news arrived courtesy of Trooper Inkster, who trotted up streaked in red mud and cursing quietly but with his customary fluency.

'Excuse me sir,' he asked after leaving off his swearing, 'but ah'm afraid tay say that ah think there are Boers oot there ahind us.'

It was Brown's turn for profanity: 'Christ! How many and how far behind?'

The diminutive Scot shook his head almost sadly and answered that he couldn't be sure of the numbers but from what he had observed, at least a dozen, perhaps a half or three quarters of a mile from their present position. He added that he thought they were looking for something rather than following their trail but whatever they were about, the rain would have slowed them up.

Slowed up or not, they were far too close for comfort and unlikely to pass by Komatipoort without stopping. Brown realised that he had to act and there was only one option. Thanking Inkster for his report, he gave orders for the advance to Komatipoort in extended order and silently prayed that they would get away safely. Inkster and Duncan volunteered to act as a rearguard that would delay any Boer pursuit and leaving the two Scots behind, complaining furiously about the weather while finding a modicum of cover for themselves and their horses, the party moved forward towards the bridge. The rain was coming down hard now and water was pooling and forming rivulets in the red earth. Brown rode close by Holgate and noticed that the black who had been speaking with him was now trotting way ahead of the main group in the direction of the cluster of buildings now shrouded in rain. Nodding in the direction of the disappearing native, Brown asked Holgate what the man was up to.

'Says he's going to make sure the men at the bridge don't shoot us' said Holgate, adding darkly: 'just hope they let him live long enough to explain and hope there's someone he can explain to, his English is none too strong.'

Plodding on through the rain and muddy ground, Brown hoped not only that the message got through but also that the men in Komatipoort would be convinced that shooting the approaching group would be a mistake. He looked along the extended line of men and horses making slow progress and could feel the tension in all of them. Johanna was helping Fitz who was still in great pain from his wound and in any other circumstance would not have been moving. The buildings ahead of them revealed nothing of anyone that might be inside, in fact, as they drew closer, Komatipoort began to look like something of a ghost town. The rain was relentless and unpleasant, soaking through clothing and boots and coursing down faces. The horses pushed on gamely, unaffected by the flashes of lightning and rumbling thunder. Unlike their riders, they at least were blissfully unaware of the danger behind and the uncertainty ahead.

They were almost upon the first buildings and Brown was searching desperately for some friendly signs or indeed just any sign of life when a man emerged from one of the nearest buildings waving his hat and yelling:

'Halt and identify yourselves.' Brown almost cried with relief, the voice was confident, arrogant even and unmistakably British.

'Brown, Major British Army.' He shouted back, 'we have wounded that need treatment.'

'Well come forward whoever you are and be recognised and be aware there are twenty rifles aimed at you right now.'

Riding towards the man who he could now see was in sodden khaki, Brown became aware that he wasn't making idle threats, there were rifles pointing at him from windows and from behind a makeshift strongpoint made out of piled furniture to partially block the trail leading toward the bridge. He made the journey slowly and carefully, not wishing to alarm any of the men holding rifles trained on him. The rain had not let up and he was conscious of the sorry figure he cut, wet through and unkempt but looking down at his opposite number, he realised that he wasn't the only scruffy soldier in Africa. This fellow had three days of beard if he had a whisker. His slouch hat was wet and crumpled and there were holes in his shirt and britches. For all that, he managed a military look, standing straight at about six feet odd and viewing Brown with ill-disguised curiosity.

Before Brown could dismount, the fellow stopped him with an oath aimed somewhere over his shoulder.

'Who in God's name is this? Major bloody Gilbert and Sullivan?'

Brown was momentarily puzzled and then realised that Von Steinaecker had accompanied him and was on his right. The only reason the madman hadn't been shot was that the riflemen facing them probably couldn't believe their eyes. Irrespective of that, Brown and Von S had gone through a lot together and Brown wasn't going to have him disrespected.

'For your information, this is Captain Baron Ludwig Von Steinaecker of Steinaecker's Horse. Now who the bloody hell might you be?'

It was bold and out of character but he was wet and tired and had not enjoyed the easiest of times. He had also noticed that the man before him was relatively young and almost certainly junior in rank. Why he had chosen to invent Steinaecker's Horse he didn't know but it was what the German wanted and he might well get it one day. It was only what he deserved after all.

It turned out he was talking to a Lieutenant Rankin of the Imperial Light Horse who made a brave attempt at a smart salute. Remembering more pressing matters, Brown told him to stop being an ass and that there was a party of Boers out there probably looking for them.

Rankin, despite Brown's admonitions against parade ground manners, was 'yessirring' furiously. faced with the news about Boers however, he looked doubtful and explained that local natives had made him aware of their fight with the Boers and he had a patrol out looking for a Major Fitzherbert and his men.

'Well you've found us, the Major is badly injured and coming in now with the rest of my chaps. So are you telling me that the men behind us are yours and not Boers?'

'Almost certainly sir. Once the black had told us that you were out there and in a fight we sent men out to find you. They're probably casting about to locate your trail now but what with the rain and all it would be hard to follow.'

'Well thank heaven for the natives then. Do you have medics with you?'

'Orderlies yes sir and there should be a doctor along in the next day or so. We're just an advance party sent to stop the Boers destroying the bridge.'

Brown looked at him in disbelief and then laughed: 'Do you realise that the last months of my life have been spent trying to blow that bloody thing up?'

Rankin looked shocked and the humour of the situation seemed lost on him as he said with delay seriousness: 'Well please don't sir, the army needs it for bringing in men and supplies from' and Brown interrupted him: 'Laurenco Marques[34] , yes I imagine so. Oh hell, just get your men to take care of the Major and for God's sake let's get out of this rain.'

Brown's dirty and weary party moved into the buildings occupied by Lieutenant Rankin's patrol with much relief. A cot was found for Fitz and a couple of medical orderlies fussed around him cleaning the wound and applying fresh dressings and congratulating Johanna on keeping 'the poor Major' alive. Whether their admiration was purely medical was hard to tell, as even wet and travel stained she was still quite the beauty. Brown took the opportunity to talk with her as they both rested with

---

[34] Highly unlikely, as British supplies would mostly flow through the Cape and Durban. The line would be needed to move men and equipment to the Eastern Transvaal, however.

tea brewed for her by kindly soldiers and shared with him as an afterthought.

The rain was drumming on the corrugated iron roof as she gave him soft smile and said: 'well you got us through, quite a feat for a shady businessman from London.'

He blushed and looked sheepish as she had hoped he would. He apologised for the deception but in his defence made the point that it had been his profession before the war. Happily she didn't press him on the circumstances that had taken him to LM but rather asked him about the future, what came next for Major Brown?

'I rather hope a return to being plain Mr. Brown and an improvement in business' came the response accompanied by a more confident grin. 'Now that the war is over, the mines here will be working again and the miners will be needing equipment. I look forward to returning to London and fulfilling that need.'

'Really Bill?' She looked almost sad and then her natural ebullience reasserted itself. 'No more soldiering or intrigue with your friend Fitzherbert? Won't you miss it?'

Brown looked at her in surprise. 'Miss it? The risk of being killed and others being killed and wounded around me? No I shan't miss that. I did what I was asked to do for my country and hopefully the country is satisfied with it. I soldiered properly once, back at the time of the first war against the Boers and decided it wasn't for me. Now the Boer Republics are defeated and Britain is the dominant power in the region they don't need me anymore.'

'Defeated is it?' Said Johanna with some fire. 'I shouldn't be too sure of that, who was it shooting at you but yesterday?'

Brown laughed: 'why some rogue band that hadn't got the news or wanted the bullion for themselves. Lord knows what stories they've been fed about millions of gold coins[35] to make them come after us. I might also point out Miss Reilly that given your involvement, an end to Boer rule might be in your interest.' Before she could interrupt, he warmed to his theme: 'Look, the Boers lived in the past, they wanted all the revenue of the mines but with the luxury of refusing the miners any rights in return and being able to sit in moral judgment over them. They treated the natives appallingly and had it not been for Britain, they would have reduced them to the status of slaves. No my dear, it's over and all of us, Britons, Boers and Blacks should be glad for a return to normality and an end to the killing. Britain will rule South Africa kindly and in the interests of all her people, not just the whites and I will be glad for the return to damp and smoky London, but never mind me, what are you going to do now?'

The question seemed to take her off guard, she said nothing and looked thoughtful before saying: 'I don't really know. There's no government to serve, and I had been so caught up in the war I hadn't given the future much thought. But here we are in the wilds near the border which we have to cross to get back to, well where exactly in order to take the next steps on our journeys, which, I imagine, will soon diverge?'

---

[35] The legend of 'Kruger's Millions' surfaces from time to time, most recently in 2001 when a family in Ermelo claimed to have dug up thousands of gold coins. There was also a 'Lost Hoard' of Kruger Ponds discovered in a Swiss bank vault and claimed by the South African Government, which might have been a residue of the treasure taken by Kruger to Europe when he fled, leaving not only his country but his wife behind.

He thought for a moment. If he could have done, he would have ridden to the nearest port of any size and taken ship for England but it set him to thinking, what indeed was the next move? The gold couldn't stay where it was and sending it to Nomahasha with Von S and his roughnecks wasn't sensible. Once again, with Fitz out of action it fell to him to take the decisions.

Thus it was that he found himself, Wheatley and Johanna plus the wounded Fitz and a quantity of gold bullion on a train for Pretoria. Rankin's medics had done a fair job of patching up Fitz and he had regained much of his old bounce even if he moved slowly and breathed heavily when he did so. They had been escorted to the railway station by a troop of Light Horse who had seen them and the gold safely aboard. Von S and Holgate had bid them a fond farewell and Inkster had offered to come with them 'just tae see the young lady safe home sir ye understand?' An offer Fitz had politely declined and Holgate had ridiculed knowing full well that charming as the young lady might be, Inkster was interested in seeing at least some of the bullion go astray.

There was no first-class compartment so Wheatley sat with them and Brown couldn't help wondering if this might not be the way of the future in a new country built on more equal lines than Britain. A thought he held until he saw the sweating blacks being harried to load coal by a white overseer at a way station in the mountains before the train began the long sweep across the flat and empty veld to Pretoria.

As they approached the city Brown remembered as a sleepy village, he wondered what he would find when they arrived. Of course, the biggest change was the influx of British and Imperial troops who were everywhere as was the Union Jack which hung from most public buildings. The city had expanded since his first visit, there was a new hotel called The President not to mention the new schools, one of which had played host to British prisoners including young Churchill. On their arrival, they were greeted by well turned out staff officers and a well-armed escort for the bullion. There were fond farewells as they went their separate ways. Fitz to the officers' hospital ward, Brown and Wheatley to Army Headquarters with the bullion and escort and Johanna to her parents. She had held Brown's hand for a time as she wished him farewell and he had felt a pang at the parting. It might have been worse had he known how she felt but he was blissfully unaware and merely conscious of a sense of ennui. Fitz and Wheatley had watched them from a discreet distance and then watched Brown's eyes follow her as she disappeared down the street in a horse and buggy.

Fitz and Johanna taken care of, Brown and Wheatley saw the bullion safely home to its new owners and accepted the faint thanks of the staff officer in charge who looked at the pair in their torn and patched khaki as if they were wayward children that needed to be cleaned up and made to do their homework. Brown's instinct was to curse the man for a pompous arse but he couldn't embarrass Wheatley and in fairness had no clue what the man may have been through in the fighting that had brought the British to Pretoria. What was more important was enlisting his help in finding accommodation for Wheatley and himself and then a ship home and a discharge.

The first item was accomplished relatively easily, Wheatley being admitted to the Sergeant's mess of the Dragoon Guards and Brown being directed to the officer's mess of an Australian Regiment. Once the Australians had ascertained that he wasn't going to look down his nose at them they were most welcoming, and he enjoyed his first evening with them even joining in the singing after dinner and learning anew favourite song they called 'Waltzing Matilda.[36]'

Good chaps as they were, Brown wanted to be on his way home and after a few days, he began to haunt headquarters and the responsible transport officers for news of his ship home. None of whom proved immediately able to help him however, promising to send word when the necessary orders arrived. He passed the time by riding out, often with Johanna who proved a more than competent horsewoman and dining in with the Australians. he enjoyed the time spent with both parties but was careful to keep them separate. However many trips he made to headquarters, his movement orders failed to materialise and he began to wonder if there was a way to circumvent the system. He also noted with rising alarm the failure of the Boers to recognise their own defeat. There were constant stories of skirmishes between British and Imperial troops and Boer Commandos with supply columns ambushed and even trains derailed and railway bridges blown. While he was in country, he did not want to be told his services were required. However, he reasoned that he had been trained to blow bridges, not to rebuild them and logically the defiance couldn't last long.

---

[36] 'Waltzing Matilda' was probably composed in 1895 in Winton Australia although the tune had been well known long before. It is entirely possible that Australian soldiers would have sung it during the Boer War.

It was after yet another fruitless call on the transport people that he wandered into the new President Hotel bar and ordered himself a beer. Quietly sipping his drink he was considering calling on Johanna the next day. Her parents weren't exactly enthusiastic about her friendship with a British officer but for the most part, they had been civil enough and she had regained all her sense of fun and mischief gently teasing him and challenging him to horse races across the veld. He was relieved that the army had left her alone after the incident with the train times. Presumably as the bullion had been recovered and only Boers were killed there was little concern. Nursing his drink, he couldn't help wondering what the truth of the matter was. Dismissing the matter as one of those things he would never know, he was pondering the wisdom of another drink before a night with his Australian hosts when a tap on the shoulder pulled him up short and he found himself looking at Major Peter Fitzherbert. Apparently as amused with the world as ever, despite the sling that held his left arm and the extra pip on his shoulder which suggested he had been promoted to Colonel.

'Fitz you must stop springing out at me in pubs' said Brown and nodding at his epaulette asked, 'or do I have to call you 'sir' now?'

'Of course not Billy but you might offer a fellow a drink.'

Emboldened by his beer, Brown observed wryly:

'The last time I bought you a drink in a bar, I ended up back in the army helping a mad kraut blow up a bridge but since I'm sure you've come here just to help me get home and out of uniform I'm going to take that chance' and laughing Brown bought the Colonel a whisky. He wasn't laughing so much after he had received Fitz's congratulations on his taking command at Komatipoort and saving both the column and the bullion. It was good to hear that his efforts had been appreciated and he didn't expect or seek more than that. Except that he assumed that his reward was a ticket home. As was Fitz's way, he then dropped his bombshell. The high command had indeed been delighted at the way matters had turned out and how Brown had behaved not only in the field but also in LM. Delighted to such an extent in fact that in view of the Boers' continued failure to stop fighting and his past successes they needed his continued service in the field.

His spirits sank as all of his worst fears came true. He could feel his ticket home vanishing as fast as Fitz's first whisky. He began to protest but it was pointless. The army embodied by the now Colonel Fitzherbert had him and could do more or less what they wanted with him. So he sipped his beer and listened as Fitz outlined his new job and tried to look cheerful. Inwardly he found himself yet again cursing everyone involved from Field Marshal Roberts down. Eventually, Fitz finished his discourse and it was a mark of the man that he managed to pique Brown's interest in the new job that would keep him in South Africa for the foreseeable future. The two men shook hands and parted company on the promise of meeting tomorrow. As he walked down the dusty street in the heat thinking how he would drown his sorrows with the Australians one last time, he realised that yet again Fitz had shanghaied him and got him to buy the bloody man's drinks as he did it.

A Note About The Boer War and Bibliography

Also referred to in South Africa as the Anglo Boer War or to be truly accurate, the Second Anglo Boer War. It was fought between the forces of the British Empire and the civilian armies of the two Boer Republics of the Transvaal and Orange Free State between October 1899 and May 1902. A war that has now been mostly forgotten by all but the Afrikaans speaking minority in South Africa and certain specialist historians but at the time, it dominated the news from Russia to California and beyond and in particular the contemporary British press.

The word Boer is Afrikaans for farmer and is the term most commonly used for the inhabitants of the two Republics fighting Britain. Many of them traced their ancestry back to Holland and they were also often referred to as Dutch although many were of German or French Huguenot descent. The Afrikaans language evolved from the Dutch spoken by the original settlers from Holland and adopted words from a variety of sources. In turn, some like Commando and Kop also found their way into English.

Many notable figures of the 19th and 20th Century were involved in the war in some way, best known perhaps being Winston Churchill who was taken prisoner by the Boers but successfully escaped. Mahatma Ghandi was a stretcher bearer on the

British side, and Sir Arthur Conan Doyle interrupted his writing about Sherlock Holmes to serve as a doctor with the British forces. Rudyard Kipling, Edgar Wallace and Roger Casement also all played a part in the conflict.

For the Boers and their descendants, the war and the treatment of Boer civilians by Britain have become part of their ethnic identity and mythology. As Afrikaners will loudly assert, It is true that thousands of farms were burned and civilians were herded into concentration camps where thousands died of disease. They are more reticent in mentioning that the farms were used as supply depots by Boer forces and that the camps were established to provide refuge and shelter for displaced Boer civilians a fact acknowledged at the time by General Botha. The war began with a Boer invasion of British territory and by doing so, at least some Boer leaders hoped to end the British presence in Southern Africa altogether. Revisionist historians have asserted that Britain forced the Boers into war but while there was little love lost between Briton and Boer, there is scant evidence of any British plot.

The war, ended in a British victory in part due to the overwhelming numbers, in part due to the professionalism of British forces against a civilian army. After the war's end, compensation was paid by the victors for property destroyed. A Union of South Africa incorporating the Boer Republics and British colonies was established under the premiership of a former Boer General Louis Botha, beginning eighty-four years of Afrikaner domination of the country. Perhaps only Britain could go to war to protect the rights of her citizens and at the moment of victory concede all of the regional power to those she had been fighting.

Bill Brown and Peter Fitzherbert are entirely fictional characters. Consul Crowe, Sir John Ardagh and Von Steinaecker were real enough as was the plot to destroy the Komatipoort Bridge. For the rest, it's a tale based on real events but intended to entertain. Modern readers may find some of the language around race and perceived racial characteristics offensive. Unfortunately, the characters lived in a less sensitive world and the language used is probably a diluted version of what they might have said.

For those interested in further reading, the following are the principle books relied upon as reference for this story.

Amery, Leo S (1902) The Times History of the War in South Africa 1899-1902 London St Dunstan's House

Angelsey, Marquess of (1973) A History of The British Cavalry 1816 to 1919 London Secker and Warburg

Ash, Chris (2020) The Boer War Atlas First Edition Pinetown KZN 30 Degrees South

Kruger, Rayne (1983) Goodbye Dolly Gray London Pan Books

McCracken, Donal P (1989) The Irish Pro Boers 1877 - 1902 Johannesburg Perskor Publishers

Reitz, Deneys; JC Smuts London (2008). Commando Jonathan Ball

Packenham, Thomas London (1993) The Boer War Weidenfeld & Nicolson

Woolmore, William Barberton (2006) Steinaecker's Horsemen South African Country Life

Printed in Great Britain
by Amazon